4/04

Library Journal—December 2003—*The New Wife*

The author of nine books, including *A Passion for More,* Barash (gender studies, Marymount Manhattan Coll.) here focuses on the role of the American wife. The book was constructed from personal interviews with women who married in each of the six decades studied (1950 to present), as well as synopses of material reflecting cultural and societal attitudes about marriage, such as novels, news stories, films, and various artistic and political statements. The end result is a small and immensely readable volume that highlights the experiences of a group of women from varying socioeconomic, religious, ethnic, and educational backgrounds, utilizing their stories to support contentions about the changing role of the wife in each era examined. Sex, abuse, finances, affairs, divorce, and childrearing are all discussed in light of the expectations these women harbored, accompanied by the backdrop of the expectations of others. Barash's conclusions are backed by statistics in addition to the interviews and cultural research. The book comes to life with the voices of many candid women and ends all too soon. Recommended for large public and academic libraries.

Lori Carabello, Ephrata P.L., PA

The author has approached this fascinating subject with great authority. Her research is exemplary, the masterful writing brings easy comprehension to a historic perspective. The American Wife of the 21st century is a new breed of woman and Susan Barash gives us extraordinary insight into the many facets of her personality.

Louise Kerz Hirschfeld
Theatre Historian
TONY Award Nominator
Television Research Consultant

A compelling analysis of wives and how important they really are. All of my wives, past and future, should profit from this book immensely.

Lewis Burke Frumkes, Author of
How to Raise Your IQ by Eating
Gifted Children

Here comes Susan Shapiro Barash, again, the immensely readable, knowledgeable chronicler of family relationships —this time with strong, new views of the American wife through the decades. If you're a wife, it will be an irresistible temptation to look yourself up and see how you compare to the other wives of your decade...and boy, is this writer on target. This is a serious and careful study and yet, the excellent interviews lend *The New Wife* a deep intimacy. It's fascinating to see how '*plus ça change, plus c'est la même chose*'. Understanding the past helps breathes vibrancy into new marriage. I'll dip into this book and probably steal from it, for a long time.

> Sherry Suib Cohen, Author of
> *Secrets of a Very Good Marriage*
> and Contributing Writer to
> *Lifetime Magazine*

We all know that the days when a wife met her husband at 5:30 with a martini and home-cooked four-course meal are a thing of the past. But do we know what it means to be a wife today, and how we got here? In this fascinating book, Susan Shapiro Barash charts the conflicting expectations of marriage and wifedom over the last half-century. She weaves the poignant voices of wives across the generations with her own trenchant observations. Barash shows how far wives— and husbands—have come.

> Leora Tanenbaum, Author of
> *Catfight: Rivalries Among Women
> —From Diets to Dating, From the
> Boardroom to the Delivery Room*

Susan Shapiro Barash writes about the evolving role of the American wife with a scholar's passion, sociologist's curiosity and writer's grace that have enlightened readers of her previous studies of relationships. *The New Wife* is a service to husbands as well as wives and the children they share.

> Sidney Offit, Author of *Memoir of
> the Bookie's Son*

THE NEW WIFE

THE EVOLVING ROLE
OF THE
AMERICAN WIFE

by

Susan Shapiro Barash

NONE
THE
LESS
PRESS

The New Wife by Susan Shapiro Barash

Printed in the United States of America
ISBN 1932053085

Library of Congress Cataloging-in-Publication Data
Available upon request

NONE
THE
LESS
PRESS

http://www.nonethelesspress.com

10 9 8 7 6 5 4 3 2 1

Author's Note

This book is based on extensive personal interviews of married and single women, and experts in the field of psychology and counseling. Names have been changed and recognizable characteristics disguised of all people in this book except the contributing experts in order to protect their privacy. Some characters are composites.

Books by Susan Shapiro Barash

A Passion for More:
Wives Reveal the Affairs
That Make or Break Their Marriages

Sisters: Devoted or Divided

The Men Out There: A Woman's Little Black Book

Second Wives:
The Pitfalls and rewards of Marrying
Widowers and Divorced Men

Reclaiming Ourselves:
How Women Dispel A Legacy of Bad Choices

Inventing Savannah

Mothers-In-Law and Daughters-In-Law:
Love, Hate, Rivalry, and Reconciliation

Women of Divorce:
Mothers, Daughters, Stepmothers—The New Triangle

For my husband, Gary A. Barash

"Well would they ever look so happy again
The handsome groom and his bride
As they stepped into that long black limousine
For their mystery ride"

—Bruce Springsteen
Walk Like a Man

Acknowledgments

I remain grateful to my three children, Jennie, Michael and Elizabeth Ripps for their love and patience. I thank my parents, Selma and Herbert L. Shapiro, as well as family members and friends. My father merits enormous thanks for his impressive research skills.

I thank Suzanne Murphy at Sarah Lawrence College, Richard Hutzler, Lewis Burke Frumkes and Carol Camper at Marymount Manhattan College. In publishing I thank Cynthia Vartan and Lori Ames. Emilie Domer, my student assistant, was indispensable.

I thank the professionals who have contributed their thoughts to this project, Dr. Ronnie Burak, clinical psychologist in private practice in Jacksonville, Florida, Dr Michele Kasson, a psychologist practicing in New York and a staff member of the Lifeline Center for Child Development, Antoinette Michaels, ACSW, founder and director of the Hope Counseling Center in Sayville, New York, Claire Owen, psychologist and professor of psychology at Marymount Manhattan College, and Jo League, psychologist with a private practice in New York City.

To the hundreds of women, married, single, widowed, divorced and remarried, who have expressed their innermost feelings about the role of the wife, I am deeply indebted. These women cannot be acknowledged by name in order to preserve their anonymity and privacy. Their adversities and triumphs are the lifeblood of this book and stand as testimony to the value of being a wife.

TABLE OF CONTENTS

1955

"I never imagined not being married, not being someone's wife," begins Alice, sixty-six. "I was married at twenty-one and at that point, I imagined that my life was beginning. Finally, I had arrived. I concentrated on decorating the house and getting repairmen to fix broken dryers and ovens, sometimes the TV antennae. It was a sign of status to live in a home with wall-to-wall carpet, so we had that. I churned out three children quickly, because that is what wives did. I made innumerable meatloaves and carpooled for miles on end. And while I wasn't unhappy, I wasn't happy exactly. My husband was the provider so he was the boss. Being a wife gave me respect. It didn't dawn on me for years that I could be something other than a wife. This is how I was raised."

1965

"I was raised to think that marriage was the goal, but by the time I reached a marriageable age, the feminist movement was beginning," Leeanne, fifty-eight, tells us. "I looked at my mother with great skepticism. I wasn't going to toss away my college degree to be someone's wife. The pressure from my family was enormous, and by the time I was twenty-four in 1968, I caved in and I got married. Then the struggle began once I had kids—the feminist teachings confused me, because I couldn't keep it up. Whatever I had learned about being on my own seemed to vanish. In the end, I worked with my husband to have a flexible schedule for the children. It wasn't a compromise, it was a sellout; I had one foot in the past and one foot in the future—where wives had children and worked."

1977

"In 1972, when I graduated college, I believed that I could be anything I wanted, even as a minority woman," Grace, fifty-two, recalls. "I won a scholarship to college and law school. I knew I wanted to marry and have a family. I thought that my husband would be understanding and fair. I imagined that we would be equals and that my career would be as important as his. I became a wife at twenty-nine and I waited until I was thirty-nine to have a child. By then I had to have infertility treatments. I was proud of my success as a lawyer, but disappointed in my marriage. I fought with my husband, looking for the romance we'd lost and somehow blaming him. When my daughter was born, I fell in love with motherhood because it had been a struggle to get there. Then my husband had an affair and I became very tired. I couldn't be a wife/mother/lawyer and hold it all together anymore. I encourage my daughter to make her own money and to expect little from marriage."

1984

"The road was paved for me by my predecessors," Karine, forty-six, explains. "Those women who had achieved success and also married and had children were my role models. I didn't believe in the downside of being a wife, I believed in romance and everlasting love. I got married at thirty-three, and kept going in my career as a stockbroker. It took me a long time to realize that women still were not treated well in the workplace and my inner voice wondered what it would be like to be a wife and mother, only that. Eight years ago, my husband and I adopted a daughter from Korea and I took time off. But I couldn't be just a housewife, so I became a powerful wife and marked my place in our community. I invested my brainpower into my job as a wife and my husband benefited from my social skills. I often wonder what is ahead for my daughter."

1993

"I was a catch of a wife when I married my husband in 1990," Carly, thirty-nine, remembers. "I had gone to the right schools and I was open to working or not working. I looked at my sister who was ten years older and she was already contemplating divorce. Our mother had been stuck in a lousy marriage. I wanted to avoid that route so I decided to focus on the marriage although I was overqualified to run a house. I opened a home office so I could keep up the house and the girls, and for a while it was enough, although I found it very lonely. I felt like life was passing me by—I was arm candy for my husband. In the late nineties I began to wonder what more there was out there and how many good years I had left, for work, to look good, to be a riveting wife. I had an affair with my plumber, and during that time I felt I was an extraordinary wife—I couldn't have been more glowing in my deception. The truth was, the constraints were too much, despite my efforts to be a perfect wife."

2002

"If I didn't marry early I would fall into the same trap as my mother," explains Deirdre, thirty. "She is divorced and has not gotten what she wanted because she tried too hard. I want to be young when I have children. I am determined to work on my marriage and to be a team with my husband. I don't want to be considered a 'wife' as much as a partner. It matters to me that we started out early. I can be anything I want to be, and I want to be Jeff's wife. I want to be a happier wife than my mother has been. I don't want to pretend things are okay like my grandmother did. I want to avoid these traps."

Preface

It is an intriguing notion that a woman's identity today remains wrapped up in the role of wife. Yet, the attitudes and expectations of this role have evolved so that a woman who becomes a wife today is not positioned in the same way as a woman who became a wife as recently as ten, twenty or thirty years ago. Although being a wife is as desired now as it has been in the past, the point of view of the wife is altered. A young wife today believes that her marriage will be egalitarian; filled with options and without complacency. Her marriage is also partly reminiscent of the past, partly unprecedented, partly a reaction to AIDS, her parents' divorce and life after 9/11. Whatever modeling she has found in her mother, she is determined to have a different experience than a wife of thirty years ago.

The new wife's sense of entitlement and power is more pronounced than that of her predecessors. This is not to say that her predecessors have not adapted to degrees. There is little question that a woman who became a wife twenty-five years ago has changed with the times, and these changes impact the young wife in much the same way as do traditional precepts of marriage. The original concepts of a wife of the past fifty years—status, companionship, family, and protection, are still valid. Yet, the balance has changed. The revised imprimatur, but an imprimatur nonetheless, of being a wife, holds fast. At the beginning of the twenty-first century, the paradigm of wife is being redefined.

It matters little to women that over the course of centuries, wives have simultaneously suffered physical beatings and commanded respect by reasons of their status. Despite an undercurrent of disparagement, including jokes, coffee klatch complaints, the commiseration of women at health clubs and at the office, women yearn to be wives. Young girls dream of it, divorced women and widows search for another chance, and single women view themselves as less, as missing something, because they are not wives. What was held up to us in the 1950s—a wife who cherished her duties at home and seemed devoid of intellectual challenges—is a stereotype long gone. A wife today does not perceive herself as a prisoner in the home, nor a mother, nor a feminist, nor an antifeminist. She is aware of the complexities of her role, and within her own tenure as wife she will change her style, she will adapt to a current trend or she will buck it. Whatever path a wife chooses, be it a power wife, arm candy for her husband, a stay-at-home wife, or a career wife, being a wife is still considered a definition of self and representative of one's acceptance in the world. Whether a woman is a wife or not, she lives in a society that considers it both an achievement and a compromise. What she imagines her role to be is represented by her mother and stamped with her own twist. The complexity of the mother-daughter role reveals daughters who repeat their mother's patterns of being a wife, choose an opposite style or a portion of their mother's style, combined with up to date mores and expectations.

As a two-time wife, and having spent my adult life at it—sixteen years in my first marriage and six in my second—I recognize the obstacles and the perks of the position. I have listened to the longings of my friends and I have eavesdropped on unknown women lamenting their fate as single women, perplexed wives, and triumphant wives. As an author who documents the lives of women, I have interviewed those who have conducted extramarital affairs, those who have divorced only to remarry the same type of man, women who have resented the husband's ex-wives, and women who "sleepwalk" through their marriages. In any of these scenarios, the concept of being or not being a wife is at the heart of the matter and remains a defining aspect of a woman's life.

Everlasting love and marriage are encouraged by our culture. Media, film, theater and literature, each use the theme repeatedly, occasionally with a twist. If we flip through the pages of *People* magazine, we are brought up-to-date on who becomes whose wife and who divorces whom, losing wifely status in the process. Recently, many wives have sympathized with Nicole Kidman, who, according to the press, was relieved of her wifely duties by her then husband, Tom Cruise. It was big news when actress Julia Roberts embarked upon her second chance at being a wife. On July 4, 2002, she and beau, Danny Moder, exchanged vows at Roberts' ranch in Taos, New Mexico. The same day Candace Bushnell, creator of *Sex and the City*, and Charles Askegard, a ballet dancer, were married on a beach in Nantucket. In both cases the press noted that the wives are older than their husbands, Roberts by one year and Bushnell by ten years. While neither wedding was conventional in terms of style, becoming a wife is time honored and prescriptive. One of the more surprising marriages is that of Gloria Steinem, renowned feminist, who at the age of sixty-six married sixty-one-year-old David Bale in 2001. According to those close to Steinem, her role as wife is exciting and rewarding.

When we think of the complicity of wives, there is Lady Macbeth, who might have washed her hands of evil deeds but was the one who had the power, good or bad, to encourage her husband all along. One of the more tenacious wives throughout history is Anne Boleyn, who convinced King Henry VIII to divorce his first wife, Catherine of Aragon, and marry her. This action on the king's part established the Church of England and allowed divorce. Anne Boleyn's marriage to the king forever sealed the fate of the wife, allowing divorce to enter the equation, so that women are free to leave a disappointing marriage and allowing their husbands the same advantage. Any woman, in fact, is able to jockey for the position of wife and she may choose to go after a married man, rather than a single man. However, this does not guarantee that a wife will be happy with her lot once she achieves it, or that she is content with her role. Current fiction, film and television series emphasize the unmarried female, characters that yearn for the right mate yet would not necessarily be able to recognize him upon arrival. This present-day barometer of women and wives points to the fact that while many paths are available to women, marriage, for women under the age of sixty-five, remains the most glorified and sought after of them all.

Each decade since the end of World War ll has altered the face of marriage to varying degrees and in the process has transformed women's lives. Portions of the original wife have remained—those of committing to one man on many levels for a lifetime, the idea of raising a family together, the recognized unit of husband and wife. While every ten years has produced major changes in the role of the wife, what prevails is a new version of the wife.

A woman who married in l955 and is still a wife today has experienced different expectations in her role over the years. Yet she is also a product of her time, so she has not adapted to all aspects of the cultural movement as it applies to being a wife. It is doubtful that she was a working mother or that her children were in day care. However, this fifties wife has adjusted to wearing trousers, she orders take-out food, she does not necessarily baby-sit her grandchildren and she has become more outspoken and independent over the years. This woman is not the wife she was fifty years ago, and the result is not only alterations in an interpersonal relationship, but the influences and customs of wives throughout the years. Her daughter is the baby boomer wife, born between 1946 and 1960.

A baby boomer wife is someone who began with an ardent idealism, the myth of the perfect wife/career woman/ mother, and has come to face reality. A population of these women has divorced and remarried, while others have renegotiated their marriages. In contrast, younger wives, in their late twenties and mid-thirties, have an aspiration and a determination that is put to the test at the outset of their marriages. One interviewee expressed certainty that when she and her husband have children, the parenting and household tasks will be shared equally. Another young wife told me that she and her husband were putting off having children until they both had established their careers. In these peer marriages, irritants such as dirty socks left by husbands on coffee tables might not exist. There is less stereotyping of wifely responsibilities and more a sense that husband and wife are in it together.

The social implications of marriage are as present today as ever before. That is, once there are children, the marriage is interpreted as a unit, that of the family. Wives become their children's mothers; husbands become fathers. Once the children are grown, the couple is left to rewrite their lives as husband and wife. Some wives find complacency in their role as wives and mothers by mid-life and accept the compromises. As one interviewee confided, "My choices are limited now that I am in my mid-forties. I have been married twice and I have children in my second marriage. What else is there at this stage but to be married with kids. So I accept what works and what doesn't." By comparison, a present-day younger wife describes the inherent status and nuances of her role. "It isn't only if you have the ring or not, but how big the ring is and what cut it is. What kind of wife you are is obvious by how you dress, where you live. Your husband's job is important. By the time you have been a wife for a few years, it isn't about your job, although it might be great. By then, everyone is having babies. That's the next step." What is notably different about a young wife today is her sense of self. She is fearless in a material world, seeing herself worthy of her demands in marriage, and capable of working or not working, as she sees fit.

For centuries women have acquired status through marriage in small villages and in high society alike. Jane Austen's characters in her nineteenth-century novel *Pride and Prejudice* exemplify the preoccupation with becoming a wife. Not that these women had much else in their lives, but what is notable is that the emphasis on marriage has outlasted a society where women were relegated to marriage as their only accomplishment. By the time that Sue Kaufman's *Diary of a Mad Housewife* was published in 1967, a wife who aimed to please could go crazy, but reconciliation, saving the package of marriage, provided the optimal condition. Twenty-two years later, with the publication of Helen Fielding's *Bridget Jones' Diary*, we are led to a goal not dissimilar from that of the mad housewife, the dream of love with the reward of becoming a wife. Despite false starts and disappointments along the way, a woman is ultimately rewarded and her suffering as a single woman is put to rest.

Marriage remains the last linkage between church and state, the one personal connection recognized by government as having validity. Marriage is looped into our system so that it is enticing for tax reasons, if nothing else, to be married. As the boundaries and rigid rules of family give way to alternative lifestyles, including cohabiting couples, gay unions, single mothers, sperm-bank babies, divorced families, and stepfamilies, it is impressive that marriage exudes hope and glamour—a safe harbor. So while there are wives who search for a delicate balance as wives, mothers and working women, few report that the role of wife is not central at all times. To be a wife is to be chosen above all others, a commitment unlike any other, and while the odds are close to sixty percent that divorce is in the future, the idea of marriage is timeless and magnetic. The role of the wife represents attainment, so if it fails the first time, according to the U.S. Census, 2000, seventy-five percent will remarry again. There are 750,000 weddings every summer in the United States according to the National Center for Health Statistics; this fact alone is testimony to the lure and fantasy of love as signified by marriage.

The stories shared by wives, who, at every stage in their wifehood, speak to the issue of how central wifing is to their essence. In this quest, I have listened to myriad accounts of wives of disparate ages and social strata. It is apparent to me that every ten years of the last fifty years of marriage are unique, yet resonant of the past. By tracing the times in terms of social, cultural and economic lineage, I have been able to hear what is collectively similar about the American wife and what is specific to each decade. Thus, my research reveals what traditions the new wives return to and hold as dear as did their mothers, and how a twenty-first-century marriage is distinctive from marriages of the past.

Notwithstanding the choices available to women today, the idea of being a wife remains compelling and significant. Knowing what women know about marriage, they enter it willingly, seek it out and remain wives through decades of change within and outside the marriage. No heightened awareness, no accomplishments made by women can negate the desire to be a wife, although societal changes affect how a woman is as a wife. While I have read treatises about women and marriage with a negative point of view, renouncing the role of wife, my research indicates that a longing for wifedom, albeit filled with preconceived notions and challenges, prevails. This book notes the progress made and queries how the past configures into the future in an exploration of the newly defined twenty-first-century wife.

PART ONE:
TUMULTUOUS TIMES

Chapter One
The Social Implications of Marriage

I think that waiting to my mid-thirties to become a wife has worked for me," begins Meredith, who married in 1990 and has no children. "I watched my friends who married early and began families and a few of them were quite dissatisfied. I knew that I had to build up my career, but I began to worry by the time I was thirty-two that I had sacrificed my personal happiness for my work. I had watched my mother and my grandmother and the message was that being a wife was the way to go; there was no other choice. In a sense I dodged a bullet since I am not like my older sister who married right out of college and has been a wife in the same way that I have been a lawyer, with little else. In fact, her marriage was one reason I waited. I didn't want to be consumed with marriage, with being someone's wife to the exclusion of all else. I thought I'd be lost. But eventually it dawned on me that my sister had something I might want after all. And I began to feel alone in the world. I knew it was time to be a wife.

"I ended up living in the suburbs because my husband loves it here and I knew that the marriage had to succeed. I suppose that I have taken on traditional responsibilities, to some extent, but I am not as into it as my sister or my mother. The fact that my husband and I keep our finances separated indicates that I am a more modern wife, one who is not financially dependent upon her husband. Being a wife gives me status in a way. I can sense it when I go places, even a simple errand like going to the dry cleaners seems to get me more respect than in my single days; there is a part of me that likes that."

The social implications of marriage allow women in the twenty-first century to still believe in the intrinsic value of being a wife and to hold out for love-based marriages. The attainment of marriage for economic reasons endures, but in many cases the marriage is not only about financial security but also about comfort, sharing, stability, commitment, sex, and the ever-present hope of romance. Even if enough of these qualities exist, over time women can lose themselves as wives. Although this has been happening to wives for hundreds of years—the last fifty years in the life of the wife in America have created the emergence of the new wife, who is a culmination of the past and a step into the future.

A fifties wife had little, if any, economic freedom. Only in the sixties did the wheels of change begin to turn and the concept of career women begins to take hold. By the seventies, women returned to the workforce en masse and were able to declare an economic independence and prove their worth as workers. This was due, in part, to the feminist movement of the sixties, which questioned the worth of a traditional wife and encouraged women to express themselves and live up to their potential. However, the conflicting messages wives have received since this social revolution have caused them to seek financial security in their husbands at the same time that they have achieved earning power. That is, wives today have discovered their empowerment through the workplace, which informs equality in the relationship, all the while keeping a foot in the door of the convention bound marriage with the husband as the breadwinner.

From girlhood onward, women believe not only that being a wife is their future, but also that they will be deficient without that experience. Yet, unhappy wives do not always remain in a less than optimal marriage. In the past thirty years, with the increase in the divorce rate close to 60 percent, as reported by the U.S. Census, women have become disillusioned with their role as wife. Thus, wives will instigate divorce in three out of four cases, according to the latest U.S. Census. Nonetheless, the illusion of marriage is riveting for women in our society today. This illusion is that wifing is tantamount to success for females, that it protects, ensures and completes them. And while the goal of wife remains, the ingredients of marriage have altered over the past five decades. Thus, for many an ambivalent wife, or for a single woman, the image of wife continues to hold a strong appeal.

Expectations of the Wife

Women are distinguished by their marital status, with marriage, at least in Western culture, considered a safe haven often envied by single women. Implicit within our patriarchy is the concept of marriage as both a goal and a solution. To catch a glimpse of popular culture, one needs only to watch HBO's series *Sex and the City* to realize how four single women approaching forty deal with conflict about their future and what marriage means to them. Whether or not it appeals to these characters to be a wife, marriage appears foremost on their minds. While Miranda and Samantha have made unconventional choices— Miranda to have a child without a husband and Samantha to continue her promiscuous escapades, adhering to the theory of men as boy toys—Carrie and Charlotte, the more traditional characters, are determined to experience marital bliss, even if they stumble in their journey to this end.

"Both my mother-in-law and my mother were examples of excellent wives," begins Clara, who at fifty-three has been married for thirty years. "Neither of them worked a day of their lives but they both encouraged me to have skills and to be prepared for the worst. The worst, in their eyes, was widowhood or divorce. And my mother had told my sisters and me when we were small that only in the worst-case scenario did we need to have a career to fall back on. The worst-case scenario, of course, was to not get married, to not be someone's wife. That was something one had to avoid, so I married right out of college, but my two sisters did not marry until their late thirties.

"I believe I am a successful wife because I watched how my mother did it, not because I had any instincts of my own. My husband has not put me ahead of himself, but I have always put him ahead of myself. That is how I was taught to be a wife—to be dutiful and to put your husband first. My mother was a good role model but she was a horrible cook and that was the one thing I decided I wouldn't be. I made certain that I wouldn't make that mistake. So my husband has had the benefit of my cooking as well. I have sat at business dinners with associates and this has furthered his career. Throughout it all, I have maintained a successful career of my own, and that has been the toughest part to do and still be that perfect wife. I have run a household, been a corporate wife and had my own business. I see myself as tired but successful."

If women know deep in their hearts that marriage is taxing, and that being a wife is a form of self-sacrifice, they push this knowledge away. As a result, each woman enters the role with a generalized expectation that marriage is fulfilling and that being a wife is important. So even when this fulfillment eludes us, we hang on because there seems to be little recourse. Isn't this what we have been looking forward to since girlhood? Such disappointment seems pervasive and a collective sensibility of the wife. As the anthropologist Margaret Mead observed, no two couples are completely similar and no two people are brought up quite the same in America. In *Male and Female* she wrote, "Every home is different from every other home, every marriage, even within the same class, in the same clique, contains contrasts between the partners...." Being a wife, one half of the marriage pact, according to Mead, is a step toward building a family, and in America this family is hell-bent on the future.

An example of this focus on the children is seen in the recent film, *Far From Heaven*, starring Julianne Moore and Dennis Quaid. In this story of the postcard family of 1957, living in a white-bread suburb of Hartford, Connecticut, a husband's homosexuality causes the family to unravel. While Moore's character, Kathy, is the quintessential fifties wife, this discovery forever alters her view of the world, freeing her to face herself. For Quaid's character, Frank, the homosexual husband, his struggle and shame are tied into the family, what this will do to his wife and children. The film presents marriage and family as sacred and primary, and the children's progress is a given. Kathy is granted the chance to stop pretending to be the ideal wife and is liberated by the unanticipated event of her husband's abandonment. For the convention-bound wife, evolution comes slowly and as evidenced in this film, in unexpected ways, but with time can form a new standard.

If fifties wives felt strained because they were expected to be grateful for their lives, always on good behavior and rewarded for good fortune, few expressed such sentiment. Self-knowledge was far from the fifties wife's realm, and many of these women seemed prepared for little more than a pleasant, breezy existence. Children were seen, not heard, and husbands sat at breakfast tables reading the paper while eating scrambled eggs with their complacent offspring. The uniqueness of each family that Mead describes was minimized, everyone appeared the same and everyone was supposedly happy. This must have been more complicated for fifties wives than they conceded, and while their consciousness was not to be raised until the next decade, some wives must have sensed the false ring of their lives ahead of the feminist movement.

"I was married in 1953, and I knew that once I was married, I would no longer work," explains Tess, seventy-one. "I expected that we would move to a suburb, close to the town where my husband and I had grown up and that we would start a family. That was what couples did. There was nothing special about me as a wife, I followed suit. We all did, we had cookbooks and station wagons, small children and baby-sitters as often as possible. We wore skirts and heels to do errands and the world seemed very civilized. If anyone had a secret, it was swept under the rug immediately. Everyone acted as if they were pleased. I doubt we were expected to think and certainly not about the world, only about our children and our bridge games. I didn't dare ask myself how I felt about life, I simply accepted it and I felt that I was well taken care of, and so were my children. I ran a clean ship and the house was always in order. No one complained about a thing back then. It is only when I put my mind to it that I can admit it was not all that it was cracked up to be. I read library books for hours on end to escape, to be in someone else's world. My husband was not a very friendly man. At cocktail parties, I did all the talking and smiling, to enable him."

The genesis of female conjugal power was elusive for the fifties wife, but has been earned in generations to follow. According to Aafke Komter, in her essay "Hidden Power in Marriage," conjugal power has been defined as decision making in the marriage, responsibility for the home and expressing one's discontent. In traditional fifties marriages, the power was the husband's, and wives felt subjugated. Betty Friedan called it "The Problem That Has No Name," which is the title of a chapter in her book *The Feminine Mystique*. The "problem" was that women remained unhappy in their roles as mothers and wives all the while being told how lucky they were. Wives have been moving away from this lot in life ever since the women's liberation movement. By the mid-sixties, even a satisfied fifties wife was forced to open her eyes to the changing world. If she held onto a portion of her fifties wife mode, she could not help but be affected by change precipitated by the second wave of feminism, which occurred with the women's liberation movement of the sixties. By the mid-seventies, the fifties wife appeared more secure in the fast-paced society that offered women choices—in marriage and in the workforce. These wives grew less timid and more accustomed to life outside the house. Their marriages were altered by a new world for women, the fact that their children were grown and therefore no longer were the focus, and their own sense of autonomy. The sixties wife, who had never experienced the constraints that the fifties wife encountered, viewed marriage in another light as illustrated below.

Marguerite, sixty-eight, who became a wife in 1965 believes these were exciting of times for women and that marriage was a part of the experience.

"I must have been married in the right decade because there was so much going on by the time I married no husband would have dared to ask for his socks to be washed. I am an artist so I was always working but I never had to face the corporate world. That was a great advantage, I realize. I saw my marriage as a union between two consenting adults, and I never felt that I had to do something for my husband because I was his wife. I was very much in favor of women having their own lives and getting their due. My husband had started life as a very traditional man but he moved with the times and he understood my way of thinking.

"We were very much in love when we married and we have remained committed to one another. We had one child, which in the fifties would have made us seem selfish, when the norm was to have at least two children, one boy and one girl. But we were so comfortable raising an only child, and she did not have the rigid upbringing girls only five years her senior had experienced. Although I have been a wife all these years, I think of myself as having been lucky enough to be with the right person for my entire adult life. Any compromises that I made were about working it out in a partnership, not about manipulating or feeling somehow stuck somewhere. I believe that the sixties did this for women and I happened to be a product of the new mold, not the old."

The focus on love and marriage, a pervasive theme in Western culture, was idealized in the fifties, realized in the sixties, and part of a new blend of work and marriage by the seventies. A woman who became a wife in the seventies was zealous in her entry into the world, firmly disdaining the stereotypic fifties wife and the open, unstructured sixties wife. While love-based marriage mattered to the seventies wife, the "deal" she struck with her husband was the predecessor of egalitarian marriages to come. However, the seventies wife was ill prepared for the constant juggling of career and family life. Without models the seventies wife became a pioneer and with her pioneerism came a steep learning curve.

"Who knew it would be so hard to manage my life because I wanted something more than to sit home and make stew and watch my children grow," remarks Nina, fifty, who was married in 1977. "My husband, Douglas, and I agreed on everything. I remember that my mother begged me not to negotiate the marriage but I felt I had no other choice. How else would Douglas understand that I wanted to work and I wanted to have a family. No one had done that in either of our families, so I had to wing it; I had to work it out with him. But it wasn't as easy as I imagined it would be. I thought of myself as a capable person and it is true, I am. That is how I succeeded at mixing work and kids on a steady basis. On weekends I would simply collapse and on Sunday nights I could never sleep because I was so nervous about the week ahead, so guilty about the time I would lose with my children and husband because of my job. I think that for me, the romance was lost quickly and there were days when I couldn't remember why it had seemed so important to be Douglas's wife. I couldn't remember how I had loved him and had to have him. That is what wanting a job and kids will do to you."

In the 1980s, equal pay for equal work and sex discrimination in the workplace became the women's rights issue of the decade. In 1984, according to Jo Freeman in her article "Comparable Worth," this issue became a partisan issue, and the Reagan administration did not support equal pay for equal work. Working wives across the country, whether they were bus dispatchers or dermatologists, were up in arms. Wives were consumed with the concept of being treated fairly in the workplace and respected for their labor. While seventies wives had been thrilled with the opportunity to become a part of the workforce, eighties wives were ready to fight for their rights. Husbands and children were supportive but, in many cases, felt pre-empted by the wives/mothers who were preoccupied with equality for women.

The feature film *Ordinary People*, starring Mary Tyler Moore and Donald Sutherland, won the Academy Award in 1980. This event delivered the message that women can leave marriages in the aftermath of tragedy, or for other extenuating circumstances. The recognition came on the heels of the 1979 Academy Award-winning film, *Kramer Vs. Kramer* in which Meryl Streep's character, Joanna Kramer, found motherhood and wifehood to be too overwhelming and relinquished both responsibilities.

"Before the eighties, I wasn't certain that I could work and have kids," begins Martine, who in 1983 became the only female partner in a company. "I wanted to work, and I knew I had a chance in a family business. But working with my brothers turned out to be worse than I expected. I found them very unsympathetic to me, pay-wise and schedule wise. My husband agreed that if I wanted to work,

I might try something that really mattered to me. So I went back to school for my MBA at night, pregnant with my third child. People thought I was nuts. But my husband was very supportive, at a time when women were still waltzing around, shopping and taking care of their children. Then I landed another job and no longer worked for the family, which was a relief. I was one of the only working wives in our town and not everyone approved. It wasn't easy, but I persevered because it mattered to me. Sometimes Jack and I would fight about it when my schedule was very demanding and he felt like Mr. Mom. I had to be careful, because I wanted to preserve my marriage and to be his wife. My husband gave me mixed messages, such as 'it isn't fair that you aren't paid as much as the men in the company for the same job and why aren't you home in time for dinner?' But we got through this and our children all went off to college, and I have never regretted those difficult times, because in the end, I did get more than most wives get out of life."

Hillary Rodham Clinton's remarks during the 1992 presidential campaign resonated with all wives, from the fifties onward. She describes a woman's life as filled with a variety of roles; women in search of a balance. At this time, Hillary Rodham Clinton was approaching her role as first lady of the United States, and had served as Arkansas's first lady for twelve years. Although her style and causes have, at times, been considered controversial, many women admire her for her commitment to children's issues and to the betterment of women around the world. Her role in public service is emblematic of the nineties, a time when wives felt entitled to pursue their personal desires to work or not work, have children or not have children. But while working women of the past two decades had clearly made their mark, there was also a return to stay-at-home mothering and a pursuit of "pink-collar" jobs which allow women to work in female-dominated professions, such as nursing, teaching, and social work with fewer hours, for less pay and a more flexible schedule for their children's sakes. If the sixties wife saw this kind of work as too compromising, the seventies and eighties wives tended to agree. Yet for the nineties wives, who appeared to have come to a quieter, more diversified place in terms of wifing and mothering, pink-collar jobs offered an opportunity for independence without sacrificing their children's schedules. It also positioned the husband as the primary breadwinner and without too many childcare demands placed upon him. For the nineties wives, who were the first compromisers since the sixties, this was an easier route.

Danielle, who at thirty-five has been married for five years, doubts that her husband, if left to his own devices, would pitch in frequently or be as much of a participant in the marriage as she would like. Her hope is to achieve an emotional equality in the marriage, if not parity in terms of household and children.

"I told my husband, Rick, from the beginning that I wanted to share a life and be close. I warned him that I didn't want to be stuck doing dishes and that my job mattered. He agreed because he is not like his father and my friends' husbands are not like their fathers either. Still if we have a barbecue, my husband grills the steaks and I end up doing the dishes. That reminds me of my childhood. On the other hand, he will do the wash and watch our sons if I want to meet a girlfriend for a movie. My friends and I are not like my mother or her friends and we don't feel the need to be fluttering around the kitchen and cutting up fruit for company. I returned to work as the head librarian in a school when my younger son turned six months old. I take my job as seriously as Rick takes his, but let's face it, he makes more money. I don't feel that I have to be a good wife and do the 'right thing'. I don't cook big meals at Easter or Christmas, and I am not missing anything by not doing it. I suppose if my mom and mother-in-law didn't want to do all the cooking at holiday time, I would feel more responsible, but it is a different world today. I am off the hook since not as much is expected domestically of working wives today.

"I remind Rick that his mother did not work and that her job was taking care of the house and kids. I don't want to be saddled with two jobs and I don't want him to be saddled with two jobs either. My solution, many nights, is having take-out food. I don't place a premium on home-cooked dinners, I'm just trying to hold it all together, my marriage, my boys and my work. And this is with a job that starts at 9 a.m. and finishes at 4 p.m., which I purposely chose because of my boys."

Since our society is steeped in love-based marriages, the actual responsibilities of day-to-day life are not the draw for women. Rather, a young woman who has never been married is looking for romance and security. Romance represents the ethereal part of the relationship, whereas security concerns practical matters, such as finances and the mundane elements of life, necessary in order to be wives. The romantic component is applicable to women of any age, from early twenties to late in life. For a woman who is a widow or a divorcee and marries a man at forty-five, the delicate balance includes her relationship with her husband, her children, perhaps his children, his career, her career, and finances. This is without the pull of in-laws, which also exists, since increasing longevity renders us with our in-laws, or second set of in-laws, for many years of the marriage.

Romance may be difficult to sustain once the tugs of work and children set in. Young wives learn that weekends are no longer times for the couple to nourish one another but to do chores and catch up with the rest of one's life if there are no children. With children, there is the constant demand of child-related activities. A wife becomes disillusioned more quickly than her husband. Her expectations are higher and women are the true romantics, raised on the myth of happy ever after. "It is a coupled world—no one wants to be alone," remarks Dr. Ronnie Burak. "So while there is a false sense of security and permanence to being married, women opt for it in many instances." A wife might be disappointed in a lack of intimacy, and overwhelmed by the machinations of day-to-day life, but she still appreciates her position of wife in a coupled society.

"For me it is about romance but my husband has to be successful. And then we have to be equals," begins Emilie, twenty-four. "Jann, my husband, and I have been married for a year and I have been guided from the start by my grandma, not my mother. I watched my mother struggle to get it right with her work, her marriage, her kids and to have equal say with my dad, and she didn't do so well. I knew I didn't want to be like that. I paid attention from the start. I only dated guys who I thought had the same goals as I have, and came from what my grandma would call 'proper families'. I know how lucky I am to have found Jann, who shares my view of life and who wanted to settle down early too. He completely supports my ambition to dance in a ballet company, and so far I've been very lucky. My dream is to be a principal dancer, but having Jann as my husband means there is room for failure. He will not hold it against me if I don't achieve this goal. Meanwhile, he works in a family business and that makes us secure financially. My mother kept telling me to play the field, but I knew this was for me, and I wanted to be set. I just couldn't live without him and I wanted to be his wife more than anything in the world. I am not cynical like the women I meet who are in their thirties and I'm not worn out like my mom and her friends. We are ideally happy, and I know it will continue."

The expectations of the twenty-first-century wife who is starting out is surprisingly reminiscent of the fifties wife, in terms of the "good provider" requirement concept as expressed by Emilie. However, the new wife brings her own ambition to the table as well, the latest spin being that she does not necessarily have to pursue her goals, that marriage is the safe haven either way. Romantic men who can provide are the name of the game, and yet these wives have had all the advantages of achieving wives of the past thirty-five years. What is notably different from the fifties wife is the expectation that the husband and wife will be equal partners in the marriage. Reese Witherspoon exemplifies the kind of wifing that these young women envision: great husbands, personal success and freedom, babies while one is young and beautiful. Peer marriage, so important to the nineties wife, who struggled to implement it, appears to be a mainstay of the twenty-first-century wife, who may be callow, but steadfast in her belief. In the year 2003, the sentiment of the new wife, as illustrated by Brianna, is that romance is not only possible but imperative. This is what she anticipates in her marriage, and her conviction propels her forward.

Neglected Wives

As Rabbi Shmuley Boteach perceives the situation of the wife in his recent book, *Kosher Adultery: Seduce and Sin with Your Spouse*, wives, particularly once children are born into the marriage, begin to feel neglected by their husbands. The rabbi sympathizes with wives, believing that they are relegated to the task of "housekeeper, mothers, chauffeurs, and organizers." His advice is that the couple work hard on intimacy and sex, as a primary component of the marriage. Wives are often not ready to shift from wife as love object to the role of mother, forever altering the fabric of the marriage.

For Ginger, who became a wife at thirty-four, five years ago, romance was a priority. However, in her case, fewer expectations meant greater success. "I expected nothing when I married my husband because I wanted him to take me away from the single scene. Even in a small town, I knew that being single in one's mid-thirties was wearing thin. I fell in love with Harrie and saw him as a protector from the other life—the continuous single parties and bar hopping from town to town. I had no idea of how to be a wife because my mother died when I was small and my two sisters and one brother are all divorced. All of this made me doubt myself, so I wanted to be led around, I wanted to be wifely. I tried to please and in return for making breakfast, I expected to be romanced.

"What I have learned in these five years is that marriage is hard work and that keeping romance alive requires imagination and energy. Even if my expectations seemed lower than those of other women, who want financial security, a big house, fancy cars, several children and becoming spoiled, just wanting to remain special to my husband is a big deal. The thing was, I wanted desperately to be Harrie's wife—I wanted, love, comfort and trust. Whether we decide to have a child or not, which we have to address soon, we are a team. I ended up with a great marriage, and I like being married."

The determination of the wife has tremendous impact on the marriage. The emphasis on romance is the wife's way of playing out her role, while, as the philosopher Friedrich Nietzsche explained it, "What woman understands by love is... not only devotion, it is a total gift of body and soul...This unconditional nature of her love is what makes it a faith, the only one she has.... As for man...if there should be men who also felt that desire for complete abandonment...they would not be men." So the wife, from time immemorial, has been looking for a return of her love from her husband according to her version of love, a version that hardly seems possible. Our culture underscores the significance of romance not only in film, television, and novels, but in real life as illustrated by the media. The glamour couple who marries often graces the cover of magazines, preserving the belief in happy ever after.

The majority of wives who believe they were "in love" with their husbands when they married them and were fairy-tale brides describe a gradual loss of self, which results in the disillusioned wife. Perhaps it is not that women want to be lost in love, as a wife or in any kind of partnering situation, but that they feel swept up in the initial romance and are subsequently defeated by the reality, neglected in the long run. "It is easier for women in our society to be in a marriage than to lead the life of a single woman. The acceptance rate for married women is high. Yet committing to this institution is not easy," comments Claire Owen, psychologist. "No one stops to ask the important questions such as is this man right for me?" And over time, the young bride becomes the wife who questions her role in many ways.

"All of my friends hate their husbands after thirty years of marriage," Veronica, fifty-four, tells us. "They are tired of pleasing their husbands and their children. By now the children are grown and the marriage is about the husband and wife. But these women have felt that they got so little back. I know how it is, because I feel the same. There is no romance, no excitement, and the trade-off starts to look shabby. Then I ask myself where can I go, what benefit is it to me to be a single woman after years of being a wife? I've invested the best years of my life in this marriage and I have been unhappy for a long time. So I join the crowd, the crowd of wives who have been at it for over twenty-five years. We know all the tricks, all the ways to get somewhere and the places where you just cannot make progress. You end up having a separate life from your husband and coming together for social occasions, dinners with friends, weddings, and funerals. This way, I still have the perks of being a wife. I don't think about love any more, and I don't hate my husband any more. I'm just doing what works for me.

"I tell my girls not to rush into anything, and to enjoy their single days. I see that they are very idealistic and believe in the same fantasy I did before I was married. I guess we can't escape it. But I want them to understand what marriage is about, what the commitment is. I think I've been a good example, because even if I am no longer crazy about my husband, I am always a good wife. Dinner is prepared, and we take vacations together. We share our daughters; this is a bond. I just keep hoping it can be different for my girls. Here I am hoping they'll have terrific husbands and then I remember that was all my mother wanted for me. My girls had better enjoy their freedom now."

Mothers today, of various socioeconomic backgrounds, varying ethnicities and religions, encourage their daughters to wait at least until their mid or late twenties to marry. According to the U.S. Census, 2000, the average age of women marrying today is twenty-five. Much of the mothers' reactions to their daughters becoming young wives are the result of their own failed marriages and the belief that they themselves married too early or for the wrong reasons. But younger women might opt for early marriages anyway, for their own reasons. "Many younger women today recognize that if they do not marry soon after college or graduate school, they might not have the opportunity," explains Dr. Michele Kasson. "So while their mothers might have married early and ended up divorced or remarried, they are also aware of a generation of women who are in their forties today who are single and without children." The idea that life can pass them by, as evidenced by this group of women, has had an impact. Thus the fear of being an "old maid," a widespread fear of past centuries, appears to be on the rise again today.

My research indicates that only half of female college students want children, but almost all female college students want husbands. Thus, women are marrying at a younger age, exhibiting a mixed bag of idealism; marrying for love and companionship, with realism manifesting in the bird-in-the-hand theory. As *The New York Times* reporter Jill Brooke explained in her October 13, 2002, piece, "A Promise to Love, Honor and Bear No Children," many young women are marrying men who do not want children, often because they are older and/or have children from a previous marriage. While some wives are content with this condition, others change their minds and divorce later over the issue. Although there is always the possibility of renegotiating one's marriage, the best plan of action for women who become wives today, whether they are in their twenties, thirties or forties, is to take a realistic view of their future role and try to assess ahead of time what they can and cannot abide. In this way, a wife feels more in control of the situation and less forgotten later on.

The Marriage Gradient

Since the inception of the institution of marriage, the idea of the marriage gradient has existed. According to Lamanna and Riedmann, co-editors of *Marriages and Families: Making Choices in a Diverse Society*, the marriage gradient applies to women who "marry up" to improve their status in terms of age, education, and occupation. However, there are also famous wives who were married off to family advantage and brought status and class to their husbands. In some cases, the marriage gradient worked both ways.

For example, when Mary Todd of the famed and wealthy Kentucky Todds married Abraham Lincoln, it was obvious to many that she was able to elevate Lincoln's status. Lincoln, a poor and shabby self-made lawyer from Illinois, offered her less tangible goods but the promise of his ambition in U.S. politics. Both benefited in this case from sharing the same dream. Mary Todd influenced her husband to run for president and furthered herself in the plan. Lincoln was considered honest, crude and gawky while his wife was known as a sophisticated, stylish woman in a society where that mattered. When Jacqueline Bouvier married John F. Kennedy in 1953, his family's ambition for him to run for President was quite obvious. As the most sophisticated and glamorous of all first ladies, Jackie

Kennedy enhanced her husband. In return, she was considered a Kennedy but later, as a Kennedy widow, she discarded this identity. This occured in 1968 when Jacqueline Kennedy married Aristotle Onassis—a Greek businessman of great wealth and importance in another sphere. Both marriages elicited recognition and prestige, regardless of Jackie's own immeasurable worth.

Every day women employ the marriage gradient in their ambition of becoming a wife. Recently the gradient has taken a turn so that it is not only applicable to money and power, but to any arena that enhances the wife and, in some instances, her husband as well. The mantra here is, "I marry you for your family's connections, and you marry me for my family's money." In these cases, both spouses are enhancing themselves through each other's place in the world.

Homogamy, a marriage between partners of similar backgrounds, ethnicity, age, education, and upbringing, has always been a mainstay of American marriages. While the marriage gradient involves one partner improving her or his position through marriage, homogamy can be mutually beneficial to the parties involved.

"My marriage was more like a merger than a marriage," begins Nora, who at forty is divorced with three young children. "I know it wasn't arranged, but had my father and father-in-law been able to arrange a marriage, they would have come up with the same plan as David, my husband, and I did all on our own. He and I were the same socially and we both benefited from the marriage, equally, because our families were so similar and quite elite, frankly. At first life was very convenient because our backgrounds were alike, and we knew the same people and everyone had the same lifestyle. But ultimately, it wasn't enough. What I found was that being in a public life, charity dinners and evenings with friends, worked. But at home, privately, my marriage was a misery. I hung in for a long time because I wanted to be David's wife and because it made sense—we had so much in common. Our families were devastated when we broke up. Our divorce was not about money or custody, like most divorces. Instead, it was about failure, despite all of our sameness. I learned that we weren't so much the same. Rather, we were brought up the same way, in the same world. I don't know if, when I marry again, I would choose someone from the exact same socioeconomic bracket or the same religion, but it made sense to me the first time. I don't think I would stray far, but I would be more aware that just because two people seem the same, it doesn't guarantee they'll be happily married. There is a value system that has to do with the heart, not where you went to college or what your address was growing up."

In another socioeconomic setting, Deandra, at twenty-seven, also feels that the theory of homogamy has been encouraged by her family. "My parents are immigrants, and they made it clear to me that I would marry someone of our ethnicity and background. Only this husband would be better, he would have a college degree and a solid job! When I said I wanted to go to college, they agreed, as long as I still would marry in my early twenties. I feel very American, but when I am with my husband's family and mine, it is a throwback to another time. We have a good marriage and I like being his wife because we have broken some of the families' rules. We look like they want us to look and live in the neighborhood and do what we are supposed to do, but we have our own world, one where we share our feelings and our hopes. My mother thinks that I married up because my husband is an accountant but I think I married an equal. That's the part my mother doesn't get, so she believes that my marriage, through my husband, is how I'll improve my life. I let her think that—the idea is that I married someone from my background and religion, who makes more money than anyone else. That is the fantasy. For me, I am lucky because I am a young wife and I love my husband. Together we have a nice lifestyle and more than I ever had growing up."

Despite the marriage gradient's ongoing influence in marriages, the appeal of marrying someone who is close to us in terms of social class remains. While the late Princess Diana improved her status by becoming a princess, her own lineage was what enabled her eligibility for the title. Similarly, Queen Noor of Jordan and the late Princess Grace of Monaco were both American-born women who became royalty through marriage but came from fine American families. In these cases, the women have "married up," yet the unions offered the husbands prestige as well.

In the past two decades, husbands in the spotlight were more likely than at any time before to have wives who were distinguished in their own right. For instance, women with established careers or those who have some type of notoriety are appealing to men. There are couples in the public eye, a part of our fame-oriented society, where each partner has retained recognition to a different degree. Famous wives include Barbara Streisand, who in 1998 married James Brolin, an actor, and Cher, who married the late Sonny Bono in 1963. She divorced Bono in 1975, marrying Greg Allman the same year. They divorced in 1977. Cher's star power exceeded either spouse, although these men had attained notoriety in their own right. In a much-publicized courtship and subsequent wedding, Paul McCartney married Heather Mills in June of 2002. In this situation, Mills, with her own recognizable career, has attained greater fame as the wife of a former Beatle. Elizabeth Taylor was a wife eight times, twice to Richard Burton, and might consider husbands to be fungible. Taylor was often more famous than her husbands, who included Nicky Hilton, Mike Todd, Eddie Fisher and Senator John Warner. In each of these instances, wives are utilizing their prestige combined with the marriage gradient.

Homogamous Versus Heterogamous Marriages

According to Zhenchao Qian's research, "Breaking the Racial Barriers: Variations in Interracial Marriages Between 1980 and 1990," homogamous marriages, where partners choose one another because their race, religion, education and social class are similar, are as follows for couples between the ages of twenty and twenty-nine: white men and women are 98 percent across the board, African American couples show 92 percent for men and 97 percent for women, Hispanic couples are at 64 percent for men and 62.5 percent for women, and Asian American couples are 39 percent homogamous for men and 33.5 percent for women. These percentages show us that homogamy is still holding true for the majority of races.

"I was encouraged to marry someone from the same background as mine," begins Christina, who, at thirty-two, has been married for five years. "My mother and grandmother, my aunts, my mother's friends, were all married to men who came from the exact same kind of families as theirs. I suppose it makes it easier and I would not have strayed because this was so ingrained in me. But I wonder about this one boyfriend I had who was Jewish and very urban. I come from a small town and everyone in our family belongs to the same church and knows all the neighbors. My mother and grandmother advised me not to marry someone of another faith or ethnicity because life is tough enough, she said. I suppose it is true, although I believe that love conquers all. When I would go to the movies or see an exotic couple at a restaurant, I would imagine that I could have had a very different life.

"My husband and I are so similar and it is cozy this way, but not exactly exciting. Every ritual, every holiday, every word, is automatically understood. We attended the same junior college and I work at a doctor's office while he is in his family's business. When we have children there will be two sets of grandmothers to baby-sit and dole out their advice. In fact, there is plenty of pressure that we don't have a baby yet and there was pressure when I didn't marry Tom immediately, but dated him for a while. Basically my marriage is safe and a known quantity because it meets the family requirements."

In contrast to the theory of homogamy is the theory of heterogamy. In this kind of union, partners are of different religions, ethnicity, or social class. The film *My Big Fat Greek Wedding* is a tale of heterogamy; a woman of working-class Greek parents falls in love with an American WASP. Her family is dismayed at first, but the father decides that things will continue to be done the Greek way and the couple concedes.

According to Lamanna and Riedmann in their book, *Marriages and Families: Making Choices in a Diverse Society*, interreligious marriages do not work as well as when partners are of the same religion, especially once children are born. When it comes to interclass marriages, there are hypergamous marriages, those in which one partner marries someone with a better financial situation and hypogamous marriages, in which one of the partners marries someone of a lower financial sphere. In either of these cases, one partner comes with more than the other and the betterment occurs for the person who is in a lower income bracket.

Religion and race can be profound issues in a marriage, although there are wives who have not anticipated this. Over time and with the birth of children, religion becomes more significant for both spouses, than does race or ethnicity. According to the U.S. Census Bureau, 2000, interracial marriages have more than doubled in the past two decades. Any idealism at the start of being a wife, according to most women, wanes in interfaith marriages, once a child is born into the family. Many wives are conscious of the fact that belonging to another race or religion can separate a wife from her husband. What might appear interesting and bold at the start of the marriage can wear thin over time. In becoming a mother, a woman might realize how important her religion is to her. Whatever differences have made the relationship alluring can be challenged on a day-to-day basis. As a result, the marriages might not last.

On the other hand, there are wives who have converted to their husbands' religion for the sake of the marriage and family. Anna believed that it was her responsibility to change her religion for her husband.

"I became Catholic in 1985, when I was twenty-nine, because I wanted to be Dan's wife," Anna begins. "I was certain that I couldn't pull it off unless there were no obstacles and it looked like the right move. Being the same religion for all these years has given us a sense of being close and united. It has helped with our two children, too. The bottom line is that I wanted to be a full partner and the religion part of it mattered to my husband. That was why I converted. I didn't think about it as a way of giving in to him, or pleasing him, because then I would have resented it. And oddly enough, I have never regretted it or held it against Dan. There have been other sources of upset and friction between us, but I never felt like I had sold my soul or somehow compromised myself by becoming Catholic. I see this as a gesture of great importance and one that I am comfortable with. It made us alike and that is an advantage in this world."

Unlike Anna, Denise, at thirty-six, feels she is unable to change her religion or lifestyle for her husband.

"I married a man who was not like our family in any way. We are not the same religion or social class," Denise tells us. "I thought at first that this was not a problem and we have three sons. At first Tom went to my church and did things with my family. His family is working class and completely unlike mine. I was so in love with him that I didn't expect anything to get in the way of this. Sometimes, though, I have felt that Tom resents my family and the holidays at their house. We do not live as well as my parents, but we do not live like his parents live. There are all these undercurrents, a sense that somehow I am superior or that being from two separate worlds is insurmountable. Finally, I decided that we needed to see a counselor. I wanted my marriage to work because I love being Tom's wife. It has become clear to me now that he has made compromises for me. So I stopped asking him to go to church with the boys and me. I levelled with the boys and told them that this is not how their father was raised. And I distanced myself from my family a bit, because it was too much in Tom's face. Some days I imagine it would have been easier to marry someone who came from the exact same background as I did. I know I could not have done what my husband did for me and that is why I stopped asking him to do it."

While homogamy is still the more popular route for wives to take, the incidence of heterogamy is increasing. "This generation of women is less fearful of what is different, of the unknown," explains Dr. Ronnie Burak. "The process becomes simplified if everyone is the same, but couples today believe they can overcome this obstacle." As our society becomes more tolerant and expansive, the taboos of yesterday no longer hold up. The sixties, with its openness and rule-breaking approach, has left its imprint here as in other aspects of a wife's life and provided the option of homogamy or heterogamy. Acceptance and choice has increased with each decade since as it applies to the marriage gradient and choices in terms of social strata, religion, and race.

Finances in Marriage

"I was married in l979," Dee Dee, forty-nine, tells us. "I was twenty-six at the time and it was absolutely the right thing to do. It was the next step for me; no other path would have been acceptable, considering how I was raised. I married an attorney with the understanding that I would work as an occupational therapist until we had children. My job clearly had its rewards, but the job ahead of me was to be a wife and mother. I worked hard at being a wife for the three years until I had my first son. Often I felt confused, was I supposed to give everything up to be a wife and mother? I did that and I raised my two boys but once they hit junior high, I went to school and got my master's in social work. Now I have my own practice and I leave wifing on the back burner. My husband doesn't love this, but he has as much of me as a wife as I will permit. I've been in and out of the full-time wifing bit for years now and I want to remain Jack's wife, but not be submerged in it. I guess this is harder on him than on me. I identify with my role of wife, to a degree, and then I just had to have something of my own, my career and the freedom it brings."

The stay-at-home versus the working-woman conflict exists for women, particularly those who took time off in the early eighties to mother their children and be full time wives. Once the children are grown, the work world offers the chance to be independent of the home and children; as well as financially independent. This is alluring to these wives. However, wives who find some satisfaction of their own in the workplace, continue to struggle with the pulls of marriage and children. The question remains, how accommodating to her husband is a wife expected to be. As Simone de Beauvoir noted in l953 in *The Second Sex*, "...Destined to the male from childhood...seeing in him a superb being whom she cannot possibly equal, the woman...will dream of transcending her being..." And so the strikingly similar need of the wife crosses socioeconomic boundaries and individual interests. She hopes to be understood and appreciated, but not to be the second sex.

The wife is positioned against the backdrop of a society that respects marriage as the highest order of commitment. The societal construct of wife and mother is strong and influential. It is only as more and more wives have pursued their careers and dreams while maintaining their wifehood that tacit approval to do so has been won.

Since ancient times, finances have factored into the marriage quotient. Families were known to marry off their daughter to a wealthy family, thus marrying up, or to families of equal wealth and social standing. While today a dowry is not expected of an American bride, confusion when it comes to finances still exists for women. The conflicting message for women since the feminist movement raised our consciousness in the 1960s causes some wives today to seek financial security, regardless of their income. Thus, for the multitude of women in the workplace with real earning power, the image of wife as merely homemaker and helpmate is somewhat outmoded, but not forgotten. Many women who marry today believe that their husbands should take care of them financially, despite their own earning capacity. This return to the Cinderella complex, the idea that men are providers and women are saved by their care and provision, is not readily forfeited. "For so long women had no choice but to stay home and then they had the choice to work or stay at home," comments Dr. Ronnie Burak. "Just because women can be the breadwinners does not mean they want to do it."

"It is just as easy to marry a rich man as a poor man," chants the mantra of our grandmothers of a variety of backgrounds. And many wives today, regardless of their personal success, agree. The media feeds us incessant images of a material world and the glitter and glamour that goes along with it. This life can be provided for by husbands we are told. In real life and throughout literature and film, we observe the lifestyle of wealthy men and their wives. Some wives are bored; some are quite content.

In the film *Unfaithful*, a wife played by Diane Lane finds her suburban existence as wife and mother to be dreary enough to embark upon an extramarital affair, despite the perks of a successful husband, played by Richard Gere. Essentially, the husband is funding the wardrobe and travel for his wife's secret trysts. In my study of wives who stray, I found that although over 60 percent of all women engage in an extramarital affair, only 25 percent of these women marry their lover. That is, women are unlikely to readily relinquish the financially secure situation her husband offers to be with her lover who has lesser means.

"I know that my husband would not have been as appealing if he did not have this fabulous career as a surgeon," admits Jenna, thirty-six. "Bill and I have been married for twelve years and I have watched him build up his practice. I know how hard he works and how well he provides for us. I think he is a great guy, but I had sexier boyfriends and young studs before we married. I remember that it was more fun but the lifestyle wasn't anything like this, nor would it ever be. So some women might say that I was calculating, but I say that I married the whole picture, the man, his means, and the life we would have together. We have a ski house and a house in the suburbs. We travel extensively and I have someone who helps me at home with the housekeeping and the children. I am spoiled, I wear great clothes and have a leisurely life. I did have a successful career in marketing but I gave that up a long time ago. I wanted to do this, and when I'm bored, I resist having a lover. But I know that I won't resist forever. What I won't do is something stupid, like my friend who is involved with her best friend's husband. I will keep it clean and free of emotion. I will never leave Bill because I'm in it for the whole picture and I like living well. I do not want to be single, I want to be a wife."

Would a wife give up her lifestyle for a happier marriage, would a husband divorce a wife when he is so successful that he will pay an enormous sum in alimony and child support? My research indicates that 65 percent of wives are discontent in their marriages but feel that the financial rewards justify remaining. In addition, the world is not kind to single women, especially divorced women. Despite all the steps forward women have taken in the past thirty-five years, a stigma of the unmarried woman remains. This supports the goal to be married and remarried, why else do women place an emphasis on this status? So while a woman might marry for the first time at forty, the U.S. Census in 2000 reports that fewer women are marrying today than in the past. The average age to become a wife is twenty-five, and fewer women are having children. This is contrary to the traditional wife's path.

For a wife today, a career represents freedom, a use of talent, and is emblematic of personal success, but it is not necessarily tied into the marriage in terms of financial contribution. This way of thinking on the part of the wife represents her double standard; work is productive and self-fulfilling, but she is not the primary breadwinner. This is especially true of the baby boomer wives who have worked hard to "have it all". Thus, the career portion of the wife's life seems to be something that belongs to her and is not necessarily a contribution to the marriage. This wife's attitude towards shared money represents her awareness of the fifties notion of wives as being cared for by husbands in exchange for their responsibility to children and household while disregarding the seventies and eighties wives who were fiercely independent financially.

Many younger women are cynical in response to their mothers' less than successful marriages and their earning power. For the daughters of baby boomers who are wives today, there is a backlash that results in earlier marriages used as a retreat from their mothers' trajectories. Baby boomer daughters observed their mothers as imprisoned wives fighting hard to have it all, denying their constant fatigue and palpable disappointment in a process for which they had signed up. This generation of wives worked hard to reach their goals, not allowing the demands of domesticity to prohibit their success in the workplace. The baby boomer wife struggled to balance her life, to assuage her guilt. The role of the wife came third, after working woman and mother. Husbands felt unsupported and marriages suffered. An egalitarian marriage began to seem more and more imperative for working wives. While they fought hard and long to achieve it, many failed in their attempts. Whatever money these women made, whatever prestige they gleaned, was hard won and they paid an emotional price for it.

"I remember how my mother raced to the office in the morning, raced to school to pick me up, raced home to make phone calls before cell phones existed and never looked relaxed," recalls Ingrid, who, at twenty-six, has been a wife for one year. "That was why I wanted to study liberal arts and did not know what I wanted to do after college. Because my mother's focus made her into a lousy wife. She married at thirty, got pregnant at thirty-four and worried she was too old for her day. I was her only child; she had no time or room for me, so whatever I could get from her, I took. My father and my mother never had any time for one another, and it's all because she was a working wife more than because she was a working mother. There was time for me, although it felt squeezed in but there was nothing left for my father. My mother traveled a lot because she worked for a bank. My father also traveled. It was like they were ships that passed in the night. I saw their teamwork when it came to me, but in every other aspect of their lives, they were on their own. I was the only common thread.

"I met my husband, John, when I was nineteen years old. My mother urged me to meet other guys, to play the field. She kept saying that marriage could be in the future, way in the future. I wanted to marry early because I wanted the security; I wanted to know that he wanted to be married to me now, not later. And I am accomplished; I ended up getting a graduate degree in business. I don't think it's at the center of my life, though. Instead, I want this marriage to be at the center. I like knowing I can work in a corporation or a business and that I can succeed. I don't have to do it like my mother and her friends did though; I don't have to prove anything to anyone. I can sit around and eat bonbons, because I am John's wife. I have more choices, but my mother worries I have married too young and have limited my options. I'm just not convinced that the road she took as a wife was so smart or that she's such a winner."

The young wife has interpreted the trajectory of her mother's life as a wife in terms of finances, among other issues. These young wives, between their early twenties to early thirties, are hesitant to repeat their mother's pattern when it comes to work. Yet the media influences remain constant and powerful; the implicit message is one of entitlement. They are entitled to successful husbands and the choice to work or not work, to do as they please without pressure or expectation. The U.S. Census in 2000 reports that today more women attend college than men and that 62 percent of married women were in the labor force by l997. According to research on the stability of marriage, conducted by Arthur J. Norton and Jeanne E. Moorman, in their essay "Current Trends in Marriage and Divorce Among American Women", marriages are more stable for women if they are in their twenties than in their teens when they marry, and being over thirty provides even a bit more security. Based on my research, young women today are more inclined to marry in their twenties than the generation before them, and less compelled to have a career or to keep going at it once they are married with children. Younger than Generation X, the baby boomer daughter, known as Generation Y, who becomes a wife will opt to not work and often deliberately seeks out a husband who provides. Curiously, these young wives' attitudes toward work and money are a mixture of their mother's philosophy, make something of yourself and their grandmother's experience, make your home your domain and be catered to and cared for.

"I am marrying Dennis in two months," sighs Reba, who is twenty-four. "We have gone to college together and both studied to be in the police force. My mother worked her way up as a secretary and became a supervisor in her job. But she was always so exhausted when she came home and she didn't care about much. She was influenced by the women's movement but definitely she was working class. She left us to fend for ourselves because she had little choice. I liked that she worked, but our father worked another shift and eventually he left; probably he couldn't take it any more. Still, I saw my mother as the good wife, a tired wife. And why not have it better than that? So I'm equipped to work and I'm trained to work, but I don't have to work. That is my view of it. I don't want to be like my mom; I don't want to be exhausted and then alone. I can do it and I don't have to do it. Dennis will make enough money and I wouldn't be bringing in the same amount anyway because that is how it is for women. This way I can count on Dennis, more like my grandma taught me. She was a lot more relaxed than my mom."

Although the traditional breadwinning husband is more accepted today than in the past three decades, the strides made by women reflect a woman's opinion that she deserves an equal partner in all decision-making in a marriage. In many cases, the new wife questions her predecessors who marched in droves to their place in society's nine-to-five workday. These wives came home too tired to cook dinner. Yet, as wives and mothers they acquiesced to the second shift even though they worked away from home as long and as hard as their husbands. An article by Laura Shapiro, "The Myth of Quality Time" in *Newsweek* May 1997 reported that women's household responsibilities had not changed although they were full-time working women. Our culture advocates for wives in the workplace. However, wives were without a clue as to how to get men to change their behavior as husbands wielding their grandiose power of sole breadwinners. The working husband continues to shoulder the stress of his financial responsibility to his family, along with the ego gratification it brings. We cannot deny that supporting a family financially is demanding and enervating yet satisfying.

The expectation that a man would be served his dinner by his wife was understandable in the early sixties, but by the eighties, when a wife was as well educated as her husband and as well paid in some cases, the expectation of serving dinner did not cut it for her. It was a slow dawning on the part of the husband, however. As Glenda, a seventy-year-old wife, views it, "The men don't change their way of thinking and acting. And that is why the progress has been so slow for the wives."

Chapter Two
The Fifties Wife:
Kitchens and Carpools

I was a typical fifties wife for five years of my life,"
begins Diana, who at seventy-two recalls her years as
a young bride. "I married right out of high school without any thought to my education. While I had friends who
were in college or junior college for a period of time, it was
only to pass the time before marriage. Once we were married, we became the ideal homemaker and housewife, soon
after to be the perfect mother of beautiful children. I really
believed that my house had to be like a television commer-
cial house, spotless and immaculate. It occurred to me years
later that this was the stuff that makes women crazy; this
standard that can't be met and can't be kept. But during my
years as a fifties wife, I was very busy taking care of my husband, house and children.

"Meanwhile, our neighborhood breakfasts and shopping
sprees couldn't fill all of our time once our children went
off to kindergarten. We were left alone at home, with our
children gone all day, and that was when it began to sink
in. Since we were taught not to complain, we were quiet.
We kept up with our houses and our superficial lunch dates
and afternoon cars games. We acted like life was complete
and were totally appreciative of our husbands as cash cows."

The post-war wife was expected to create a wonderful
home environment for her husband and children. The wife

had a very specific role in this time period and was expected to be pleased with her lot in life. Not expected to challenge her role as wife and homemaker, she replaced any intellectual pursuit with P.T.A. meetings and volunteer work. The media had a strong influence upon women in this decade and was reflected in how wives conducted their lives. This era, as described by David Halberstam in his book, *The Fifties*, was a time of "general good will and expanding affluence." Americans were taught to believe in what was "reflected back at them." This included information gleaned from books and magazines, and from television, which held the greatest power of all. Television shows, family sitcoms, such as *Leave It to Beaver* and *Father Knows Best*, emphasized home and family as the ultimate contentment.

The set example was that of home and hearth, and implicit within this theme was the idealized wife. The coupling of American women was a goal, and to be a single woman was to be incomplete. With this focus, women became wives who were encouraged by the media to have the latest electronic appliances, including wall ovens and refrigerators. These were considered status symbols and wives believed they needed these things integral to their role of wife. Again, television was a powerful influence through its advertisers, who directed their attention to wives, their primary target, convincing them of what was required in their impeccable homes. This way of thinking pervaded the decade. No one questioned the cultural standard of the fifties wife, or her investment in the technological age, vis-à-vis her state-of-the-art kitchen. There was an increasing emphasis on buying goods, thus unwittingly contributing to the growing materialism of Americans. It was not until Betty Friedan published *The Feminine Mystique* in 1963 and described the fifties wife as being held prisoner in her sparkling kitchen of her spotless home, that women came to question the status quo.

Romance and Sexuality

The age-old concept of romance equalling love and marriage pervaded the fifties, mixed in with a puritan ethic of virginity and a chaste quality to the wife. Fifties wives did not have as many requirements as wives have today and there was no heightened sense of self. The fifties wife's job was to run the home, care for her husband and her children, that was her realm. Since the majority of fifties wives did not work, they did not need a husband who understood their careers. If any expectation of the wife included romance in the early stages of marriage, the underlying message was that romance existed during the courtship, with love as a practical means to an end. The end result, what won the day, was marriage, and with marriage came an expectation of sex to procreate and satisfy one's husband. Romance was understood to be found in gestures as prosaic as red roses on Valentine's Day, accompanied by a Hallmark greeting card.

In the film *The Hours*, Julianne Moore plays a fifties wife who is dissatisfied with her lot in life and finds her husband lacking despite his feeble gestures at romance. This is manifested in a brief scene where he makes breakfast and brings her flowers, although it is his birthday, not hers. The wife finds not only a dearth of romance in her marriage, but suffers from a general and non-specific melancholy. She defies the standards of the fifties wife because she has all that she could possibly expect—a doting husband, a devoted little boy, and a second pregnancy underway—yet finds all of it so unsatisfying. Had her husband been more romantic would this character have stayed and not walked out, devastating her husband and son, and forever rejecting her baby daughter? An anomaly for the decade, Moore's character shows us the dark side of a frustrated wife, who cannot be wooed by romantic gestures or a comfortable life.

What is interesting about the Julianne Moore character is that there is no specificity to her unhappiness and not a drop of sexuality to her role as a wife. Perhaps this is because wives, by definition, were not sexy and because there was no psychology attached to the role of wife in the fifties. After all, marriage was what every woman strived for, and the notion that it might be less than optimal had yet to be recognized. In fact this would not be realized until future decades, catapulted into recognition by the sixties wife and the feminist revolution. A fifties wife had a mission, and digging into her past to understand her future was not a part of this mission. Nor was it possible for a fifties wife to be contemplative about her marriage, contrasting and comparing it to other experiences, either positive or negative, because no other experiences existed for her. The fifties wife married at nineteen or twenty and essentially began her adult life at that point.

"I was fortunate because I was madly in love with my husband when we married in 1956," begins Cynthia, who married at twenty. "I had gone to high school with Ray and we had been high school sweethearts. I knew I wanted to be his wife and it was romantic and also very heated sexually. We were expected to be virgins when we married and that was why we married early, in order to have sex. You could be sexy with your husband and that was okay, but not beforehand. Everyone worried about birth control. No one could become pregnant without being married, and everyone counted the months when someone had a child not a year into a marriage. Everyone was watching everyone else to see whom he or she married, where they lived, when they had children. There was nothing else to think about, really. It was like a contagion; everyone wanted to be married. After twenty-one, you were over the hill. It put such a limit on women; few of us finished college. Some of my friends attended Katherine Gibbs secretarial school. Both secretarial school and college were just a place where women bided their time until they were married. And we wanted to be married because we wanted to have sex.

"A big part of being married was the sex. You were only supposed to sleep with one man and that was your husband. The girls who slept around, and there were plenty of them, were considered tramps and promiscuous. Sure, they became wives too, but they did not pretend to be virgins. I would say that 90 percent of the women I knew were virgins when they married because our mothers taught us to save ourselves for our husbands. We were young and married and wanted lots of sex. We also expected a quality of life, provided by our husbands. That, and sex, made it important to be a wife."

A fifties wife's physical desires were legitimatized by marriage—a bride was a virgin and thus could never be a whore. Sex was circumscribed by marriage for the "good girl/young wife". Romantic love for women was sexual and passionate, and husbands were, naturally, the sole source of this. The good news about romantic love as observed by Robert J. Sternberg in his book, *The Psychology of Love*, is that romantic love will become compassionate love over time. "Passion may be replaced over time by long-term and deeply felt commitment," he notes. For the fifties wife, the sex and passion were important, as evidenced in Cynthia's interview above. Yet it was only a part of the package. While compassionate love sounds like an alternative as one ages, a fifties wife discovered that romantic love was interrupted by her duties as wife too soon. The inevitability of being wife and mother/ caretaker and organizer took over.

The other factor for wives in the fifties was a lack of birth control. Margaret Sanger, who was in her seventies in the fifties, had spent her entire life fighting for a woman's right to control her own body. However, the Pill had yet to be discovered, and diaphragms had an abysmal success rate. Wives were taught to want to have babies, it was an important purpose, but the fact that there was no way to control how many children one had and how often one could be pregnant was a deterrent to sexual freedom. Once a wife became a young mother, her view of sex and the end result was altered. The explicit message was that sex was for the beginning of marriage, when one was not only young but also compelled, before the business of real life set in. The fifties wife was feminine at all times, and this mattered more than being sexual. Part of being feminine was encompassed by sexuality, if only designated for the marriage bed. But being feminine meant being a fixture at home, not only a superb wife but also an exemplary mother.

"I loved being a wife," begins April, who married in 1956 at the age of twenty-four. "I was a bit old for those days, to be a bride and a virgin, and my mother acted like it was a huge relief to marry me off. No one stressed sexual relations or any kind of intimacy with my husband, not my mother, not my older sisters. Instead, I was supposed to be a caretaker and I was supposed to be 'wifely.' I was very happy because my husband was considerate of me and we had very traditional roles. But it wasn't sexy; it was never about sex. Nor did I feel that I was a sexual being. I was a wife, what my mother had raised me to be.

"My husband and I lived in a small town for our entire marriage. In the fifties, we did what couples did until we had children. We would go out on occasion with friends and I worked as a nurse in a doctor's office. I would meet my best friend during lunch break, she was a secretary, and we would giggle about our husbands, mostly about how cheap they were and about how often they wanted sex. Then we both got pregnant, and we did what wives did once they had children. We quit our jobs and watched our babies and clipped recipes from the local paper and from *McCalls'*. Sometimes I would get a baby-sitter on a Saturday night when my three children were small, and my husband and I would go to movies or to dinner with friends. But not often, because we really couldn't afford it. My life was about taking care of the house and making life comfortable for my husband and the children. I never complained that I was tired and I was always available to my husband for sex. In truth, I was exhausted, and I couldn't be sexy if I had wanted to be, if I was supposed to be. When I look back on that time, it feels like I was being told what to do and how to act. It was lucky for me that I wanted to act that way, like a conventional wife, someone who does her duty gladly. But sex wasn't stressed as sex; it was just a part of being a wife."

The message from television and film was that one could either be a good wife/ feminine and pleasing or a sex kitten/ feminine and forbidden. Television offered the fifties wives examples such as Harriet in *The Adventures of Ozzie and Harriet,* a sexless, sterile sort of wife whose efficiency and subordination in the day-to-day grind of life was impressive. Another show featured Lucille Ball as a wacky wife whose interesting spin was that she was not happy in her lot as housewife and yearned to be a movie star. Her husband, on and off screen, Desi Arnez, played a musician in the show, who wanted "a wife who's just a wife."

It was Hollywood that offered the complexity of sex kitten versus wife, especially in films featuring Marilyn Monroe and Kim Novak. Marilyn Monroe played the sexy roles with a certain vulnerability that had universal appeal and achieved stardom in such films as *The Seven Year Itch* and *Some Like it Hot*. In her personal life, her short marriage to Joe DiMaggio failed because DiMaggio sought a conventional wife, not a sex symbol. But Monroe was unwilling to trade her fame and ambition for home-cooked dinners, despite her feelings for her husband. Although Kim Novak rivalled Monroe, she never achieved the same status. As Jackie Byars describes it in her essay "Struggling Over the Feminine in the Star Image," Kim Novak represented a fifties woman in terms of femininity. Novak starred in successful films such as *Picnic*, *Pal Joey*, and *Bell, Book and Candle*. While the image of a glamorous fifties star might have been evolving, it did not sway the fifties wife into adopting this mode. If anything, it drove home the fact that movie stars such as Monroe and Novak belonged in another world.

The Hollywood star who was popular with the fifties wife was the all-American Doris Day. In retrospect, the idea of Doris Day and Rock Hudson as a perfect "Hollywood couple" seems ludicrous, since we now know that Hudson was gay and thus posturing in those films. Yet the image projected in the fifties in the film *Pillow Talk,* for example, offered a happy ending for a non-married working woman. Doris Day portrays a single woman who in the end discovers romantic love, after a series of misunderstandings and humorous episodes. Rock Hudson plays an impressively eligible man, who becomes the object of her affection. That these two find one another is a promise of marriage for the audience, in keeping with the fifties tradition.

In the squeaky-clean climate of postwar America, the wife as homemaker, social secretary, and mother left little room for sexual desire. If a wife felt dissatisfied, or worse, without personal satisfaction, she kept it to herself. The message was that any kind of stress, sexual or otherwise, should be pushed under the rug. The dire results of such efforts on a wife's part can be seen in the recent film *Far From Heaven*, starring Julianne Moore. In the case of Moore's character in this film, her husband's preference for men could not be hidden, despite her efforts to do so. So this fifties wife, beautiful and composed, suffered from sexual rejection at a time when wives were available as their husbands' required it. Early in the film, Moore's character invites several women friends over for a card game. At this gathering, the women confide in one another how many times a week each needs to have sex with her husband. It is obvious that these women believe that they are servicing their husbands, and that it is a chore. While the others giggle, Moore's character squirms. The writing is on the wall, and soon after, her husband, played by Dennis Quaid, rejects her for a man, a totally foreign and unacceptable alternative in the fifties, where no one lived outside the box in any way.

If a husband had an affair with a woman, that was horrid enough. However, it was understood that it was purely for sex, and usually on a business trip where there would be no fuss or evidence. Some wives even understood that they were not sexy enough and that was the only reason for a husband's tryst. But rarely was this discussed—the pretense of fidelity was too important to a fifties marriage. This was before husbands divorced for their mistresses' sake, which would occur in the decades to follow. The thought that a husband would leave his wife to be with another man, as shown in *Far From Heaven*, was absolutely disastrous for the family in mid-century America. This is not because husbands with such longings did not exist, but because society did not permit them to exist.

When Alfred Kinsey came out with his shocking survey of sexuality in America, his findings seemed contrary to the image projected by the happy couples that abounded. Kinsey reported in his study, *The Sexual Behavior in the Human Male*, that 80 percent of married men engaged in extramarital sex. This book was followed in 1953 by publication of *The Sexual Behavior in the Human Female*, which reported that 29 percent of married women admitted to marital infidelity. In the patriarchal climate of the fifties, where husbands were heads of households and wives secondary, the straying husband was somehow excused. But the notion of a cheating wife was antithetical to all that a wife stood for: devotion, loyalty, altruism and repression. Not surprisingly, the percentage of straying wives shocked the public and disavowed women of their gratitude and total satisfaction in marriage. The feminine wife who had become a sexy adulteress contradicted all that the fifties wife represented. This conflicted with Hollywood, television, and women's magazines, and with the society at large, which emphasized the dichotomy of wife/mistress. It was difficult for the public, women and men alike, to comprehend Kinsey's study. As Billy Graham declared of Kinsey's research, "It is impossible to estimate the damage this book will do to the already deteriorating morals of America."

"I had an affair from the beginning of my marriage because I was unhappy," begins Rachel, who was married in 1957. "In another era, I would have left my husband but in the fifties, no one got divorced. You toughed it out; you made a life of it. But there was very little sex in our marriage and I wanted more. The rest of my marriage was okay, not great, but we had these two children and a life. My husband was moderately successful, so it came down to sex. I had married very young, at twenty, and I expected something more.

"My lover was a friend's husband, since I knew no other men outside our circle. We lived in a middle-class suburb and had these potluck dinners at each other's houses on Saturday nights in the summer, and one thing led to another. I wasn't the only one who was fooling around. We all seemed to be restless, and somehow another man made a difference. So even if as a wife I wasn't supposed to be sexy, as someone's lover, I could be. I liked that, even though I knew nothing of sex; none of us did. We were naïve, young married women with our lives ahead of us and plenty of rules. The rules were all about being a good wife, a good mother, a good girl. I guess I rebelled. The affair lasted a long time but I never left my husband. I felt guilty at times but I was never strong enough to go. Where could I have gone anyway?"

While the fifties wife lacked the introspection of wives in decades to follow, she did have a beginning level of awareness of her own needs. However, not many wives at the time fully recognized their sexuality, nor were they encouraged to do so. Romance was not a part of family life. The wife's responsibility was to care for a husband, home and children. The consequences of expressing one's longings were implicit, and wives, good girls that they were, steered away from this unknown path, remaining aligned with what the culture allowed. Yet, as Jessica Benjamin notes in her book, *The Bonds of Love*, mothers are supposed to be nurturers, and to be appreciated as mothers, not as sexual beings. The fifties wife was caught in a web of expectations that limited her own voice and desires.

Financial Inequality

The majority of fifties wives did not work for a living, nor was this expected of them. If a wife did work, it was out of economic necessity, and other more fortunate wives/ mothers either frowned on her or cast their pity her way. The concept of combining career and marriage was unthinkable and for the most part, women who worked were single. Single working women bore the stigma of not being wives, and therefore had to support themselves. In this way, the societal message of the fifties was not much more advanced than the turn of the century world of Lily Bart, the lead character in Edith Wharton's novel *The House of Mirth,* which was published in 1905. Lily Bart was reduced to life as a working girl because she did not make the right choice to marry and therefore attain a husband/provider, and a place in society. For Lily, work was beyond being a compromise, it was stooping socially and without dignity.

For those wives who had worked during the Second World War, the return of their husbands from the war and the subsequent economic growth made it so that both partners did not have to work. According to David Halberstam in *The Fifties,* eight million women entered the workforce during the war, but two years after the war, two million women had lost their jobs, replaced as the men returned. Not only did society discourage working wives, but there were few career choices for women who wanted to work. The circumstances that required a wife to work were almost shameful in the cookie-cutter climate that enveloped the fifties. The acceptable route for a wife who worked was to leave her job once she became pregnant and begin her destiny, that of raising her children.

But few questioned their isolation. When the ideal fifties family had left the city for a split-level house in the suburbs, young wives, filled with sexual energy and talent, found themselves hidden away, relegated to carpools and coffee klatches, where they shared recipes for dinner casseroles. No confessions were shared among women. Rather, there was a pretense of life as happy, fulfilling. Talk of money was virtually absent as well because it was assumed to be everywhere, every wife' s husband brought enough home to make life comfortable. Although there were different social strata, money was not a concern because husbands had substantial work and the economy was booming.

"I depended upon my husband financially from the time we had our first baby," begins Agnes, who married in 1955 and had her first child a year later. "I had worked as a teacher, but I knew that once we had a baby, I would stay at home. I took good care of our house and I never said a word to my husband about how much money he gave me for food and errands. The only problem was when I wanted to shop. He saw no reason why I needed nice clothes to be alone with a baby all day. I sort of ignored him at first and made do. When my mother came to town to visit, she would take me shopping and she warned me not to be demanding of Stan in terms of extras, like a few new pieces of clothing each season. Three years later, my second son was born, and that was when I realized I had to be resourceful to make ends meet. I would buy meat on sale at the butcher and I skimped on everything else. I practically starved myself in order to have enough food for everyone else. All this so that I could buy myself a hat and some pretty sweaters. Stan was the one in control. He would go out with the men in his office for steak dinners and for drinks at expensive places but he wouldn't be easy on me about shopping.

"When our first two children entered grade school, I found myself out in the world again. Not as a teacher, but as a mother who dropped her children off and attended school meetings and bake sales. I had to look a certain way. I asked my husband, who had been promoted at work about my working part-time. We lived in a four-bedroom house on the right side of town and the mortgage was small. We took a trip as a family once a year and at Christmas; everyone got lovely gifts. I thought that Stan was being unfair about my wanting to work, so I found a college student who would watch my baby daughter and I went back to teaching. I wanted my own money. I believe that some of the other mothers in town raised their eyebrows at me and maybe whispered behind my back. But I was a teacher and that worked so well with the children's hours that they couldn't damn me too much. The best part was that I had money for myself. I kept it separate and Stan continued to pay for our family. For years I harbored a grudge against him because of how he treated me over money, especially when he made enough to help me out. On the other hand, I loved not being one of those women who whispered at some school meeting that her husband wouldn't give her any money to spend."

Agnes' independence and survival techniques are impressive, particularly at a time when most wives would have suffered in silence without such resourcefulness. According to my pool of interviewees, many women during the fifties became skillful at finding ways to get spending money from their husbands without returning to work. Others had husbands who were less controlling than Agnes' husband. Yet the power of the husband because he was the breadwinner cannot be denied. As Dr. Ronnie Burak views it, "Enough women during the fifties were happy to do just what they were told. Some were content and some were unfulfilled but certainly there were not many decisions to make. The rules made it easier, these wives knew the way it was supposed to be."

Consistent with Dr. Burak's remark is Lillian's experience as a fifties wife. However, in contrasting Lillian's role with Agnes', we see that the way one's freedom is played out depends upon how the husband reacts to his wife and the relationship the couple share.

"I was married in 1950 to a man whom I had loved since grade school," begins Lillian. "We were in a rush to be married, and being his wife was all that I cared about. I didn't think so much about having children, like my sisters did or some of my friends, I just knew it was part of the deal. Unlike my friends, we waited for four years before our first child was born and traveled quite often for his business during those years. My husband's family had more money than mine, and he had grown up in a beautiful home. He worked with his brothers and they did quite well.

"From the beginning he was generous with me. I was a conventional wife in every way. I did not have a checkbook until 1972, depending upon Harry for anything that had to do with money. I did not work although I had some talent as a painter. I did it as a hobby. It was clear to me that Harry wanted me at home and I accepted this. In a way there was a trade-off, he took me wherever I wanted to go and bought me whatever I wanted—clothes, bags, jewelry, shoes—before our children were born and afterward. In exchange, I was a really good wife. I don't think I was as quiet as some of my friends, not quite as docile, but somewhat spoiled because we had a housekeeper. But I was pretty honest about what things cost and what I wanted. I never had to sneak around to buy a dress. I also knew that it was not a hardship for Harry to support me in this style. He was a very successful businessman and his family had money. In exchange for his generosity, I ran a tight ship and our home was an oasis for him."

Lilian's marriage, to an extent, represents the marriage gradient, discussed in Chapter One. Although Lillian speaks of romantic love for her husband, it also seems a plus to have "married up" in terms of finances and therefore status. While her role as a mid-century wife was not altered by this fact, her wifely duties did not include housework and cooking. She was less a prisoner of the home and she was indulged materially, which she acknowledges. But the home that she describes as an "oasis" was definitely a significant aspect of marriage in the fifties, whatever one's financial status. Although Lillian was given more money to spend than a wife whose husband earned less or whose husband was less generous, still the fact is, fifties wives depended upon their husbands for economic security.

The husband worked until five o'clock, the idea of being a workaholic had not yet infiltrated the culture, and returned in time for a family dinner. The wife was delighted to have her husband home from his busy day. Her life, if stressful with children, their needs, homework, after-school activities and the responsibility of running the house, was not to be emphasized once her husband walked through the door. Instead, the husband's reward for his work was to be appreciated by his wife and family. "The Good Wife's Guide", often attributed to Helen B. Andelin's book, *Fascinating Motherhood*, and just as often relegated tot he urban legend junk heap, made the following suggestions. The wives were expected to cook sumptuous meals for their husbands, and creating these meals was a way to show their care. The wives were to appear attractive and upbeat when their husbands arrived home from work. The children were also expected to be exemplary, scrubbed, and smiling for their fathers. Even if a wife wanted to discuss certain immediate matters with her husband, she was expected to defer to his choice of conversation. All of this was because he was the "master of the house."

A fifties wife was encouraged to be subordinate because she was not economically independent. The children and the wife/mother were a showcase for the husband's success in the world outside the home. The wife was expected to excel in the microcosm that her husband retreated to after a day of toil in order to support his family.

At a time in America when the family was revered and marriage mandatory, wives kept fairly quiet about their husbands' finances. As the late Daniel J. Levinson wrote of it in his study, *The Seasons of a Woman's Life*, the "traditional marriage enterprise" consisted of wives who were mothers with domestic and household duties. With men as "heads of households," women had limited means and little power. In this structure, the man is independent because he makes money and is the financial provider for his family. Levinson also recognized the tension of home life for the wife, who had to balance caring for her children and keeping close ties with the family and extended family. For example, an extended family had much more significance in the fifties than it does today and most likely, was located within close proximity to in-laws and adult siblings. The wife's interactions with her mother-in-law were constrained financially as well. Unless her husband approved of a day of shopping with her mother-in-law, she would have no means for such an outing. Yet these women, as housewives, connected by the husband/son, did spend time together and were supposed to, as their roles dictated.

There were exceptions to the rule that young women worked only until marriage. While wives did not pursue a career, an aspect of caregiving—nursing, teaching, or secretarial work was acceptable. There was the sense that wives who worked were set apart, along with the realization that they had achieved wings by making their own money. It was a bold path to choose, yet some fifties wives found satisfaction in this way.

As Suzanne, who was widowed in 1956, tells us, working came as one of the most pleasant surprises of her life. "I was a traditional fifties wife to my first husband. I had two young boys and I wanted to be at home with them. I took care of my children and did charity work. I was happy because I didn't know anything else and it seemed a good life to me. But I had gone to college and I was always interested in the outside world. My husband asked me to help him out in his office in an emergency situation. A single woman who ran the office had quit and he couldn't find a replacement and was in a bind. I agreed, and at first I did it part time and for free, because I was just helping him out, not really contributing to the workplace. I thought that I wasn't equipped to do office work or help run a business because wives didn't do that. I watched the single women in his office with envy and I wondered that I couldn't do all that they did and more. When they had conversations, they were about the work and not about children's schedules.

"The world was divided into interesting women, it seemed to me, who worked in Dave, my husband's office, and women who were mothers at the school fairs, who were boring and knew nothing. So I had to wear two hats, the hat of wife and mother and the hat of a working girl, which no wife and mother was in those days. I had a keen business sense and Dave saw that. Still, he hired someone else in the middle of it, because he was so confused about having a wife who could succeed in the business world. Then he was unhappy with my replacement and he asked me to come back.

"This time I demanded to be compensated for my work. I hired someone to be at the house when my kids got home from school so I could put in a full day of work. It took my husband months to pay me for my efforts and once he did and I had a salary, I realized how good that felt. Now I was worthy because money talks. I continued with this career in the sixties and seventies and I became well known. Having my own money and not being like my married friends who asked their husbands to pay for even a shoemaker's repair made me happy. I'm not so sure my husband liked it as much as I did. And the more established I became, the less he had a traditional wife. I loved it, every part of it."

That a wife was subordinate because she had no economic freedom in the fifties cannot be disputed, as evidenced in Suzanne's experience. That mid-century wives expected their husbands to pay for everything, from children's needs, to groceries, to a new car, is both chilling and an understandable reflection of the times. Wives did not view this as a sacrifice as much as a duty. The more prestigious the husband, the better off the wife was in terms of the perks for her duty. It seemed less self-sacrificing to be relegated to the home and children when there were fur coats and jewels in store for the wife instead of a day of housecleaning. As psychologist Claire Owen views it, the financial control of the fifties husband was what kept the women there. "These women were falling into a trap with nowhere to go. They had happy husbands and beautiful homes, perfect children and no way out. If these women felt crazy, and diffident about how they lived, they dared not say." After all, how could they escape without money, and the money belonged to the husband.

Mothering and Wifing

Mothering and wifing went hand in hand for the fifties wife more than at any time in the past five decades. Wives had no other commitment or expectation than to care for their children and husbands. There were no other tugs or distractions, no priorities other than to be a mother and a wife. The mother/wife was young, in her early or mid-twenties when she had her children, because the average age to marry was twenty, according to the National Center for Health Statistics. A young wife had plenty of energy for carpooling, after-school activities—ballet and piano lessons for her daughters, Little League and Boy Scouts for her sons—as well as bake sales and school meetings. At home there was the constant upkeep of a pristine home and delectable meals. Children were to be seen, not heard, as evidenced in *Far From Heaven*, where Julianne Moore's character reproached her children whenever they attempted to speak. There were also children who could be a bit mischievous, as exhibited in the popular television show, *Dennis the Menace*. The common characteristics of the fifties child, however, were that of an obedient daughter or son, who had gendered interests and good manners. For the most part, mothers were not troubled by their children;

rather, they were in control. Few children were expected to exhibit unique abilities; every child was expected to be obedient, unchallenging, and remarkably the same. If there were any problems, the family kept it a secret and not much, if any, psychological help was available to address a challenging situation.

For Deidre, who had a daughter with disabilities in 1950, it was exceedingly uncomfortable. "My two daughters were fine and then I gave birth to Molly, who was mildly retarded and could just get by. I saw that my friends pretended there was nothing wrong with her. My husband counted on me to take care of her and to deal with the school and the special ed. department. We rarely referred to her in any way that was different than the other girls and yet it was apparent to both of us that she was not all right, that she would not lead a normal life. When she was a teenager, it had to be painful for her because her sisters had been very popular at the same age.

"I think it was a mistake not to face these problems head on. Instead, we acted like it was all all right. I look back now and I realize that by acting like Molly was okay, we hurt her chances of getting ahead. We wanted her to be like us, we wished she was like us and we didn't pay enough attention to who she was. The reason that my husband and I treated our daughter this way is because that is how it was in the fifties. No one was allowed to have a child with problems; it was embarrassing to have this in your life. We all boasted about our children and our lives. There was no place to go with it."

Mothering was not only intrinsic to the role of the fifties wife, but idealized. The same approach that applied to wifing in this era applied to mothering; no issues, no fuss, no muss. Anything that was more demanding and required more attention, or that delved beneath the surface, was somehow annoying to these women. It was not only annoying to the family, but it was shameful. One might imagine that the fifties wife was intolerant of a child who had special needs, but the flavor, based on my interviews, seems to be more about how taxing it was. A mother was a good mother in a prescribed manner, but there was no prescription for mothers with impaired or troubled children. The couple needed to work together for the betterment of the child and to address the problem. Yet, the lack of communication that existed between husband and wife in the mid-century made this difficult to achieve.

"No one talked about anything," recalls Helen, who, at seventy-two, has two daughters whom she raised in the mid-fifties. "We acted as if life was perfect. My husband was happy this way. If either of my girls had a problem or needed something, they had to come to me before 5:30 when their father returned from his office. Once he was home, I had to be all his and they came second. This wasn't easy and it made me feel torn, but it was how we were supposed to be. My younger daughter, Anne, was nine when she began to have headaches and epileptic fits. She definitely needed my help after my husband got home from work and she couldn't be on a schedule of 'time for children versus time for parents.' At first I was afraid to even tell my husband about her. But I was also worried about her health. I took her to the first specialist by myself, a few towns away. Once I heard the word 'epilepsy', I knew I had to tell him and I knew he wouldn't be pleased. I wanted to keep it a secret from my friends, too. But one of my closest friends' daughters was in my daughter's class. She was there one day when Anne had a seizure and I came to school to pick her up. After that, the entire neighborhood knew. My friends called me, more out of curiosity than sympathy. I think it was because everyone was so afraid of having a child like mine, and no one knew what to do."

In part, it was not only that women were impractical when it came to complications in their lives; they were unskilled. Wives were not able to share their problems with their friends, let alone their husbands, because they were not supposed to have any problems. The magazines did not address issues, but focused on an ideal family, free from worries and trouble. "What women were taught was to marry and to have children and to lie happily ever after," comments Dr. Michele Kasson. "No one was told it might not work out or that the dream of a beautiful family may be shattered by reality, for example, a child with issues or infertility."

If a fifties wife did not have children, she was not fulfilling her duty as a wife. The discovery that she was infertile was not only shocking but devastating. It appeared that the husband kept his end of the bargain whereas the wife felt she had failed because she was not producing children. In these unenlightened times, fertility doctors told women to go home and take their temperatures. There was no technology to detect what the problem was and no in vitro fertilization or other options for infertile couples. Nor were the couples aware that they were infertile; rather, the wife believed that there was something wrong with her and her alone. In a conventional marriage of the mid-century, there was little else for a wife to do but raise children. A woman's disappointment in not having children was only exacerbated by the societal expectation that she could not live up to. Not surprisingly, she began to doubt herself—after all, her efforts as the good wife who deserved to become the good mother had failed her. As authors Belenky, Clinchy, Goldberger and Tarule explain it in *Women's Ways of Knowing: The Development of Self, Voice and Mind*, women looked "outward for self-knowledge", which is partly why mothering was underscored. This manifested in a "self-definition based on the social expectations that define concrete social and occupational roles"—in this instance, being a wife and mother. It was all mapped out for the fifties mother/wife, as long as she followed instructions and did not change the rules. For those wives who did not have a choice, either could not become pregnant on their own or had a child with problems or a disability, it was doubly arduous because of the strict rules of the culture.

"I was raised to be married and have children," Dana, who married at eighteen, tells us. "I married before my older brothers because, if the truth be told, I wanted to escape from our family. In those days, marriage was the only way to be on your own. I went from my parents' home to my husband's arms. Part of the deal was that we would have children, but Steve and I agreed to wait for a few years. We were both so young and we knew having children would curtail our freedom. So we waited, and then I did not become pregnant. We saw some doctors and they were useless. Meanwhile, my brothers had both gotten married and already their wives were pregnant. I had to watch while my sisters-in-law had babies and moved to houses in the suburbs. We stayed in town because we had no children. All of my friends were married by then and had kids. It was very hard for me and I felt embarrassed. I was having fun with my husband, but there was always that lingering doubt, would we ever have a family of our own?

"In 1956 we adopted twins, a boy and a girl, and suddenly we had our entire family. I felt like I fit in better and I did everything that my friends did, invited people over on Sundays with their kids and served chicken, potato salad and coleslaw. But I was the only one in my group and in the family that adopted and I secretly felt like I still had failed. I had these kids, but not like other women had them. Then, my daughter had trouble with her eyes and my son had some health problems and doctors asked us about our own medical histories. Our histories had nothing to do with our children's problems. It seemed like we couldn't escape the fact that we were different. It felt lousy to be different in the fifties."

Wives as mothers abided by the carefully drawn societal map of how to be a mother during these times. Women felt they were dissected in their dual roles, and anyone who fell short was uncomfortable. There was little sense of self or of individuality for women. All eyes were upon them. There was little escaping the life one was destined to lead. It is little wonder that Dana did not find herself readily accepted once she adopted her children. Those wives who had whispered about her when she had no children now felt entitled to whisper about her because she had adopted her children. It was not enough to adopt her children and to have a family; by these means Dana was not adhering to the established structure. Due to the enormous pressure to conform, any wavering from the construct left a wife floundering and uncertain. David Halberstam points out in his research on the fifties that wives were "uneasy and lonely and largely without guidance." It is this lack of models that caused wives to be taught how to lead their lives through magazines and television.

This uncertainty can be recognized in the fifties wife's take on mothering. There was little room for a baby derived outside one's biological make up and this product of the marriage had to be flawless. In the case of wives who were able to conceive, there was an emphasis on having done it all to perfection. Wives at this time were not, for the most part, childless, and so the advent of a baby was expected and mandatory at once. The amount of raised eyebrows for childless wives was excruciating. Once a wife had children, she was in her glory, and the wife/mother duties never conflicted for this era of women. Rather, they blended together to make the wife's life complete. With small children, the role of mothering was a consuming task, but as the children grew to school age and became more independent, the fifties wife found that she had free time with no real abilities or interests of her own.

The idea of free time was unfamiliar to this period of wife because her obligations had filled her day. While she did not operate at a harried pace, the steady crawl assigned to her schedule suited most wives. These wives did not imagine themselves beyond their duties. With older children who entered school and eventually grew up, another adjustment in terms of time and scheduling began. Neither sports nor health clubs were in vogue for women of this era and charity work had its limits.

My research indicates that it was once the children no longer had immediate or constant needs, that the fifties wife had several choices. Although two children were a common theme—one boy and one girl—some fifties wives had two children in the early part of the decade and a third as the decade neared an end. Having a child at this stage ensured them a secure place as wives and mothers for another ten years, at least. It was definitely in vogue to have one boy and one girl, if possible. The other accepted family consisted of three or four children.

"I deliberately became pregnant when I was thirty, which was unheard of in my day," begins Darlene. "I did it because I had gotten married in 1949 when I was twenty and had my first son in 1950 and my second son in 1952. I had always wanted a girl, so in 1959 I decided to go for it. All of my friends whispered about how it was a mistake and how I'd been sloppy. I didn't dare tell them I wanted a baby later in my marriage. I wanted to try for a girl, and I was lucky, and I wanted to stay a mother. What was I going to discuss with my husband once the kids were grown? We'd spent years worrying about our kids and now it was looking to me like it wouldn't last forever after all—the kids were getting bigger.

"So I had this baby and, in a way, I was a better mother to her than to my sons. I'd been too young with the boys. At thirty I was ready to have a baby. Whatever I did when the boys were little was hit or miss. I tried so hard to be a good mother and a good wife. Then I saw them get busy with school and they were gone all day. There wasn't much for me to do and my friends were nice but no one was very interesting, really. I played cards on some afternoons and I did volunteer work at the local hospital. My husband refused to let me get a part-time job. I could see that things were going to get boring and I knew a baby would hedge my bets. I did it because I had nothing else to do but make dinners, raise children and keep house. That was how it was then. Besides I got my girl this way."

Repressed Emotions

The wife's personal desires were not addressed in the mid-century, nor was society equipped to consider her yearnings. The wife's life in the 1950s offered no ambition beyond being wife and mother. The common wisdom was that a woman was not only fortunate to be a wife by the age of twenty, but designed to be a wife. As evidenced in my pool of interviewees, few other areas of interest were open to women.

But the salient question becomes, what did these women feel and what was their emotional state? Even if a wife was overjoyed to have a baby or to be a wife, profound emotions were not encouraged. While most wives felt close to their children and invested great energy in them, closeness with their husbands is not often described. No one—not the wife, her mother, her best female friend, or her sister—was meant to reveal herself. This explains why if there was a problem, an unhappy marriage or a child with special needs, there was little recourse.

Wives at this time were subordinate to their spouses, and with subordination comes distance. Without parity, it is difficult to feel as connected to one's partner as if there is equality and teamwork. This did not exist in the fifties marriages, the concept was unknown. Thus wives were separated by their designated roles from their husbands. Ironically, the entire goal of a fifties wife was to be a companion to her husband and to nurture her children. An excellent and inspiring example was Princess Grace of Monaco, an elegant wife and great beauty. Granted she was married to a Prince, but she was a wife who stood by her husband's side and raised her children. She had given up a glamorous career in Hollywood to marry a man and have his children, what more could one want from life?

If wives were undernourished emotionally, they had little recourse or ways of self-expression. As Claire Owen, psychologist, remarks, "The fifties wives bought the myth that they were happy while in truth they were discontented. It was devastating to have their children go to school and be left behind in these houses, with nothing to do." It seems that the unrest and lack of direction had not dawned on the fifties wife before the decade had closed and the sixties were upon them. These wives did not convey their feelings about their lot in life. However, closet drinking manifested as a way to manage the day for fifties wives.

"My friends and I would start drinking before our kids returned from school," Gwen confesses. "We got through most of the day, but by 2:30 or three o'clock, it wasn't working. Because we had to prove our devotion to our children, we would stay at home waiting for the school bus to drop them off but we would have had one drink already when they arrived. Once the kids turned on the television and had a snack, we would sneak into our bedrooms with another drink and call each other on the phone to have some company. I always washed my mouth out with mouthwash before Ted returned home at 5:30. And by then the drinks had worn off a bit. But I did it because it made me feel less alone. Even though I never confided my misery to my friends and I couldn't sort it out by myself—I had this nice house, a cleaning woman once a week, my own car, my two kids—there had to be some kind of unhappiness that we all had, five of us, in order to drink together over the telephone.

"I was very frantic about keeping our house clean, it seemed very important to me. I felt like I was pretending that this was satisfying because everyone else was saying so. I had time on my hands but everyone else acted busy.

In reality, no one was busy, not once the kids were gone all day. I just wanted one friend to admit it. No one admitted anything; we'd been raised to keep quiet and we were wives, weren't we? We had no thoughts of our own; we just kept things going. It was almost like if you didn't feel, you wouldn't suffer. Except we were all suffering and didn't know it, or didn't say it."

The media repeatedly told women they were happy in their lives. June Cleaver in the popular television series *Leave It to Beaver* was a happy wife, who said little of consequence to her husband. In real life, without any level of communication, marriages turned stale, even if the wife was relieved to have a husband who was not critical or unkind and who paid her way.

As psychologist John Gottman indicates in his book, *Why Marriages Succeed and Fail*, positive communication is necessary for a marriage to survive. If the fifties wife was able to recognize the lack of communication in her marriage, she was not going to act on it. The culture did not believe in divorce, which was a stigma even greater than that of a troubled child or an unsuccessful husband. Only a handful of miserable wives were willing to seek a divorce even when the marriage merited it. Instead, these women worked hard at making positive impressions and hoped for their children's happiness. What was lacking was self-esteem and self-knowledge for these wives, who were repressed, yet schooled at maintaining their lives, without interruption or any upset along the way. These wives had little reaction to the political climate, to McCarthyism and the Red Scare, because they were not encouraged to be free thinkers. Even the college-educated women who had become wives and mothers were caught up in this limited realm of being set aside in the suburbs.

Yet there was a price to pay for not expressing one's feelings and instead perpetuating a kind of sleepwalking to get by. Indeed, this behavior resulted in more clinical depression in many women as they denied their own needs in order to fill a prescribed role in society. The curious part is that a collusion existed when it came to a wife's lot in life: between husbands and wives, wives and wives, wives and their own mothers. These women were not willing to reveal their inner sadness or sense of loss. They were supposed to be happy, they were fortunate to lead these lives. That was the current way of thinking.

Sharon, who was married in 1955, witnessed her friend's depression once she was married and had children.

"I had a good friend, who had a nervous breakdown, with three kids in a beautiful suburb in the Midwest. Her name was Rose, and we had gone to junior college together. We had also taken a secretarial course after college. I finished it, but Rose got married before it ended. She married a nice guy, Butch, who was a salesman, and who seemed to love her. No one could believe that she had this breakdown and had to be institutionalized because she seemed so happy. I was really upset by this since Rose was the one who had the most successful husband. She had gotten married with all these ideas about being a wife, like recipes and curtains and a den with books in her house. I think that Rose actually snapped from trying too hard to be happy. Her husband travelled for business and she was left alone with the kids.

"She described her life to me, how she would read books for days on end and would forget to do the wash and to make dinner. Her husband had a fit. I do remember her once telling me that she could not talk to him about anything and that she was relieved when he was on a business trip. Who would listen in those days? She would call me and talk for hours, as she missed having adult company around. She had sisters, but once they moved away, she couldn't cope. They used to bring casseroles over to her house and help her out a little. No one discussed what happened to her after her breakdown—I called Butch and her oldest sister. I once called her mother to suggest that Rose go to art class because she had loved to work at a kiln—like we did in college. I thought it would be almost like therapy, I guess. Her mother told me to stay out of it. I felt like I was pushed away when I wanted to do something. Soon after that, she got divorced, and had another breakdown. That life was too much for her and she was too smart for it, in a way. I bet she lost her mind from the boredom. The rest of us weren't like Rose, so we didn't mind it."

If large numbers of fifties wives were frustrated with their lives, they did not express it. The nice-girl image that was mandatory for the mid-century wife could, in some cases, enervate the wife. It wasn't easy to keep up appearances at all times, and there were those who were more successful at it than others. The degree of happiness depended upon a woman's ratio of personal happiness to her required behavior and responsibilities. For example, if a wife was disappointed in her life and had false expectations of what it would be like to be a wife and mother, it was not something that could be addressed. If a wife was delighted with her assigned role and did not scrutinize her life, she was better situated. One wonders how these women escaped at least a modicum of dissatisfaction.

Levinson writes of the fifties wife in *The Seasons of a Woman's Life*, "The men the women knew were not especially loving or heroic. For the most part, they were politely distant or sexually demanding. Neither partner was ready for a more loving, intimate relationship. Marriage as a concrete way of life was still rather unreal." The distance between wives and husbands that Levinson describes did not improve but was diffused for a number of years once there were children. The day-to-day demands of mothering sufficed for most wives for a period of time. If these wives were fortunate enough to be in successful marriages, they could look forward to a future with their husbands once the childbearing years had ended. Not that many wives thought this way or saw that far ahead. The majority of fifties wives with whom I spoke said they had no such vision of life after their children were grown.

"I was prepared for nothing when I married at nineteen," begins Ruth, who has been a fifties wife for fifty-one years. "No one prepared me for marriage or childraising, but I sure knew that it was my lot in life. I married a fellow I knew from the next town and we moved to the city together for his work. I was thrilled to have four children, three girls and one boy, and I worked hard to raise them to be solid citizens. My husband and I were not exactly close, and I doubt that I ever expressed my feelings except when my parents died, and later when my sister passed away. Besides that, I just focused on the kids and he worked at the office and expected that life at home was settled. I was wise enough to know that this was my life, and not to look for more. I told myself to appreciate what I had and not question any of it. What was the point? Our lives were in a mold. We got a sitter on Saturday night for the kids and went out with friends who had the same lives as we did. My children were disciplined and polite because my husband and I agreed that we did not want our children to be problematic.

"I went out of my way, from my years as a young wife, to avoid feeling much of anything and therefore avoided any incidents. Everything seemed a process—getting the kids through grade school, high school, confirmation, college. Part of my job was to always invite my in-laws and my parents for Sunday dinners. So there I was—a good wife, good daughter, good mother, good daughter-in-law. I hated those Sundays. I wanted to rest and be left alone instead of doing dishes for the family. I kept my mouth shut if something bothered me. In those days I liked and even loved my husband. I had a few friends who I think despised their husbands."

Ruth describes herself as wife, mother, daughter, and daughter-in-law, each role necessary to the successful fifties wife. Her connections were many, since there were always female friends in the mix, but the level of attachment was minimal. Thus, if a fifties wife looked to female friendships to fill the void, there was not much hope. These friendships were maintained on a surface level and usually were based on common ground—that of husbands and children, and similar socioeconomic bracket. It would not be until future decades that wives sought female friendships that actually enhanced their lives. The admission that husbands were deficient had not yet been addressed in the 1950s—wives did not even know what they were looking for, only that there was an emptiness. Therefore, the emphasis on female friendship in the fifties was on a par with mothering and wifing, circumscribed by a repressed society of women.

The socialization of the wives at this time and the lack of self-fulfillment extended to female friendships. How could these women recognize their isolation when there was no one with whom to communicate their thoughts? As Dr. Ronnie Burak points out, from a psychological point of view, women might have been depressed, but maybe not only about the marriage. "Perhaps women were just depressed in those days, as they can be today," remarks Dr. Burak. "Or these wives might have felt limited in other ways, not only by the marriage but because of the limitations of the times."

The more successful wives were the ones who assessed their situation, found their husbands pleasing and their children enjoyable and made the best of it, shopping and lunching with friends, running their homes without being consumed by it. While these women might have realized their situation, they found a separate sense of contentment. This is the case of Gina, a widow after twenty years of marriage, who viewed her marriage as one that required diplomacy.

"I met my husband during the war in Europe and we escaped to America together and were married in l950. It was a big romance, and knowing him during the war helped me get through it," Gina tells us. "I came to America and I became a wife; it was similar to my friends' marriages, women who had been here for some time. I also made friends here and they did not seem happy. For me it was a lifestyle that I accepted. I knew that there were two ways of thinking for husbands and wives and that marriage for me was not the same as marriage for my husband. I knew that it would not be easy some days but that I wanted to be a wife. We had no children, which meant that we had to face each other at a time when everyone hid behind their kids. My husband and I worked together on the marriage, and while other couples might have done the same, we had more of a consciousness about it.

"I never said a word if he worked late, if he came home late. I never asked where he had been or who he had been with; I didn't want to know. I saw that he gave in his own way and while I never said all this to him, I think that he gave 30 percent and I gave the rest. It was the only way. I was compromising but I was always conscious of my role as his wife, always. It was a deal and I was careful not to think only of myself, but to think of him. To think of him first, and myself second. It is difficult to be giving all of the time, but it is a better feeling, and that way I know that I did all that I should do.

"I would tell myself, as long as we shared values and a way of looking at the world, we would be together; I saw this in the marriage. I never told my husband, but I knew I didn't need a man to be complete, although I loved my husband. I knew that I wasn't like other wives my age; I understood my husband better than they understood their husbands. I knew that real freedom, as a woman and as a wife, is to have independence. I knew this in the fifties, when no women were thinking this way. Once my husband died, I knew I could never have something this special again. I never remarried."

In Gina's interview we recognize a wife who is both convention bound and a free thinker when it comes to her position in the marriage. That Gina did not have children set her apart at once and what she had endured in Europe in World War II also influenced her thinking. Her assimilation in her role as a fifties wife was only partial, but with a heightened self-awareness that is unique for wives of this period. In a sense, she was a rule breaker, but also highly satisfied with her marriage. For the many fifties wives who did not have Gina's breadth of experience or philosophy of life, the repression was rampant. No one considered independence, which Gina talks about, to be an important ingredient in a marriage.

In the hectic, reformational decades to follow the fifties, wives had more opportunity for self-reflection and more options in the world. After enough decades, the life of the fifties wife, in all its simplicity and restraint, came to symbolize an easier world for women, even in a period when women were anesthetized in their role. The 1950s represented the first decade in the life of the modern wife, even though a strict societal structure existed. Within the constraints, there was an individuality, as well as a collective behavior. The fifties wife, whether she knew it or not, was the bridge to the world beyond wifedom as martyrdom. It was the far-off rumblings by the end of the decade that set the stage for what was to follow in the life of the American wife.

Chapter Three
The Sixties Wife:
Hell Let Loose

I was married in 1962, when Jackie Kennedy was our idol and we wore sleeveless dresses that just covered our knees," begins Jane. "I was not quite a virgin when I married Tom, but close. I'd had one boyfriend in college and then I met Tom. I quit school to marry him and we moved to another state. No one in my family paid much attention to me once I was married because in their eyes, I had done the right thing. I doubt I paid much attention to Tom's character, but once we were together for a year or so, I realized that he wasn't who I thought he was. I felt I had no options, so I took care of my children and waited, wondering what I would do. I was someone's wife and I had these children to care for. I had the right clothes and the right friends, but I was miserable.

"And then the world began to change. In the fifties this marriage to a man who turned out to be quite cruel would have been my fate; end of story. But after five years and three children, one daughter and twin sons, I knew I couldn't remain with him. Although there had never been a divorce in our family, I declared I wanted a divorce. I thought I could make it alone better than in this marriage. The women's movement was beginning and I read books by Friedan and de Beauvoir. I decided that I could go back to school and finish my degree; that my college education would not be a waste; and I would complete it. I moved into a small rental house and enrolled in a junior college. My mother was still asking me if I wanted to reconcile with Tom, and I was hoping that I would never see him again. By the end of the decade, no one seemed to care half as much about being someone's wife as they had in even the early sixties."

There is little question that the sixties was a decade of tremendous change and turmoil, not only for wives, but for all Americans. The Eisenhower era ended in 1961 when John F. Kennedy took office and Camelot, with JFK as our handsome, regal leader, began. Kennedy's term in office was cut short by his tragic assassination in November of 1963, and the remaining portion of the decade was under the helm of Lyndon B. Johnson, followed by Richard Nixon. Much had been put in motion, including the civil rights movement, the space program, the Peace Corps, and ultimately the Vietnam War. These events were momentous, and it was impossible for the sixties wife to not be influenced, and ultimately altered, by them.

Unlike the fifties wife, who was remarkably unchanged in rhythm or style from 1950 to 1959, the American wife in the early sixties was not the same as an American wife at the end of the decade. Important issues that directly affected the sixties wife were the women's liberation movement, the sexual revolution, the civil rights movement and the Vietnam War. During these tumultuous times, peace activists, the drug culture, hippies, Twiggy, Barbie dolls, the release of six James Bond films, the Beatles, the evolution of rock musicians and Woodstock penetrated the culture. For the sixties wife, the world was filled with a newness that society had never anticipated and had yet to envision; it would manifest in freedom and equality that had not been considered for women before this time.

The birth control pill gave the sixties wife control over her destiny and a sexual freedom that her predecessors could not have dreamed about. These women were no longer beholden to their husbands but suddenly had a say about sex and its consequences. The option of family planning gave wives—the only women who so far were supposed to have children—control over their destinies. The sixties wife was a woman in a sea of newness, and how she acclimated was partially circumstantial and partly personal—the possibilities were unprecedented. An early sixties bride who wore the vestiges of the fifties wife could well find herself a bra-burning feminist by 1969.

Early Sixties—Still Earning That MRS.

The 1960s rolled in within a climate that was similar to the fifties when it came to the life of the wife. Mimi Eisenhower was still first lady, a woman who had choreographed her life according to her husband's career and was, in this sense, a perfect example of the martyrdom of the wife of previous decade. While she reaped the rewards of a husband who was elected president of the United States, she was, above all, an example for the fifties wife and living proof that one should stand behind her man. Therefore, it was a shock to the system and a delight to American wives to discover in 1961 that their sophisticated, beautiful new first lady in was also quite clever. Once Jackie Kennedy began tours of the White House and helped her husband write (some say she actually wrote it solo) *Profiles In Courage*, it became clear to wives everywhere that this was a new wife for a new decade. That Jackie Kennedy enhanced her husband was natural, but she was a talented woman in her own right while also a devoted mother who believed in family. Jackie Kennedy achieved a balancing act; her accomplishments were impressive, yet she also sustained the imprimatur of the quiet, secondary spouse, regardless of her own allure. Thus, Jackie set a wifely example and substantiated the message of marriage as greatly rewarding. Wives at the beginning of the sixties were as hell-bent on getting married as their fifties predecessors.

"I began college in 1959 and my mother and grandmother made it very clear that I was going there for one reason and one reason only," begins Patricia, who married in 1963, a month after her graduation. "My sister, who is four years older, had not graduated from college when she married, but I wanted my college degree. I'm not sure why I knew somehow that it was important, but in the back of my mind, I wanted it. There wasn't a girl in my class at our college, a state school, who wasn't engaged by the middle of senior year. When I went home at Christmas without that ring, my mother hissed at me, under no uncertain terms was I to return without it by spring break. I felt the pressure and I felt somehow like I was failing my family. I remember going food shopping and running into two friends from high school. One worked at the food store and the other was a manicurist. They were both married already. They were not impressed with me, with my being in college; it was only about getting married.

"I did not disappoint my parents, and I was engaged by mid-January of my senior year. I had been dating Rich, my husband, for a year, so it was the right next step. We rented an apartment for the first two years of our marriage and he worked in the family business. I thought it would be different somehow, but really I was doing everything exactly as planned and exactly as my sisters and parents expected of me. The only thing I did that was unlike them was that I had more spunk, kind of like Alice Kramden in *The Honeymooners*. But basically, I was still a passive wife."

The concept of winning a husband in college had not lost its magic and the customs of the fifties were firmly imbedded in the consciousness of the women at the dawn of the next decade. Little girls were already in training: orchestrating pretend weddings for Barbie and Ken. "I remember getting my little sister a Barbie and we sewed a wedding gown for her," Marcia tells us. "It was a way of teaching her about her future."

The sixties version of Barbie dolls were extremely popular, and collected by young girls across America. The implicit message was one that concurred with the fifties—that Barbie was an eligible single woman, as evidenced in her physical demeanor, created to be Ken's wife. In her essay, "What Barbie Dolls Have to Say about Postwar American Culture," Miriam Forman-Brunell describes Barbie as unable to walk in her high heels and as confined to the home so that she could be a full-time mother and wife. Along with Barbie and Ken, there was Alice and Ralph Kramden. Few episodes of *The Honeymooners*, starring Jackie Gleason as Ralph Kramden and Audrey Meadows as his wife, Alice, ended without her having the last word. Nonetheless, Alice Kramden was a convention-bound wife who tolerated her husband's foolish schemes, but was always attentive and wifely.

At the same time that the early-sixties wife played her role much like a fifties wife, one feminist treatise was already published and awakening women in some far recesses of their brains. This was *The Second Sex*, written by Simone de Beauvoir, who lived by her convictions as the lover, not the wife, of philosopher Jean-Paul Sartre. Her life and work epitomized that of an independent, free-spirited woman who would enter the decade later through the feminist thought of Betty Friedan and Gloria Steinem. The call to arms of *The Second Sex* directly addressed the limitations of marriage. As de Beauvoir writes, "...woman has always been man's dependent, if not his slave; the two sexes have never shared the world in equality. And even today woman is heavily handicapped, though her situation is beginning to change..." This promise would be a slow dawning for the sixties wife, who seemed to have a case of "the devil you know'" theory, thereby sticking to what was familiar, if deficient. These wives remained in search of marriage and the purported safety of home and family.

Poet Sylvia Plath, who committed suicide in 1963, was an anomaly for her time. Plath's writings suggest that she wanted a husband and children, which she had as the wife of poet Ted Hughes and the mother of two small children. However, Plath also struggled with the inner meaning of life for women at the time and did not plan to be only housewife and mother. Were Plath's suicidal tendencies heightened by her domestic responsibilities? Was her marriage so unhappy that there was no way out? Plath's book, *The Bell Jar*, and her subsequent death would come to represent the desperation of a young wife and mother who was also a unique talent. The tragedy is that had Plath lived on through the decade, she would have witnessed some of her issues addressed by the feminist movement. Instead, she became an icon and symbol of domestic suffering on the eve of women's liberation.

Generally, wives did not contemplate suicide in the 1960s. It was not a part of their repertoire, because they were still determined to have the dream—that of marriage and family. The dream was less antiseptic than in the fifties, but the goals were similar to those of the past decade. Now, a wife who wanted to be a wife, and to have children, might also consider part-time work, pink-collar work. Schedules were set around the family, and few wives dared to work while their children were still at home, before they began kindergarten. Once their children were off to school, a few brave wives picked up the pieces of their old jobs—not exactly careers, but something that filled a day or two a week in a familiar work setting.

As Melissa, who was married in 1964, explained it, there was an implicit approval for women to do this at the time when the feminist treatises were beginning to gather steam.

"I don't know how I heard or thought I could work just a little and be married, but I did it. I was a teacher when I was single, so I decided to be a substitute teacher. That way, I could always say no if the day wasn't right when they called me, if my children were sick at home or something. My sister married in 1959, five years earlier. She and I were similar in how we acted as wives and mothers. Being a wife was the most important job in the world, until you had a baby. Then your child was the most important job in the world. I had dated my husband in high school and I knew that I would be his wife. I was friendly with his sister and I used to whisper to her, asking her if she would mind if we would some day be sisters-in-law. We both came from very traditional middle-class families where everyone did the same thing. No one strayed from the standard—to get married and have children. The only thing I did that was a little unlike everyone else was the substitute teaching. And my sister, a fifties wife, said she would not have done that to the family. I didn't look at myself as having many choices, so this was just something I could pull off that got me out of the house."

If the idea of working outside the home was appealing to an early- to mid-sixties wife, she often put it off in favor of the fifties mode of wifing. She was simply not confident that this was a right choice for her, so it was easier not to have the option at all. In the early sixties, a wife might be found vacuuming her living room in a pair of high-heeled shoes, as seen on television in shows like *Leave It to Beaver* and *Donna Reed*. In these shows, June Cleaver and Donna

Reed were featured as busy housewives in the beginning of the decade. Marital equality was not in the picture for the sixties wife, in spite of the fact that de Beauvoir and Friedan had spelled out the situation for women. In the early years many wives turned away from this radical mode of thought. Not all movie stars were committed to long-standing marriages like Joanne Woodward and Paul Newman, who appeared as teammates. As in the fifties, most movie stars were exempt from the mundane existence of one husband per wife; but sexuality did not exist much outside of Hollywood. Those marriages could be tantalizing and dicey; for example Liz Taylor's stormy marriage to Richard Burton, which was of great interest to women in the sixties, but nothing to emulate and far from the realm of an ordinary wife. The fact that Audrey Hepburn was married to Mel Ferrer, twelve years her senior, was again a distant reality.

None of this mattered much to the ordinary wife of the sixties, except as curious magazine reading in the beauty shop. As long as everyday women in everyday lives sought the role of wife, the taboo of having sex before marriage stood the test of time. Most of my interviewees indicate that until mid-decade, women pretended to be virgins, with a handful of them telling the truth. The best of friends lied to one another about their virginity because a premium was placed on this status. But pregnancy remained a nagging problem, because along with the fiction of remaining a virgin came a single woman's lack of access to the Pill. For those young women who lost their virginity with a boyfriend, not a husband, the taboo of no longer being a virgin on one's wedding night began to subside. Single women were realizing that they could have sex before marriage, but they were on the fringe. The pervasive message was that women were to save themselves. Virginity was something one saved for her husband, while scholarships and schooling were forfeited for her husband. All this sounds very fifties, but slowly the norm began to shift to a point where a woman could be a wife and not a virgin on her wedding day. She could hold on to her schooling with the idea that, perhaps in the distant future, exempt of husband care and childcare, there was a degree that was all hers.

"I gave up my scholarship to journalism school," recalls Darcy, "and I was a virgin when I got married. I went to secretarial school instead because I was married and it was more practical. When my friend, who was two years younger, didn't give up her scholarship and was not a virgin when she got married, I understood that I had somehow blown it. What was the point of giving up so much, school and fun, just to be married? I realized that she could have a big wedding and a husband, just like I did, without so much sacrifice. I didn't realize that I would think that way by 1966, having gotten married in 1963. Things were changing, I guess, and it was hitting me that the rules were not worth following; they hadn't done so much for me. I wanted to write for a newspaper or freelance, not be a secretary until I had kids. I did it the way I was supposed to, but I thought to myself, at least my girls will have more options."

Being a wife remained a goal for women, but somewhere in the recesses of their minds, the women of the sixties knew that the rigid and binding life that they were expected to lead was a trap. The sixties wife was set apart from the fifties wife by her ability to see this, even if it took the first half of the decade to reach that point. While her life appeared remarkably similar to that of women in the previous decade, the outside world was no longer the benign post-war climate of the recent past. The newly agitated and raging world beyond every wife's home could not be ignored. By 1963, President Kennedy had been assassinated and a world of violence had begun. The Vietnam War and civil rights had become a part of the country's reality, and the sixties wife could not hide behind the facade of home and family.

The Advent of the Pill

The puritan ethic of the fifties put a kibosh on sexy wives and this concept remained for the first half of the sixties at least. This is true even though birth control pills became available in 1960, representing a medical miracle for women. As reported by *FDA Consumer Magazine*, by 1973 ten million women used the Pill and today almost eleven million women use this form of contraception. The advent of the Pill offered wives control over their destinies. Not only was the birth control pill an improvement over the diaphragm in terms of comfort and ease, but it had a success rate of 90 percent.

Of course, the fear was that with the Pill women would not have to marry to have sex because they no longer would risk becoming pregnant when they had sex. On January 24, 1964, *Time* magazine declared the Pill the "New Morality," recognizing how far-reaching the consequences were in terms of sexual freedom for women. As Paula Kamen points out in her book *Her Way: Young Women Remake the Sexual Revolution*, "For many traditionally oriented women, however, the sexual revolution has meant a loss of power because sex is no longer a bargaining tool for a long-term commitment." While in the fifties and early sixties, wives used this tool to snare the man for the big deal—the goal being marriage—the value of sex was diminished once a woman's ability to use it as she pleased became a part of her existence.

The Pill obliterated the rules of sexual conduct as soon as it became available to any woman, married or single. Coinciding with the birth control pill was the publication of Helen Gurley Brown's book, *Sex and the Single Girl*, a revolutionary publication for its day. The book disclosed a single woman's life as adventurous and worthy, and advocated sex and career as a healthy part of it. For the buttoned-up wife of the early sixties, this information was shocking, but combined with the availability of the birth control pill, it was the beginning of the demise of the virgin wife.

"At first I was this young wife, we had a big wedding and I thought it was love ever after," recalls Lucinda, who has been married since 1964. "Everything happened according to plan. I got pregnant and had a baby right away, but then I decided that I didn't want another one so fast. That was when I went to the doctor and got the Pill. Then I was at home with the baby and it was lonely. I loved my husband, Clyde, and I loved my baby daughter, but I felt like something was missing. I could never have told my husband or my mother, and certainly not any of my friends, about my feelings. I ended up having an affair with a former professor of mine. I found him comforting and kind to me. I loved how he spoke of books and how he knew so much. It was something I missed in my life; I had always been a good student and liked going to school. This affair lasted a year, until he moved to another area for a new position. I would never have done it if I wasn't on the Pill because I knew how easily I could become pregnant. The Pill gave me freedom in the marriage and outside of the marriage, which I knew wasn't supposed to happen. I never did it again, but having this professor in my life when I was young and unhappy helped me. I stayed married, so no one is any worse for this. In my mind I was doing what men had done for ages."

As evidenced in Lucinda's experience, the Pill allowed women to question the values of traditional marriages, and suddenly the wife had more opportunity and liberties than a husband could ever have imagined. The goal of raising a family and being chained to one's house might have amused a sixties wife, despite her training for marriage and motherhood. The days when husbands were confident that their wives were content were gone. As Germaine Greer points out in *The Female Eunuch*, it was the very family structure itself that was not truly set up for paternity to endure. Wives were on their own, and it was implicit that they were trustworthy.

Films released in the late sixties reflected the impact of the Pill on society. In 1968, a comedy, *Prudence and the Pill*, starring David Niven and Deborah Kerr, showed how women's lives were altered by the new universe of birth control pills. In 1969, *Bob, Carol, Ted and Alice*, starring Natalie Wood, Robert Culp, Elliott Gould and Dyan Cannon addressed wife-swapping, another phenomenon that became a part of the sixties and lasted into the seventies as a definite by-product of the Pill. It was monogamy with a twist, an answer to being condemned to life with the same partner for the rest of one's days. The sense of adventure brought about by wife-swapping could prove particularly appealing to a sixties wife who had begun her tenure as a virgin and was now essentially testing other waters with her husband's consent. In both of these films, it was the sexual facileness that created a new kind of wife. "Women in general became restless with appointed roles," explains psychologist Claire Owen. "This manifested in several ways; women were discontent and they began to change their lives and how they acted as wives."

For other sixties wives, the responsibilities that came with marriage and children were less influenced by the changing tide and any philosophical questioning of what a wife's life is worth. Working-class and lower-middle-class wives did not have the luxury of asking themselves what they were missing sexually by being attached to a husband. For them, other considerations, such as family planning and finances, prompted their quest for the birth control pill.

"By the time I went on the Pill, I had two children and an unhappy marriage," begins Marie, who was married in 1962. "I got married right out of high school and was a working girl. We had no money, so I had to have a job. For me it wasn't about getting married and having a nice home, it was about getting married because I was pregnant and then trying to make it last. It wasn't easy because I was too young to be married and I knew nothing about the world. I worked, and my mother watched my babies. But I wasn't like the other girls I'd known in high school who were wealthy and had a chance to go to college. They married too, but it wasn't like when I got married. I had to be married, and even if they had to do it, they lived in pretty houses and had clothes, a car, all of that stuff that comes with marriage. I had a husband, which I thought was a good thing in the beginning, and babies, and a mom who helped me out. I lived in fear of becoming pregnant again, so the Pill was a necessity for me. It gave me a chance to work and raise my two kids without being deathly afraid of any more coming along. I had a cousin who had an abortion and she almost died. The Pill was really the only chance for any woman, rich or poor."

The Pill had the potential to save middle- and upper-middle-class, and minority women from feeling caught with babies and unwanted pregnancies. Yet for lower-class and minority women who had husbands and children, the trappings of marriage were different. These women usually worked for a living and depended upon a family member to help care for their children. Their husbands were often not as reliable in terms of financial support, so these wives often found themselves alone with children and jobs—

something that would affect all classes in the future decades. In the sixties, abandoned wives were ashamed of their situation, and ill-equipped to manage. As these women tried to maneuver their lives, the Pill was one method of control in a world where they felt virtually powerless.

Unmarried women had less access to the Pill than did their married counterparts, and less justification in the eyes of a profession consisting of predominantly male gynecologists. Single women who were faint of heart did not venture out to endure the judgment of a male physician to procure a prescription. With few female physicians in the United States in the 1960s, it was unlikely that a single woman in search of the Pill would find a sympathetic same-gendered doctor to administer the medication. As several wives recalled their own experiences in getting the Pill, this was not a comfortable situation even when they were married. In many cases, these wives felt scrutinized by the very doctors who had delivered their babies. That women reacted this way is a reflection of their lack of confidence and lack of entitlement. Having the courage to demand a prescription for the Pill, take it to one's local pharmacist, and thus declare one's future when it came to pregnancy, was intimidating to many wives. The "good girl" facade was slowly being tossed to the wind, and with time a wife might reveal her needs. This was heavy stuff for a wife in the sixties who had been convention bound and reminiscent of her fifties predecessor. As psychologist Jo League points out, "Before the Pill and the idea that it was there for women, these women were figuratively and literally non-orgasmic. Their lives had little that was about them and not simply about others."

War Brides and Lost Dreams

Frequently the sixties wife's life was entwined with the Vietnam War. By 1965, according to Joan and Robert Morrison's book, *From Camelot to Kent State*, 170,000 servicemen were stationed in Vietnam; by 1967 there were 464,000 troops. Amid antiwar demonstrations, young wives saw their husbands off to fight a war that few believed in.

By the end of the Vietnam War, 58,000 American soldiers had died. Director Michael Cimino's film of Vietnam and its aftermath, *The Deer Hunter*, epitomizes the legacy of the war for its survivors, both husbands and wives alike. The film tells the tale of young men from a Pennsylvania coal-mining town who became soldiers and the women who loved them. It begins with a wedding (and farewell party) for the groom and his two friends, who leave the next morning for Vietnam. The pregnant bride and her friends plan to wait for these men, but the groom returns a paraplegic.

Other real-life scenarios that occurred during and after the Vietnam War included young wives who became widows, wives of activists who fled over the border with their husbands in protest of the war, and wives who welcomed home heroin-addicted husbands and bitter men who no longer held any illusions about war or America.

"I was married in 1966 and Terry, my husband, and I considered going to Canada to hide," begins Adele, who has been married for thirty-eight years. "I remember that we talked to his father and decided against it. Terry enlisted so that he wasn't drafted and he was obligated to serve for three years. He spent the first eighteen months on the front and that really frightened me. I lived at my parents' and went to work as a medical technician. I didn't even feel like we were married, except that we had been having sex for a few months before he left. In a way I wasn't much different than my aunt who eloped during World War II, and lived at home while my uncle was overseas. He returned two years later to be with her. Sex was the thing—it was forbidden, unless you were married, and I thought that you had to be married to have it. That was one reason I wanted to marry Terry so much, and later, while he was in Vietnam, I learned from my friends and from one of my sisters that everyone lied, everyone had it before they got married. I guess I was a traditional bride with a soldier for a husband.

"It never occurred to me that we could have protested against the war, which was happening around the time that Terry was stationed over there. I came from a simple family, religious and respectful, and this is what young men were doing—they were going to Vietnam. I worried about him, and I waited. The night he came back I became pregnant with our first child."

It is interesting to note that wives of drafted and enlisted men did not have the same degree of raised consciousness as university students on campus. Across America young women and men had begun to actively protest the war. In spring of 1965, there were 12,000 protesters at an antiwar demonstration held in Washington, DC, and the following fall, fourteen thousand protesters marched in New York City. Yet for the wives of soldiers, the unrest over an unpopular war was little consolation. While a sixties wife whose husband was in Vietnam might not have wanted to face all that ailed America, it was difficult to completely block things out. By the mid-sixties, according to Morrison and Morrison, "the ranks in Vietnam were filled disproportionately by black soldiers." "Black Power" became evident, as the peaceful marches of Martin Luther King began to seem remote and unsuccessful. An early-sixties wife had been concerned merely with her role as wife and young mother—and perhaps about keeping her job—until the turbulent times began.

"I know that my husband felt he was drafted because he was black," begins Chandra, who was married in 1963. "But in 1967, everyone we knew was being drafted. There wasn't any choice. But we also knew the war wasn't right. My brother went over and so did my cousins, and then my husband, Thomas. I was heartsick because we had two little children and another on the way. I had read about draft card burning, about women holding peace rallies, but it was like another world to me. At the start of the war, Thomas and I had talked about it. We knew if he got drafted, he'd have to go. He had a high number and I was relieved. I kept pretending life was the same as before the war, with him and me and our kids. But the war dragged on and on. I began to dread hearing that he would be called. I kept thinking there was something special if you had a wife and kids. But he got drafted anyway.

"It was a nightmare for me. I moved back into my mother's house because I couldn't afford our apartment. I waited for him to write, to hear any word from him. I would read the newspapers and I was so afraid. After a few months, I asked a woman at work about getting involved in some anti-war protests. She told me what to do. I felt much better once I was protesting. When Thomas came back, I told him and he said I did the right thing. He said it was a useless war. But he was there and it changed him, made him kind of cold and not the same. That war hurt us as a husband and wife."

In contrast to World War II and the belief that America was right to be at war, the Vietnam War evoked strong anti-war feelings, both for those whose loved ones were in Vietnam and for those who were opposed to the war politically. There was little consolation for the wives of servicemen, who suffered desperate nights and tearful days despite the sense that they were not alone in their feelings about the war. Those young sixties wives who had believed in marriage and family now witnessed their husbands departing to fight a senseless war. These women were anxious and disillusioned. While wives waited at home for their husbands to return, the air was filled with protest songs, race riots, and the beginnings of the women's liberation movement.

"It all turned for me the day my husband was drafted and I knew that there were no certainties anymore," recalls Carol. "We decided to get married right before he was shipped out. I remember how we planned a quick wedding because I was dying to marry him. My mother had trained me to think this is what I should do and no war was going to stop my plans; that's how I was in the beginning. I hated that the war was going on and I thank God that we got through it, but I didn't expect everything to change so much while he was away. I watched the war protests on television and I was someone who should have done something, but instead I thought the world was divided into those who didn't have to go and stayed home to protest and those who had to go—and what could be done then? Nothing.

"There was so much going on in the time that Marty was gone. He came home, I remember, and I went to meet him at the airport. Instead of being respected for being in a uniform, it was like he was a pariah. I think that by 1968 the entire country, even those who believed at first that we should fight, had changed their minds. I remember that it was no longer a good thing to say I was married, let alone that I was married to a Marine. It was like a double whammy—by the end of the sixties, you weren't supposed to want to be a wife, and definitely not to someone who had been in Vietnam. But it wasn't his choice to go; it wasn't something we wanted. It happened to us."

The idea of a wife of a military man, which had been so prestigious during World War II, was blemished by the war in Vietnam. The dream of a simple life as wife and mother was disrupted by the reality of Vietnam and its atrocities. The emotional price of the war and the altered state of those men returning home was profound. Wives of Vietnam vets had to contend with a variety of returning soldiers, some bitter, others hooked on drugs, others maimed or disoriented. Wives with injured husbands had a sense that they had been cheated of a whole life. Veterans themselves came back to a turbulent end of the decade, with a palpable lack of welcome and no acknowledgment for the service they had provided. Wives, as well as their husbands, were baffled by the prevailing unsupportive attitude toward those who had served in Vietnam.

"It is as if the soldiers themselves were being punished for a useless war," Diana recalls. "My husband came back in 1968 and after that I had to live as a military wife on a base for fifteen months. We lived down South and I hated every minute of it. If we went off base, even in the South, he was given a dirty look for being in uniform. I expected this in cities where there were hippies and antiwar demonstrations, but not down South. There were other military wives—all of our husbands had served in Vietnam. For that reason, I thought everyone would be friendly, but no one was friendly. I was pregnant immediately and even the other pregnant wives would not befriend me. I don't know why it was like this—I mean we were all in it together, first waiting for them to get back and then the sheer happiness of having our husbands with us again. No one talked about Vietnam, none of the men, and I thought that was really weird. Then I learned that no one's husband was ever going to talk about it.

"I felt like my whole idea of how my husband and I would lead our life together didn't matter anymore. Whatever we had planned before he left didn't make much sense; it seemed trivial. I was glad to be pregnant though, because that made us real, and the future real. It was something we would have done without a war. But I saw that the wives of the vets had to adjust, along with the vets themselves. That took some time because the world had changed while the men were gone."

The Rise of Feminism

Essays on Sex Equality, written by John Stuart Mill and Harriet Taylor Mill in 1869, addressed the subjugation of women a century before the second wave of feminism began in 1968. As Alice Rossi points out in her 1969 introduction to the book, it took thirty more years after the book was published for another book in defense of female parity to come out: Charlotte Perkins Gilman's *Women and Economics*. After that, there was another long wait of sixty-three years before the issuance of Simone de Beauvoir's *The Second Sex*. The concept of equal rights for women had manifested in the fight for the right to vote at the beginning of the twentieth century. This was known as the first wave of feminism. After the suffragettes' long fight, this right was awarded to women in 1920. After this victory, feminism was dormant until the 1960s, when radical feminists, who believed that men had all the power in a patriarchal society, became prominent. This "second wave" became known as the women's movement, which on some level raised the consciousness of even the most placid wives of the decade.

It is interesting to note that a population of young women today, including many students, view feminism as a negative cause. The reality is that without this movement, women today would not be established in the workplace, experience egalitarian marriages, or have a heightened awareness of date rape and domestic violence. Before the advent of the second wave of feminism wives were docile, and even when they recognized the inequality of their gender, they said little about it.

As mentioned, the backdrop of the women's movement was the civil rights movement and the Vietnam War. For wives married to servicemen in Vietnam, the reality of an unfair world for women was a slow dawning. This was partially due to an awareness that women who involved themselves in protests were not equal to the men who led the marches, and partially because women began to see another evolving social system in America—one that fought for equality for minorities, including women. For wives who were traditionalists, at home with their children while their husbands worked, the value of being a wife remained important. But the word on the street—that women were as entitled as men to their rights—was thrilling.

"In some ways, by the end of the sixties I was no longer the same person as I had been at the beginning," Suzie tells us. "I had gotten married at twenty, in 1962, and I had two small children right away. I had given up college and had no degree. I stayed at home with the kids. My husband did not get drafted, and that was lucky. He was a typical husband, who worked hard and expected me to run the house. It wasn't what I wanted. I don't know if I realized this on my own, or if it was because everything was changing in America that I realized I needed to change. Probably I was never the most conventional of women, but when you are young and doing what you are supposed to do, you don't have to face that. The war and the drug culture changed my attitude. Or maybe I had no attitude and then I finally developed one, and learned how strongly I felt about certain things. I began to read books that made me think differently, like *The Yellow Wallpaper*, by Charlotte Perkins Gilman. I saw that women were not treated fairly, and that made us think we were less. I began to talk about it with other women and soon we had our own consciousness-raising group. It was really exciting. Somehow it gave meaning to mothering and wifing. I could do that, but secretly I believed in women as deserving more in life and in their independence. This was amazing stuff. I remember my mother warning me that this could be dangerous for my marriage.

"Basically, I had two lives and it worked. I was a good wife like I'd been taught, but I had this other side of me— a new side—that read literature about how the patriarchy had kept women from reaching their full potential. I believed this. I had no idea what my future would be. It was up to my husband to an extent, since I was changing and I wanted him to understand it—to understand how women had been treated—and to be the kind of man who believed in equal rights. Deep down I knew that if he didn't accept the feminist ideology, eventually I would hate being his wife. These were scary thoughts, but I had them."

Wives who began to fathom the social hierarchy in the sixties had a great deal to absorb. The fifties wife, who had an easy time of pretending because it was a quiet time in America, was long forsaken. Even for a sixties wife who held tightly to a gentler time, there was no escaping the daily news. By the late sixties, there was the Democratic National Convention, the Chicago Seven and the rise of the Black Panther party. College campuses abounded with students experimenting with drugs, mostly marijuana and hashish, and Vietnam vets, emotionally scarred and clashing with the drug and hippie culture. In addition, a faction of women who were in college by the end of the decade had little interest in pursuing the early-sixties dream of earning their MRS. by the time they graduated. The credo of the feminists was infiltrating their lives and they embraced it. The faction of women who still sought their MRS. by the end of college was the precursor to the seventies and eighties wives, who believed that they had options; being a wife among them. Whether women appreciated the mantra of the women's movement or not, it could not be ignored. What had held the 1950s wife in her position had dissolved.

As Michael S. Kimmel remarks in his book, *The Gendered Society*, "...the 1950s pattern of family life—characterized by high rates of marriage, high fertility, and low and stable rates of divorce" was over, and "this 'traditional' family began to crack under the enormous weight put upon it." The issues of the sixties contributed to the end of the complacent, housebound wife who was replaced with the working wife. The U.S. Department of Labor, Women's Bureau, reports that in 1960, 37.7 percent of women were in the civilian labor force, but by 1980, over 50 percent of women would be a part of the workforce. These statistics were a result of the women's movement and its influence upon wives.

By the end of the decade, the leading women of the early sixties had a new style, too. Jackie Kennedy remained a fashion icon but the fashion had changed and she was no longer wearing pillbox hats to match her suits. Instead, she wore sleek trousers and fitted sweaters, her hair was longer and she appeared freer, less studied. Jackie Kennedy had been a widow for five years when she married and became a second wife to Greek shipping magnate Aristotle Onassis. If Onassis was not the appropriate choice for JFK's widow, according to the Kennedy clan, as documented in Randy Taraborelli's book, *Jackie, Ethel, Joan*, it represented a departure from her past. Jackie Kennedy Onassis, always an icon, showed the sixties wife that it is never too late to reinvent one's life. While the act of remarriage was not a feminist ideal, the act of seeking one's own fulfillment, in this case Jackie's choice of a husband, represented both individuality and thereby a new and enlightened way of thinking for wives.

By 1962 Marilyn Monroe had died a mysterious death and was deemed an icon of another sort. Although her breed of sexuality might not have set well with the feminists, it was indisputably a kind of power. In a less glamorous style than Monroe's, women were going braless and sporting unshaven legs. Single women seemed to cotton to this theme sooner than married women, but wives were not immune. How far a wife would go was entwined with her husband's response to the feminist revolution. If a wife had an "enlightened" husband, there was a chance that the couple would dabble in feminist beliefs and an alternative lifestyle.

"I was from a middle-class family in a suburb of a mid-size city in the Northeast," begins Brenda, who had married in 1966. "I had a big wedding with lots of guests, and Bert and I counted the checks that we received as wedding gifts until dawn. It was natural that we would move to an apartment at first and then, once Bert finished business school, we would buy a small house and start a family. But the Vietnam War was going on and one of my younger brothers was drafted. That was the first blow to my fantasy of how life should be. Then Bert and I needed more money, despite our wedding gifts, and I went out looking for a better job and got to be manager on a floor of a department store. I really liked it and I liked making money. Then we experimented with pot and we liked that much better than having a drink now and then. Slowly we began to change our buttoned-up way of dressing. I was no longer wearing preppy skirts and sweaters, but going braless and wearing bellbottom jeans. At first no one could believe us, but we were having this metamorphosis.

"Bert was different, too. He'd grown his hair long and was very interested in protest marches and world peace. We began to think that we had too many possessions, that we were too materialistic. After the Democratic National Convention in 1968, we packed up a few things and moved to a commune. I look back at it now as a stage we needed to go through; it shed the past, the way we'd been raised. It made us reconsider our belief system and made us more equal than if we had stayed in the kind of marriage we had married for. There was free love and open sex on the commune and trust became a big issue between us. That we moved home after a year together is a miracle. We adjusted to life after the commune with another point of view."

Not only was the concept of a wedding as the symbol of all that the couple stands for being discarded, not as many women were getting married right out of school as in the past. According to the U.S. Census in 2000, the median age at which women married in both 1950 and 1960 was 20.3, and steadily rose from 1970 on. The fact that women were becoming wives at a later age was an indicator of how women viewed their lives. "It appeared that women were questioning every single institution after the National Democratic Convention," remarks psychologist Claire Owen. "For the wives who had popped pills and were closet drinkers at the start of the decade, there was a movement that made them aware of their own needs. They stopped feeling this low-grade malaise and began to understand themselves better."

In the beginning stages of the feminist movement, minority and working-class women were kept out of the loop. However significant Betty Friedan's work was, it spoke to white, middle-class women. As Rosalinda Mendez Gonzalez notes in her essay, "Distinctions in Western Women's Experience: Ethnicity, Class and Social Change," initially the women's groups "attacked institutions and ideologies as patriarchal without distinction as to class or ethnic inequalities." The battle for women's rights was full fledged by 1970, but it took time for the ethnic female voices to be heard. Gonzales reminds us that "women's struggles to change the conditions of ethnic class, racial or sex discrimination," came later in the movement.

"The women's liberation movement didn't affect me, not at first," begins Kora, who was married in 1965. "I didn't go to college and I hadn't read books about it. I didn't think that my husband and I were not equals. I was too worried about having a job, raising our kids and being treated like I counted outside of our home to think about that stuff. My fear was more that my husband would leave because there were too many responsibilities for him to handle. My sister's husband left, so I knew how easily it could happen.

"It took a few years for me to understand that this movement would help me out. I was very hopeful when Martin Luther King was preaching. I liked his way of doing things and I agreed with what he said. Once he died, I knew we were going to suffer. But I believed in family, I wanted to be married and I wanted to be paid for my hard work. My husband and I didn't have time to work on what they called 'feminist issues.' We were too busy trying to hold it together. Sure, I wanted to be treated better by everyone, my husband, my employer, other women. I had little faith, though; I was just trying to get through."

The assassination of Martin Luther King in April of 1968 and the assassination of Robert F. Kennedy two months later left the world bereft and at a loss. Americans who had been naïve and true believers only a decade earlier now had to face a world filled with gratuitous violence. It was disheartening to recognize that the death of these men proved that a bias persisted against leaders who believed in civil rights. "As a feminist, I knew what we were up against the day that Martin Luther King died," recalls Laura, who became a wife in 1964 and a feminist in 1968. "I saw that bigotry and intolerance still existed, despite all the work that King had done, all that Bobby Kennedy had spoken about. That affected women, too, because we were also trying to be equals in a society that didn't want to let us in." Against the backdrop of the many events and movements in America in the sixties, the women's movement had a deliberate style, and worked hard to have a voice.

The issue of abortion became a prominent and heated topic. The National Organization for Women (NOW), which had been formally incorporated in Washington, DC, in 1967, made its stand on the issue of abortion clear in 1968 when members demonstrated for abortion law repeal. Kate Millet carried a sign: "Nobody Should Legislate My Rights To My Body." At this point, wives jumped on the bandwagon and began to attend "Women's Liberation Groups" around the country.

"I was pregnant when I got married in 1967," begins Ellen. "I knew I had to get married because I didn't want an abortion. In the end I miscarried, but by then I was already married. No one seemed to think about marriage in 1968 and 1969. Girls I knew in school who wore their boyfriend's fraternity pins were out marching for women' s rights. Phrases like "sex discrimination" and "it's my body" were common. Suddenly it all made sense to me and I thought to myself, 'Why did I marry Rob? Why hadn't I just tried to get an abortion? Why couldn't I join my friends with these groups of women?' I realized that because of the women's movement I had become an antiwar activist, and I was for civil rights. I'd never really thought outside myself before. Part of this thinking made me feel younger and more sure of myself, like I didn't have to get married and have kids yet. I could get the Pill and have sex because I wanted to. I could go out and get sex. Wow, it was incredibly unlike anything I'd ever thought before."

Sexual pleasure had not been something women dared to consider before the birth control pill was available. Wives, the only women entitled to have sex, were to have a limited experience while husbands were permitted many sexual experiences in the first part of the sixties, much as it had been in the fifties. But with the drug culture and the sexual revolution, a woman's sexual experience broadened. No longer was reproduction at the heart of the matter, enjoyment for women as well as men became the focus. The new and surprising message that caught on quite rapidly was that women did not have to marry to have sex any more than men did. As Michael S. Kimmel points out in *The Gendered Society*, "Ideologically, feminism made the pursuit of sexual pleasure...a political goal. No longer would women believe that they were sexually disinterested, passive and virtuous asexual angels." The women's movement, the Pill and the availability of abortion made marriage less necessary at an early age for women. The feminists were eager to achieve equal rights for women and were not concerned with the direction of the recent past, which included marriage and families. This is not to say that feminists did not have male partners, if they so chose, but such relationships were of the moment, not a means to an end, and not simply to win a husband.

Early feminists saw themselves as either radical or liberal in their approach. Radical feminists were those women who viewed the gender divide as very important. They believed that men dominate women and that society reinforces this tradition. Liberal feminists are less extreme in their approach, lobbying, for example, for women to have opportunities equal to those of men. Although radical feminists were significantly removed from the life of the everyday wife, their message filtered in to the extent that even a wife who resisted the call to arms could not help but question her life.

Among this substantial group of sixties wives who adhered to the convention-bound lifestyle, even if they identified on some level, few seemed ready to give up their safe havens during this turbulent era. This way of thinking is exemplified in the 2003 film, *Down with Love*, a comedic sixties tale of work versus love and marriage. In this movie, Renee Zellweger plays an author who writes a book about how women can work and not marry, and have sex without love. Although she rises to fame as her readership embraces her philosophy, deep down, Zellweger's character is conflicted about the demands of a career and the conventional path of wife.

A conservative view of marriage persisted in strongholds around the country. This group of women resisted feminist precepts for at least another several years, but eventually saw the benefits of the movement. As for those wives who were swept up in the initial wave, feminism spoke to them of a better, freer life. Psychologist Jo League views it as "a wonderful explosion" for women and wives who had been conformists. "It was intoxicating for women to talk about how they felt after having been so bolted up and powerless for so long," she remarks.

"I knew about the feminists' revolution," begins Doreen, who married in 1966. "I thought it was great, it was about some important things: abortion, sex discrimination at work.

But I was just a working-class wife. I married my high school boyfriend. We had two children under three, what could I do? How could it change my life? I asked myself all the right questions, but I still had the life I had. I worked hours around my kids' and my husband's schedules. Mostly I was a wife and mother. I wanted to bake cookies and had visions of my daughter joining the Girl Scouts. It seemed like a better idea than to join a women's group and complain about how we had been treated for centuries. That was how I first acted when Gloria Steinem and Kate Millet were out there, getting women to join in.

"Then my sister was raped and my mother and I had to do some serious legwork to get her an abortion. That was when I saw how women were treated. It finally dawned on me how women need to have choices. This meant in marriage and outside of marriage, it meant women everywhere. That was when I sort of crossed the line. I said to myself, why not be a part of this great plan for women, the end of women as second-class citizens? I'm married, but it isn't the end all and be all, there are other things. I even realized I wanted to go back to school, get my degree, no matter how I'd been raised, how my husband thought."

As Estelle B. Freedman notes in her book, *No Turning Back*, "The Civil Rights Act of 1964 outlawed racial discrimination but also banned sex discrimination partly at the urging of the lobbyists from the aging National Women's Party. The act established the Equal Employment Opportunity Commission (EEOC) to hear complaints about discrimination based on either race or gender." While in theory this made absolute sense, the world did not change overnight, and it was only through repeat performances and radical statements that all kinds of women heard the voice of the feminists. Alas, here was the early-sixties wife who resonated with fifties concepts, blended with a bit of courage and wiliness, now being given the chance to fight for equality. She was not a frontrunner for the cause. Rather, she was someone who would tread lightly into the next decade. The feminist revolution required a huge adjustment on the part of the population, female and male alike, and this took time and effort.

By the late sixties, wives who had held on tightly to the traditional code of the fifties and early sixties recognized that women were the largest minority in the country, if not in the world. Not every wife was up in arms, however, but many were becoming educated about the feminist treatises. Some women were making headlines, such as Pauli Murray, a black civil rights lawyer, and feminists such as Gloria Steinem and Betty Friedan. Despite the importance of their message for all women, they continued to address mainly upper- and middle-class, college-educated women.

For Randy, it was the very voice of Gloria Steinem that caused her to re-evaluate her marriage and her life. "My husband, Sam, and I had always been secret revolutionaries and removed ourselves from the standard way of living," begins Randy, who was married in 1968. "So the women's movement was a perfect place for us to work together toward a common goal. As uptight as we'd been in high school was as loose as we became by our last year in college. I had joined a women's lib group and Sam decided to make tie-dye shirts after graduation. We felt that we were very politically aware. Even though we married early and marriage was a respected institution, we were different from other married people. We experimented with drugs and wild sex and we lived together for six months before we had our wedding. This really upset our families, but we did get married. Sometimes I think it was just to please our mothers because we were Catholic. I was on the Pill, which also bothered our mothers, but I felt incredibly empowered.

"I look back on that time and I realize that Sam and I grew up together in our marriage. We loved each other— not by playing roles of husband and wife, but by being who we were. It was a marriage with a solid base, without any future career for him or for me, for that matter. We stuck to this plan for two or three years. By the early seventies, we both got graduate degrees and respectable jobs. We did not have children, but we had and still have a great marriage. If the sixties were a time to learn and experiment, it was successful for us. We went to Woodstock together and it was one of the best experiences of my life. The entire country was trying things on for size—most of all, the women's movement helped me be a good wife because I was able to be myself."

The Woodstock Festival, held in 1969, was a departure from the past in many ways, and boasted of a world filled with free love and music. For those wives who attended with their husbands (certainly not a majority of the attendees), the atmosphere was filled with experimental drugs, rock and roll, protest songs and sex. Woodstock had an appeal even for a wife who was steeped in tradition. This is shown in the 1998 film, *A Walk on the Moon,* starring Diane Lane and Viggo Mortensen. The film, which takes place in 1969, is about a young married woman, played by Diane Lane, who senses her life is passing her by when she breaks the rules and has a torrid affair with Viggo Mortensen's character, "the blouse man." They meet in the Catskills where Diane Lane's character, her mother-in-law and children are summering. Her husband, played by Liev Schreiber, is hard at work in the hot city. The affair is a sexual awakening for this wife, who married in the early sixties because she was pregnant, and a foray into a world of music and tactile sensations. The action culminates when she and her lover sneak off to attend Woodstock. Lane's character epitomizes an early-sixties wife, who eventually has a sexual awakening and realizes her own needs, separate from her marriage.

As these wheels of change were churning, Hollywood continued to offer a varied menu for the culture to contemplate. In the film *Rosemary's Baby*, released in 1968, Mia Farrow's character, Rosemary, was a sweet, innocent housewife who did not work and desperately wanted to have a baby. The underlying message, that mother love is the most potent love of all, cannot necessarily be construed as a political statement because the movie was so macabre and filled with evil that it defies most norms. However, the fact that Rosemary's husband sold his soul for an acting career and rapes her in the process, while she is dimwitted about the entire episode, is disturbing for a wife during any decade.

Actresses, women with too much sex appeal to ever play anyone's wife, continued to appear on screen, as the sixth and last James Bond film of the decade, *On Her Majesty's Secret Service*, was released in 1969. Sean Connery, as Bond, was not only a brilliant secret agent but also a great womanizer who viewed women as sexual objects, even in the face of the ardent feminism that was sweeping the country. A 1967 film that addressed the reality of race discrimination was *To Sir With Love*, an emotional movie starring Sidney Poitier as an engineer who is unemployed because he is black. He takes a job teaching high school in the West End of London, where his students come to respect him and his unique way of teaching.

But it was *The Graduate*, released in 1967, that raised serious questions about marriage, motherhood, betrayal and a woman's enduring sexuality. Each of these films depicted a slice of life at the time, and evoked a strong response in wives, even if some were hesitant to react.

A part of the feminist message was that wifehood and motherhood were overrated, and it was only through the sisterhood that women would be propelled to the point where they deserved to be. In decades to follow, feminists would be questioned about this stand, concerning motherhood in particular, and some recanting took place. Yet, in the sixties, at the beginning of the second wave of feminism, the slighting of motherhood was partly in retaliation for the consuming and limiting life women had led for hundreds of years. With this diminishment of motherhood came a diminishment of the role of wife on the most fundamental level as caregiver and mother.

In some ancient cultures wives had, in fact, had equality, and this might have inspired the feminist leaders. For example, ancient Celtic women had an impressively advanced status when it came to marriage and finances, resonating with the goal of the feminists of the sixties. As Peter Berresford Ellis writes in *Celtic Women: Women in Celtic Society and Literature*, ancient female Celts were able to participate in government, become judges, and were permitted to own property that could not be taken away once they were married. If husbands mistreated them, these women had the right to divorce and could claim damages. In contrast to the liberated life of the Celtic wife was the Greek wife of Homeric times. Greek heroes interpreted women as prizes when they left Troy, and marriages were about family status and political connections. If sexual attraction was the reason for marriage (which was not often the case), it was the man who had the option of being attracted to the woman and not the reverse, as reported by Pauline Schmitt Pantel in *History of Women in the West: From Ancient Goddesses to Christian Saints*. It is interesting to compare these two ancient societies to modern times, specifically the 1960s, when women were fighting against the treatment that Greek women received in the time of Homer, and moving toward the kind of consideration Celtic women experienced centuries ago.

"I had to work on my husband to get him to understand what it was that I wanted, not only as a wife, but as a woman," Rebecca begins. "I had been a good wife on the surface, I did all the things I was supposed to do. But what I realized once the feminists made themselves known was that I'd been waiting for this my whole life. The other parts—marrying, cooking, getting pregnant—were all what I was supposed to do. The idea that I could work if I wanted, that men should make way for women at jobs, that I would not have to stay at home the rest of my days and pretend that it was fun, sounded fabulous to me. But I needed my husband to be on board. I wanted him to think that this made sense because I respected him and I wanted to be his wife. Only, better than a wife, I wanted to be his friend. I wanted to share with him and to be important as a person, not a wife only. I think he was baffled, but so much in our society had changed by then, that he had to be open-minded. I felt like he'd been stripped of his power as a husband and a guy who was on the straight and narrow. Too much had changed in our country for him to keep that part up. He had to have a new part and I had already chosen mine. We grew together in a way, something that would not have happened in the early days, when we were a typical young couple, insulated from the world."

Linda Nicholsen sums it up in her introduction to *The Second Wave: A Reader in Feminist History*, when she remarks that the 1960s were a time when the public was beginning to question gender roles. It was this heightened awareness that caused major changes and a point of view regarding gender that still influences people today in both the private and public sectors, according to Nicholsen. This translated into a re-evaluation of one's role as wife. Whether a wife implemented this by the end of the sixties or not, it was a simmering pot, a constant march, a slow dawning, even for those who preferred denial. By 1969, it could not be refuted; women in America had elevated their status, wives included. Equality for women was an honorable cause.

The closing of the 1960s revealed that more major changes had come in a ten-year period than in any previous decade or any to follow so far. The decade was outstanding for its breadth and depth of fresh ideologies and, most significant of all, the push for human rights and egalitarianism. These changes in the American landscape and lifestyle affected people collectively and individually. The majority of my interviewees express adaptation to a new way of thinking brought about by feminism, abortion and birth control, even if they were initially hesitant. The value of being a wife was held dear by most women in the sixties, yet the manner in which one was a wife and the average age of becoming a wife would evolve. This was a by-product of the women's movement and would be realized by the 1970s. Since it takes years for institutions to change, and any departure from the norm is approached with skepticism by the masses, persistence and one's belief system must prevail. For these reasons, the sixties wife was not diminished by the innovations of the decade, but her familiar standing was modified as she became part of her own reinvention.

Chapter Four
The Seventies Wife: Blazers as Armor

W hen I was married in 1972, I knew that I would have a career," Sara tells us. "I had no expectation of what kind of wife I would be, but I knew having children was a part of the package. I loved my husband, Ken, and I wanted to be his wife. Part of the appeal was that Ken was ahead of his time in many ways. But he definitely wanted to raise a family with me. I never planned on having children, and once we were married, I put it off as long as possible. I was in law school and it was pretty gruelling. I began when I was pregnant with my first child, and that was when my husband came through for me. His mother was dead-set against my doing this—becoming a lawyer—but he defended me. He understood. On the other hand, Ken was not around for the day-to-day of raising three boys, all born in the seventies, a time when few women went to law school, and the idea of childcare as a means to have both children and a career was not on everybody's plate. I saw myself as torn in many directions, but also as someone who had an opportunity. I really wanted to be a lawyer and I loved having children, once I had them. I knew I was responsible for them, and I knew that my husband felt less so. Yet, I still see him as ahead of his time because of his support of me.

"The most threatening thing to me was to become a stay-at-home mom without a career. It was something that I dreaded, and I recalled how my mother did nothing but raise me and that her life appeared empty to me, looking at her days and how she had no interests. I did not want that for myself. I was thrilled that she was behind my decision to be a lawyer, but it only drove home the reality that her life was missing something. During my days in law school, I found myself pushing very hard to achieve. Then, when it was finished, I chose an area of law that was not too demanding. I wanted an easy practice, where I could work four days a week. This was because I was married with kids."

The seventies were an exciting time to be female and a challenging decade in which to be a wife. When the Vietnam War ended in 1975, with Gerald Ford as president after Richard Nixon's resignation in 1974, the unified voice of the women's movement was beginning to take effect. The workplace beckoned women, and wives and single women alike were ready to reap the rewards of the fight for equal rights. The earliest baby boomers, true believers in love, romance, marriage and career, marched forth in pursuit of "having it all."

While the role of wife was compelling, the workplace was also seductive. Women with either an undergraduate and/or graduate degree were ready to use their education in a practical way. This was a time when women donned shoulder pads and wanted to dress like men, the standard against which they were compared. It was not until 1982 when Carol Gilligan published *In a Different Voice* that women would realize, at last, that they were compared unfairly to a patriarchal standard of the male, and that they were separate but equal. In the 1970s, wives were determined to set forth in the work world without any modelling for how to balance marriage, mothering and career.

It would take the entire decade for women to recognize that they had only partially arrived in the world by entering the labor force, and that discrimination in the workplace was still rampant. Progress was slow and steady, with many steps backward along the way. The start of the decade was quite promising, with women struggling to be heard. In 1970, thirteen women were elected to Congress: twelve to the House and one to the Senate. The same year, fifty thousand women, single and married, marched down Fifth Avenue in New York City to celebrate the fiftieth anniversary of the Nineteenth Amendment, which granted women the right to vote. The Professional Women's Caucus sued every law school in the country that received funding for discrimination against women. Books were published addressing subjects that had never been contemplated before. *Sisterhood is Powerful: An Anthology of Writings from the Women's Liberation Movement*, edited by Robin Morgan, and *The Female Eunuch*, by Germaine Greer, were both released in 1970, along with the Boston Women's Health Book Collective, *Our Bodies, Ourselves*, a definitive book on how women were to take care of their bodies and their special needs.

While women faced their responsibility to create a better world for their gender, men too were struggling to find their way. For example, in the film *Five Easy Pieces*, released in 1970 and starring Jack Nicholson, a new human condition, a result of the Vietnam War and drug culture—that of running away from one's own heritage in order to find oneself—became known.

The entire country was not in favor of the beliefs of the feminists. *Time* magazine published a lead story on Kate Millet on December 8, 1970, stating that her bisexuality could discredit her as a spokesperson for the feminist movement. Earlier that year, Dr. Edgar F. Berman, a friend of Hubert Humphrey and a member of the Democratic Party's Committee on National Priorities, asserted that women could not hold important jobs because of their "raging hormonal imbalances." The National Organization of Women (NOW) and other feminist organizations forced Dr. Berman to leave the committee. Thus, despite progress, there was a population of Americans who did not rally around the promise of a new universe of equality for women. A survey conducted by the American Association of University Women indicated that 60 percent of men and 43 percent of women were advocates of women as stay-at-home wives and mothers. In this mixed framework of promise and the continual endeavor to be recognized, the seventies wife began her journey.

Wifing Plus Working

Working wives put in long hours only to arrive home for the second shift, that of household duties and managing young children. Quality time versus quantity time for working mothers/career wives soon became a mantra. What faced the working wife in terms of compounded responsibilities was unprecedented. Thus, the decade of the seventies became a time of trial and error. Yet gearing up for the common goal of a dual working couple made sense even if it was a new dimension in a marriage. As Carol Tavris writes in *The Mismeasure of Women*, "unromantic explanations—such as through structure of work—are better predictors of how men and women will get along than are explanations based on male and female 'nature'." The salient question in the seventies was: did wives and husbands on the eve of women penetrating the workplace realize the value of a married couple where both partners worked?

Women began to enter professions that had historically belonged to men, with the percentage increasing exponentially throughout the seventies. In *Feminism in America: A History*, W. O'Neill found that in 1960 only 230 women in the United States were attorneys, but by 1982 twelve thousand women were attorneys, a jump from three percent to 33 percent of the population. Similarly, while only three percent of the population who held medical degrees were female in 1960, females with medical degrees comprised 25 percent of the population in 1981.

By 1975 the working women who were wives were pioneers who had yet to discover that the glass ceiling was real and that their husbands were as responsible for creating and perpetrating it as were other men. Meanwhile, these seventies wives and mothers forged ahead in the workplace, sporting blazers laden down with shoulder pads, on occasion even wearing trousers to the office, in search of perfection. Women had progressed in their thinking and way of envisioning themselves, as evidenced in Barbara Grizutti Harrison's essay, "What Do Women Want?" "In 1959 for every four Smith alumnae who were teachers, there was one in business. In 1979 there were four Smith alumnae in business for everyone in teaching," writes Harrison.

"I was encouraged to have a career in case I never got married," recalls Dorothea, who has been married for thirty-four years. "When I got married in 1970, I only knew about being a dutiful wife. It was almost as if the sixties and all the rebellion had passed me by and the only thing I was prepared for was to be a wife. It hardly mattered that I'd gone to college on a scholarship and that I was fairly talented in the sciences. I was taught that my husband came first and he did. He would have been the most traditional of husbands but we needed money. So he looked upon my taking a job at a science lab as a way to make money for our family and I looked at it as a golden opportunity to use my skills. I have always seen myself as more accommodating toward him than he is toward me. I see myself as someone who bends to his schedule, his corporate travel, his clients. But in the beginning, in the seventies, when we were first married and had two small children, my going to work was a necessity. He had to climb the corporate ladder and build his career. This took a long time in a big company. Today he is successful, but for years, I was the one who was more successful.

"We never talked about how successful I was. That was because I'd been so well trained by my mother and my grandmother to defer to the man. I knew, and the people at the lab knew, that I was excellent at what I do. I was lucky and had flexible hours when my girls were small. That was due to my kind and sympathetic boss who needed me there. He was willing to bend the rules because I did some important things at the lab. As a child of the fifties, married at twenty, I knew that the rules were changing and I was the beneficiary of a decade in which women went to work. I'd observed how my mother and grandmother handled their husbands, and I never let on that I loved my job or how much it meant to me. That way my husband got to think it was all about him. Meanwhile I was ready to march for women's rights. I kept my politics silent, along with my abilities at work. I acted like an old-fashioned wife, but I was definitely one of the trail-blazing working wives. I was never depressed, like my mother and her friends. But I was much more tired than they were. I admit, I was pulled in many directions, but I also had this fabulous career."

In the midst of the roisterous decade of the sixties, wives did not consider the workplace a career, but tried to navigate their path as best they could; it was all about change and equality. The seventies wife was exempt from this kind of thinking, and was receptive to her role as wife, mother and career woman. It all seemed exciting and hopeful. Yet, as in many cases with wives of any decade, how the husband reacted to his wife's style was significant. Plenty of husbands in the seventies admitted that the world was new and filled with options that had not existed before for wives.

These seventies wives felt very fortunate, at the cusp of something fresh, far from the kind of ambivalence and regret that would come to haunt future decades of wives. The idealism of the seventies wife can be compared only to the idealism of the eighties wife. This is perhaps because it took more than a decade for it to sink in that wives were not being treated fairly at work or at home, despite their ambition and their ardent and zealous efforts to be working women and mothers. They had yet to realize how much they were up against—not only husbands who were not trained or particularly educable in terms of sharing childcare after work hours, even with the best of intentions, but also a corporate structure that allowed women in, but not as equals. While wives in the seventies were just beginning their entry into the work world, it seemed to them that it would only be a matter of time before the bias against women, the power structure whereby men ruled American business, would recognize their value and treat them accordingly.

Being a wife seemed, naïvely, all the more interesting because the seventies wife saw that she had superseded the fifties way of thinking, when wives had no careers or aspirations beyond raising their children. They had also gone beyond the sixties wife by putting their money where their mouth was. Liberated sixties wives had demanded entry into the world of commerce, medicine, science, law, advertising, journalism, publishing and the arts. Now the responsibility of the seventies wife was to show their predecessors that they had not fought in vain. The seventies wife was the one to make it a reality.

"I began my marriage working for Beau, my husband, in 1973," Polly tells us. "He needed an office manager and I took the job. We met in a Midwest city and settled on the West Coast. I doubt I was ever in love with him but I admired him; I respected him. There was never going to be enough money and that made me want a better job. Not for anyone's sake but my own. It isn't so much that I was a part of the movement, this surge of women workers. It's just that it was a chance for me to get the right job at a time when women were making progress. So I ended up as an administrator at a college. It was so much better than running Beau's office or teaching, which I'd done years earlier. It made perfect use of my skills. Every morning that I went to work, I felt important because I had this job. I made money, which was amazing.

"Then I had a baby and I felt I couldn't stay on full time. I promised Beau I would cut back. I worked three days a week and left our daughter at my mother-in-law's house on the days I worked. What I learned was that this balance pleased me. Had I wanted more time at the office, a full work week, it would have bothered my husband."

In the early seventies, when wives with and without children were penetrating the workplace, the country was beginning to comprehend the value and abilities of women. Dr. Juanita Kreps became the first female governor of the New York Stock Exchange in February of 1972 and Shirley Chisholm was the first black woman to run for president, supported by NOW, the National Organization of Women. Stanford University conducted a survey reporting that less than one out of twenty-five women graduating from the school expected to be stay-at-home wives and mothers. This was heady stuff and quite unlike the prior decades. Gloria Steinem was the editor and Pat Carbine the publisher of *Ms.* Magazine, which hit the stands in 1972 with articles by Kate Millet, Angela Davis (who had been found not guilty of murder and conspiracy charges by a California jury the same year), and Alice Walker, who published a fiction piece. Women were expressing themselves, taking steps into the unknown in search of personal gratification, with the intention of being both seen and heard. As Katherine

Graham, publisher of *The Washington Post* from 1969 to 1979, viewed it, it had to be enjoyable for women, as well as gratifying. Beyond fun, work was beguiling for women and entirely separate from their marriages. Marriage was only a part of one's destiny for the seventies woman, albeit a substantial piece.

In spite of the mounting proof of women making their mark, sexism persisted, in marriages and in the work world. As Florence Howe points out in her essay "The Proper Study of Woman: Women Studies," in 1975, ten volumes of *Female Studies*—a journal that considered the status of women—were written and distributed in universities. Women in academia hesitated to pursue a doctorate and prestigious positions at this point in time, even with the encouragement of other women. The belief was that women were not supposed to be professors, they were meant to be mothers or to work as teachers or secretaries, regardless of their brainpower. The women who did not fit the mold were considered odd, perhaps even suspicious. Once they hit the workplace outside of academia, they met with less than rave reviews, and much bias. In 1972, NOW and the Urban League filed a class action suit for sex and race discrimination against General Mills.

"Maybe I was unaware of how it would be for me, working and being married at twenty three," recalls Claudia. "I gave up graduate school not for my husband but for a terrific job in magazine publishing. It didn't occur to me until years later that I could have been married, gone to school and worked. I was too new. This was 1976 and I had finished college and landed a job. I got married ahead of most of my friends, but my husband knew my ambitions and it was a good thing, or so it seemed to me. I was moving up the ladder fast when, after three years of marriage, I found myself pregnant. I knew I couldn't have an abortion, not because I didn't believe in abortion, but because I was married and one day we were going to have a family anyway. So at twenty-seven I ended up giving up a career I loved for my baby. I wanted a part-time job, but the company wouldn't consider it, so I began to freelance. At first it was a shock to my system, because I had worked hard every day at the office, late hours, and had never spent much time at home. Suddenly I was a wife and mother and not a career woman. This wasn't an easy adjustment for me. Had I been at it longer or understood how confusing it was to thread it all together, maybe I would have come up with a better solution, like finding help or somehow convincing my boss that I deserved to stay. Ironically, my boss was a man who got it, but couldn't implement anything with this big company. I did get maternity leave, which was beginning to happen in some businesses.

"What I believed in is that I could have a great career, a husband, and eventually children. I was just beginning to see that, no matter what we heard about fair play, it didn't exist. After a year of missing work horribly, being unable to attend even the Christmas party at the company because it depressed me to be so out of the loop, I began to make a career for myself as a contributing editor to several magazines. This worked for me in terms of being available to my baby and my husband. What surprised me was that as much as I loved my baby and my husband, I didn't see how I had to be a martyr. It was a necessary compromise for me but as soon as my son began kindergarten, I resumed a full time job in my field."

While Claudia's efforts to balance children, work and marriage were not always a perfect blend, many seventies wives chose pink-collar jobs that contoured to their children's schedules and reduced their workload once children were on the scene. Pink-collar jobs allow a woman fewer hours and, in some cases, summers off. The jobs work around their children's school hours and school vacations, with the obvious examples being schoolteachers, librarians, college professors, consultants, and freelancers in various fields. For those wives who did not opt for the pink-collar route but remained in their high-powered positions in banking or law, 80 percent of my interviewees reported that if there was a sick child at school, she was the one to leave the office, not her husband, to fetch the child. As Alix Kate Shulman explains it in her essay, "A Marriage Contract," she and her husband could not abide by a verbal agreement, and had to create a formal agreement, "based on a detailed schedule of family duties and assignments." Even with this specific agreement in hand, and her freelance writing job, Shulman describes the difficulty of shedding ten years of "traditional sex roles".

As women combined their work as wives and mothers with their careers, the responsibilities of caring for home and children, undervalued but mandatory in the fifties, questioned and disputed by the late sixties, was invisible work in the seventies. A wife, with or without children, would be ashamed to be at home. Housework remained imperceptible to the outside workforce, and even to the wives themselves, who no longer settled for being at home. The snag was how seriously they were treated in the workplace—the real world of ideas and a vehicle for making money and gaining economic independence. Economic independence was appealing, but women still were not paid fairly. To this day, women receive 73 cents on the dollar for their endeavors, as reported by the National Council of Women's Organizations. For wives and mothers who gave up precious time with their children to be working and building a career, if they were welcome in the workplace it was not readily discernible. These wives required a suspension of disbelief in order to forge forward. According to Concoran and Duncan's 1979 study, the reason men were paid better than women was because they had on-the-job training. This was a Catch 22 for women, for how could they be compared to a man who had been there for decades when women were only beginning to fill positions in the seventies?

"I married in 1975, and it was my goal in life to be a wife. I grew up in a very religious family and this is what was stressed," begins Bethany. "Still, it was the seventies, and I knew that this was the time for women to get great jobs and to do what men had done. I was aware of the feminists and what was now available to women, but all I wanted to do at first was to be a wife, to stay at home with the kids. It was my husband who pushed me, who thought that having a job and getting outside of housewifing and mothering would make my life more interesting. He encouraged me to get my Master's degree and to get a job in advertising. I did this more for him than for me, but once I got there, I saw how important it was for me to be working and for other women to be working. I always felt secure because I had a husband and I knew that he made more money. But I also felt good about myself because I was working, and doing something that I liked. I became stronger because I worked and was more aware of how women lead their lives.

"I think that if I had stayed at home, it would have been so different for me. My life would not have had as many dimensions. I had a few female colleagues and that was fun, even though it was also competitive. Mostly there were men in the office and that wasn't easy. They weren't always nice or fair, but my feeling was that women were just starting out, so nothing had been established yet. No one knew the rules. After I'd been at it for fifteen years, I knew that it was a deliberate bias against women, and that being married made it even harder. I kept waiting for it to get better because more and more women with husbands and kids were working by the end of the seventies and in the eighties."

The trajectory of Bethany's experience, first as a traditional wife and, soon after, as a wife/working woman who became invested in her career, is an example of how a group of seventies wives began their tenure. Women were facing a world that had changed, and they needed to have an independent identity. Although these wives had a heightened sense of awareness when it came to women's roles in the workplace, they also wanted the role of wife, albeit a brave new wife who could have it all—marriage, children and careers. As Dr. Michele Kasson points out, "Women did not give up their identity as wives but added to it. They knew the world was not the same as when their mothers were wives and that they had to move with the times."

Discrimination in the Workplace

Discrimination was reported continually from women in the workplace—as wives, as mothers, and simply for being female. Not surprisingly, there were still many more female teachers than male, and many women preferred a profession where they could avoid prejudice. After all, not every wife was anxious to be a trailblazer. One group of seventies wives understood that their sanity depended upon a manageable life. If these women were intrigued with the workplace and the chance to spearhead, their instincts led them to a gentler area of work. This still included the realm of teaching and nursing, but at least these women had jobs, and had not forfeited them for husbands and children.

"When I got married in 1970, I did not know that I would work. It seemed like an outrageous thing to do," begins Andrea. "It wasn't what I thought my marriage was about, and I very much wanted to start a family. I had my first daughter by the time I was twenty-six and then another girl almost three years later. My husband urged me to go into his business and I thought it would be easy, because I could create my own hours. In 1975, I began to work because my children were in school and I had time. I pretended I was a teacher or a librarian in terms of my hours. I would work until three in the afternoon and would take lots of time off in the summer, around their camp schedules. But as the girls got older, the company grew. I ended up running a very successful manufacturing business with several offices. By the mid-eighties, it was more than a full-time job. It was terrific to see how my ideas came to fruition.

"I don't know if Hank, my husband, would have been as supportive of my work if the business had not been ours. I know that he could count on me and that I did a good job. We ended up having a better lifestyle because of my running this leg of the company. I was sensitive to being available for the girls, but their schedules usually blended with mine. When they were in junior high and high school I was at my busiest, and they were very independent. So that sort of worked out. I had flexibility because I was the boss and, if there was something the girls needed, I did that. I was very fortunate because I did well and also served as a role model for my daughters. Today they are both married and work with me. I never encountered sexism and discrimination because I hired women and it was my show. I think my daughters are sheltered from that also, because they are in our business. I wonder if I would have been as successful or fearless if I had gone to work for a big company like some of my friends did."

In contrast to Andrea's experience is Loretta's decision to work for a family business and her subsequent collision with her family's brand of sex discrimination.

"I doubt that my father ever wanted to hire me but I did get my Master's degree in business and he really couldn't turn me down,'"

begins Loretta, who married in 1978, but had worked for the company for four years prior to her marriage. "I appreciated that I was treated like an equal when it came to vacation schedules and other office rules, and I was a good producer. Once I had a child and we bought a house and renovated it, I needed some extra time, and my father and brothers were not very nice to me. My brothers felt that I was asking for special treatment because I had a baby. Of course, I was. I didn't see either of them running home to take care of their children, because they had wives. I had no wife; I was the wife and the worker. Bending my career around my children's and baby-sitters' schedule was necessary, even though I had a job that was as big a deal as theirs. I felt I had to defend myself, but no one gave me any privileges.

"The message was, you're one of us, one of the guys, so don't go acting like a girl since you wanted to be one of the guys. I began to think that if I worked in a business that was not my family's, I would simply follow their rules and ask for special compensation if I needed it. Then I wouldn't have to face this side of my brother and my father. After eight years of this and two children later, I went to work for my husband, who is a physician, and I ran his office. He was kinder to all of the women who worked there, actually, and it was a much better environment for me. He couldn't be sexist; the office was sexist by nature since all of the women worked for him and he was the boss. On the other hand, it wasn't overt, they were nurses and managers and he was the doctor who everyone came to see. Basically, I've worked my whole married life, but never in the capacity I deserved."

By 1976, when *Redbook* magazine conducted a survey of discrimination against women in the workplace, 90 percent of the young women responded that they felt it was a "serious" issue. At the same time, *The Washington Post* conducted a study with the Center of International Development at Harvard University and learned that men were equally supportive of feminist goals as were women. This applied to a young contingent that was under thirty years of age. For women and men over forty-five, the surprising discovery was that 39 percent of men and 25 percent of women believed that careers came before family for women. These contrasting studies convey the discrepancies in public attitudes and perceptions in a shifting universe for women at the time.

"My husband, Rob, was totally supportive of me," explains Belinda, who was married in 1977, at the age of twenty-six. "He had a job with a construction company as an administrator and I had a job at a bank. I dressed for success every day. We both believed in teamwork and the idea of raising children in an equal partnership. We both saw my career as important and practical—the salary mattered and I was doing what women were getting a chance to do, have a good job. Rob and I agreed on the Equal Rights Act and what feminists believed in. When I was passed over at the bank after six years of hard work and dedication, we both saw it as discrimination and as a way to keep women from getting ahead. It took me double the time it would have taken a man, but I did eventually get the promotion. I think that my husband's constant belief in me made it happen. There were no other women around, only men once I was promoted."

Not only was it not easy for women to climb their way to the top in the seventies, but even *Ladies' Home Journal*, a magazine that devoted itself to housewives, had only given the position of editor-in-chief to a woman once in its ninety-year history when Lenore Hershey was awarded the position in 1974. The appointment of Lee Anne Schreiber as sports editor of *The New York Times* in November of 1978, at the end of the decade, was further proof of women getting ahead. Not only did Schreiber have fifty reporters answer to her, but she ran the Sunday Sports section and Sports Monday as the first woman in this position. This was the same year that women were denied disability pay for pregnancy by the U.S. Supreme Court. And while sexual harassment would not become breaking news until the Anita Hill-Clarence Thomas debacle in 1990, in 1975 the Working Women United Institute's research indicated that 70 percent of its respondents had endured an incident of sexual harassment. The survey also indicated that this was not specifically targeted at women of a particular age, and that it did not matter if women were single or married.

Discrimination against wives in the workplace had not been addressed before, but prior to the seventies, minorities and the working poor were not treated fairly. The slow recognition began when women stepped forth to fight for their rights, paving the way for other minorities to do the same. As Marilyn French points out in *The War Against Women*, "War against women in the workplace may have a single main intention—to keep them in an inferior economic position." According to French's research, it is not only discrimination against women, but racial discrimination against women. "Twice as many black women as white are killed at work," she notes, based on a *New York Times* article from August 16, 1990, which reports that murder is the leading cause of death for women in job-related injuries. The seventies working wives were not only not yet cognizant of this fact, but were too invested in the idea of work to give up on their hard-earned progress, even with such knowledge.

It is not that the seventies wife did not recognize the layers of prejudice—for being married, for being a wife who had no children, for being married with children. Male bosses could raise their brows at any status of women and many of them believed in the old school of thought—that a woman worked until she became a wife, or as a wife until she had children. It was unprecedented to leave one's babies at home to forge a career. In fact, if a wife had children, the boss was waiting for a shoe to drop—some kind of child-related emergency to reinforce his expectation that he could not count on this wife/mother/employee to show up. There were school concerts, Little League games and other activities that the wife/mother/employee had to attend. Husbands/fathers/bosses did not have to attend these events to the same degree, at least in the opinion of male bosses. That had been the norm. Ideally, the wife and her husband would share their attendance at the obligatory school/sports events for their children. Yet, when push came to shove, it was the ever-acrobatic wife who ended up the spectator for her child. Fathers were excused because of work, while mothers did both things full-time.

"It wasn't that my job didn't matter compared to my husband's job," begins Ellie, "but I had two jobs and my husband only had one. My jobs mattered greatly, both of them. All day long I worked for the Board of Ed, and all night long I did the wash, helped my kids with homework, and made dinner. At night, my husband, Ted, basically watched sports and read the papers. I would be in the kitchen alone, cleaning up, wondering if it was worse to be discriminated against at my office job, or in my job as a wife and mother. My office was becoming modern, and I liked the work. It took years for me to be heard by my husband, who did not get it. He did not see why it was so hard for me to work and run the house. He didn't have to get it because it wasn't his problem. It made me feel alone and angry. I decided not to give up on either mothering or working. I decided if anything had to go, it was the marriage. Subconsciously he must have figured it out and, eventually, we found a common ground."

The seventies were faster-paced, with fax machines and computers beginning to edge their way across the horizon, along with the idea of the workaholic. Many seventies wives were determined to make a success of their careers, especially those who had attended law school, medical school or business school, as soon as the doors were open to minorities, including women. The chance to work in these fields had not been available to women previously, so they were going to make it into something very real for themselves. As Marion Velez, social worker, notes, "Married women had little idea how complicated it was going to be to raise their children and work in these demanding careers. In the seventies there was no one who had been there before and they had to figure it out for themselves." The idea of having a career was like a contagion for women, and wives constituted a large part of the working population. The big question that wives asked each other by the mid-seventies was, what field are you in, not how many children do you have? While the answers varied, the majority of women were making an effort to incorporate work into their lives as wives and mothers. Economic freedom, even for those wives who made less than their husbands, was an exciting element of the seventies marriage.

Romance and the Seventies Wife

Famous and diverse wives were emerging in the seventies, some with careers, some without. Each of these wives was visible through the media, and wives who watched from afar had a sense that romance was a part of the quotient. This group of seventies wives included Yoko Ono, who married John Lennon in 1969, thereby forming a prominent seventies couple who participated in peace sit-ins and cut several albums together. In 1971, Tricia Nixon, daughter of President Richard Nixon, became the sixteenth bride to be married in the White House. Only two years later her mother, Pat, a dedicated wife, would find her husband, Richard Nixon, disappointing due to his involvement in the Watergate scandal, and become emotionally distanced from him. This exhibited what can happen to even strong, successful marriages that are placed under enormous strain.

Mick Jagger and Bianca Perez were also wed in 1971. Actress Joan Collins' third marriage began in 1972 when she married Ronald Kass, a music and film producer. Princess Anne, the only daughter of Queen Elizabeth of England, married Captain Mark Phillips in 1973. In 1975, Hillary Rodham married her fellow Yale law school classmate, William Jefferson Clinton, and an ambitious political couple was born. Lisa Halaby married King Hussein of Jordan in 1978 to become Queen Noor. Actress Elizabeth Taylor was married to Richard Burton from 1964 to 1974 in their first marriage, only to remarry him in 1975. The second time lasted less than a year. Laura and George W. Bush married in 1977 at a small wedding with only seventy guests. Patricia Hearst married her bodyguard, Bernard Shaw, two years after she was released from prison in 1979. Perhaps not all of these wives were starstruck with the role. Yet the fact that so many famous couples chose to wed supports the sensibility that everyday women shared— marriage continued to matter, and being a wife remained a substantial role.

As noted by Juanita H. Williams in her essay "Sexuality in Marriage," "shifts toward greater power and participation for women can now be seen in the personal, social, political, and economic sectors of their lives. These changes affect sexuality in marriage either directly or indirectly." In fact, most wives in the seventies were beginning to feel freer sexually, and more in touch with their own desires. When Marilyn French published the novel *The Women's Room* in 1977, wives were exposed for what they suffered not only in the late sixties when the book begins, but through the seventies, as wives pushed through the disappointments of husbands, children and romance in order to define themselves in a world defined by feminism. A year before *The Women's Room* hit the stores, *The Hite Report: A National Study of Female Sexuality* was published. Written by Shere Hite, the book is considered a classic feminist view of sex as women experience it in their frustrations with their partners and their own inner yearnings.

Love was riveting, and the myth of romantic love remained as popular in the seventies as it had been in the past two decades, particularly the fifties. But now there was a new twist—that of discarding love, if it didn't seem right. This applied mostly to single women, who seemed willing to take chances in order todo it correctly. Hollywood offered an example of this in the 1976 Woody Allen film *Annie Hall*. Annie Hall, played by Diane Keaton, wore male-type clothing and did not marry. She was independent, at times confident, and distinctly not a wife. Many wives of this era experienced a combination of ambition in a career, mothering and a faster-paced life than in previous times. If the fifties had been tranquil to the point of boredom and closet drinking for wives, and the sixties so turbulent that marriage existed without much attention being paid to the institution, the seventies marriage was a main event, made all the more appealing because it could be coupled with a full life, including a career and independence.

"I had a career, and I liked being married," begins Louisa, who was married in 1976. "I didn't marry to have status and I didn't work to have status, but I saw that both did that for me. It was romantic to get up and travel on the commuter train to work with my husband. I felt important and like I was appreciated. I put off having kids as long as I could and I worked on myself and my marriage. I loved it. I remember when we were first married, I could not wait to be Joe's wife. Then, within a year, I saw there were shifts in responsibility once I became a manager for a chain of health clubs. Suddenly Joe knew that I had a good job and a place out in the world. I think he liked it, and it was romantic to be working all week and have these great weekends together. We were experimental, because it was a new era. We went to parties that were practically orgies, but we were always a couple. There were few disruptions in our marriage in the seventies because we had no kids yet and we had enough money so that we weren't stressed about that. We concentrated on the relationship, and I think that made it work."

In 1977, Plato's Retreat, a swingers club, was opened by Larry Levenson, a former fast food manager on the Upper West Side of Manhattan in the Ansonia Hotel. This popular club, exclusively for married and committed couples, reflected the sexual curiosity that existed within some of these partnerships. Levenson had plans to open Plato's Retreats in cities across the country, but sex clubs came to an abrupt halt with the discovery of AIDS in the early eighties. Of course not all seventies couples were in search of Plato's Retreat, complete with orgies and optional nakedness on the dance floor.

Earlier in the decade, Eric Segal's soapy novel, *Love Story*, was released as a film starring Ali McGraw as Jenny and Ryan O'Neill as Oliver. The movie took a stab at the life of the elite versus the working class and made much of romantic love and marriage for this ill-fated couple. Bold in its exposé of the class system, the movie was filled with the idea of marriage as romantic more than sexy. Jenny's career, although she had graduated from Radcliffe College, was that of a schoolteacher, while Oliver was, naturally, a lawyer. The main obstacle for the couple was that Oliver had been cut off from his father for marrying someone "beneath his station," socially speaking.

By 1978, 64 percent of the population was married, according to the National Center for Health Statistics. While women might have felt fortunate to be wives and career women, the Women's Bureau of the U.S. Department of Labor reported that they still were not paid fairly for equal work. This affected close to half the population of wives, who were in the labor force, but not the other wives—those who did not enter the workforce and were at home with their children. Although this latter group constituted half of the population, they were perceived as a minority, not as forceful as the working wives of the seventies. Many members of this group of wives were disconcerted with the times and perhaps slightly bored at home, while their peers were out in the real world. The suburban wife of the seventies was hip and more open sexually than her predecessors, but not always content. This slice of life can be seen in the 1999 movie *The Ice Storm*, an Ang Lee film that takes place in 1973 in New Canaan, Connecticut. Ben and Elena Hood, a married couple, are losing their way against a backdrop of Watergate, marijuana for adults and children, and their defiant teenagers. In the fishbowl existence depicted in *The Ice Storm*, there are wife-swapping parties (as there were in the sixties), and it is not uncommon for a wife to conduct an illicit affair with her friend's husband. Only when tragedy strikes this community do wives and husbands re-evaluate their lives.

"I know that my ambition dissolved because of me; no one else is to blame," begins Jane, who became a wife in 1974. "I married a man who wanted a wife, not a working woman who could sometimes be his companion. He seemed like he believed in the new age of women working but I learned after we were married that he disdained women who wanted to get ahead. It was strange because I was not one of those women who were fixated on being married, like some of my friends had been. Growing up, I had a friend who would fantasize whenever she had a date about which guy she would marry. I wasn't like that. So finding out that my husband didn't advocate for my working or working women in general was a bit of a shock. But I decided that I had married the right person and that I would make this work; he just needed to be educated. I agreed to be a stay-at-home wife once we had kids and worked hard until then in my career. Once we had two children, I found my life as a wife and mother to be more demanding. That was when I decided I would give the kids until kindergarten and then go back to get a great job. I wanted a life beyond what I was doing. When I explained my plan to my husband, I realized how much we cared about each other. But it requires constant work, even if the love is in place, to have kids, a job and a husband."

Women who felt successful in the seventies faced two components, career and romance, that had not been emphasized by their predecessors. Children as a part of the marriage were, for the most part, expected, and remained an age-old reason to be married. Career and romance, as pieces of a marriage that lasts beyond the early days, were enticing for the wife of this decade. It was as if the post-war wife of the fifties and the developing wife of the sixties who gained the right to birth control and women's rights culminated in the seventies wife, who was out there for the first time, brought to that place by the radical sixties and complacent fifties women. If romance had seemed almost beside the point in the fifties and was sidetracked in the sixties, now was the chance to have romance in one's marriage *and* to have a career of one's own. It was challenging, but seventies wives were very idealistic—it was the lack of modelling that caused them to be this way. They were beginning to believe that they could "have it all," a mantra that would come to haunt the eighties wife and send the nineties wife spinning in all directions. Yet in the infancy stages of "having it all," it was a bewitching premise. As Antoinette Michaels, relationship expert, points out, women have a much more idealized concept of life than do men. "In the seventies, women were trying to weigh both their careers and their marriages. The energy they put in sometimes ended up tipping the scale," she observes.

For Alison, who became a seventies wife in 1975, there was mutual respect for "hers" and "his" business obligations.

"Sometimes I think it was because I was not fixated on being married that it has worked out so well for Tad, my husband, and me. When we first married, I worked for him at his office. That was okay, but a bit old fashioned, and it wasn't really what I cared about. It was still about him. I left and was able to get a job in fashion, which was interesting to me. I made a career of it, and kept my energy up for the marriage, and we always traveled for his work or mine. These trips were busy but we made an effort for them to be romantic too. No wives had traveled for work in the past, and it was a whole new thing. Sometimes we were on a business trip for Tad and sometimes for my work. When it was my office, he was the wife. When it was his business,

I was the wife. We would make sure that one night was just for the two of us, no matter what. Our lives required the same amount of energy to be poured into the marriage as into our careers. We shared the same values and that is why it worked. We were smart enough to stave off any complications by assessing our marriage like we assessed business plans at work. That's how it stayed romantic."

The notion of a romantic marriage became commingled with the notion of a working wife. It struck a wife's fancy that, as she put on her navy gabardine jacket and matching skirt, medium-inch heels, and white shirt with a scarf tied to resemble a man's tie, she was in love with life, with her husband, and with the possibilities in store for her. At this juncture, wives began putting off having a first baby for a few years, a trend that steadily increased per decade until infertility crept into the modern wife's reality.

The seventies wife did not entertain these thoughts—she was just starting out, and life was rich with options. As the late Stephen A. Mitchell viewed romantic love in his book, *Can Love Last? The Fate of Romance Over Time*, it is the couple themselves who are guilty of destroying the romantic element of their love. According to Mitchell, people feel off center when they are head over heels in love, but then the partners tend to make it mundane as a way of controlling the situation. The romance becomes ordinary, not extraordinary, taken over by the day-to-day life each partner leads. While marriage creates stability, it also squashes the initial excitement. The seventies wife was able to avoid this trap for some time by virtue of the teamwork she and her husband built together. Husbands were changing at this time in history, too, and the seventies wife welcomed a husband who understood she had no time to cook dinner, who realized her value in the workplace and her individuality. How could she not be in love with a supportive husband who treated her like an equal—or so it seemed.

Mothering and Work

Whether they have careers or not, it is a hard lesson for wives to learn that babies change everything. The fifties wife and the traditional sixties wife went after childbearing without much thought and little choice. By the end of the sixties, radical feminists were dead-set against babies, viewing them as a form of stymieing women. Although this is not the long-term message from the feminists, it was conveyed to women at one time. Whether it was taken literally or merely as food for thought, the message caused women to consider themselves and their lives, not just the lives of those around them—those of husbands and children. An inexperienced seventies wife adhering to the model of children and work anticipated that she could succeed but was missing the logic to analyze the situation. Thus, it was a rude awakening to learn that finding dependable childcare and leaving one's young children to go to an office would be so complicated. This issue would loom large for the decades to follow, without any salient solution.

Even with undeniable setbacks due to childcare glitches and part-time versus full-time work, the statistics from the U.S. Census still revealed that close to 45 percent of the workforce was comprised of married women with children by the end of the seventies. From 1960 to the 1970s, married women were responsible for close to half of the increase in the labor force. Clearly, the shift had taken place. Wives no longer left jobs when they got married, and not as often when they had children. Instead, they modified their work hours, if at all possible. According to Leibowitz, Waite and Witsberger in their study, "Child Care for Preschoolers: Differences by Ages," women who were better educated and paid higher wages were better at finding reliable childcare. By 1975, 36 percent of women with preschoolers were in the workplace, as were 52 percent with children under eighteen, according to the Childcare Action Campaign. Yet the dilemma for working mothers was very real, and many of them equivocated over what was right, mothering full-time or working.

The seventies was the first decade for wives to wrestle with this large, unrelenting issue. In her essay, "The Mommy Wars: Ambivalence, Ideological Work, and the Cultural Contradictions of Motherhood," Sharon Hays writes: "Leaving one's child with a paid caregiver for hours on end is therefore a potential problem not only because that other mother may not be a good mother but also because the real mother misses out on the joys that come from just being with the child.... This is a heartrending issue for many mothers who work outside the home." The argument for ambitious women with children was one the seventies wife could only envision, but not yet know (as those working wives of the following decade would) for certain; if one takes time out from the fast track to be a stay-at-home mother, the momentum is lost. In other words, society does not make allowances for working mothers; it caters to men who have no such conflict.

"I finessed the marriage part and managed to stay happily married while becoming a physician in the seventies," begins Jaycee. "And I did well in medical school, my internship and in my residency. But once I had a baby, it was really crazy. My husband was also in medical school, so we were on very similar schedules with similar demands. Neither of us was able to take care of a baby full-time because we were so preoccupied with getting somewhere. That is the nature of becoming a doctor. I asked my mother-in-law and my mother to help out, but both turned me down and thought it wasn't necessary for me to become a doctor. They were only proud of me after the fact, but didn't get what it entailed or why I couldn't make a schedule around their schedules and the baby's needs. It was not easy because I couldn't get support anywhere. Some of the other female doctors didn't even understand. I felt so alone and so tired. My husband, Gary, thought that now that there was a baby we were not on the same path. I was the one who was supposed to put my life on hold, not him. I didn't love him as much any more, or my career. I was in love with this baby but I needed help. In the end I used nursing students and found someone to live in our house and that worked. I relaxed eventually but then I felt guilty because I'd be leaving for hours at a time to go to the hospital. It wasn't easy. I don't see how it can be easy, even if more wives are doing it nowadays."

The seventies wife who had kept the romance alive a bit longer than her predecessors was genuinely baffled when a baby arrived and confounded an already intense schedule. Romance had lasted longer only because the seventies wife was so pleased with herself, and therefore could afford to be a benevolent, rather than resentful, wife. Until the baby arrived, the seventies wife did not believe that the bubble would burst because she did not know what mothering entailed. Her mother, a fifties wife, had appeared bored to her, with time to herself, and there was no modelling for a working wife such as Jaycee, who was in her residency when her baby was born. Many seventies wives, especially toward the end of the decade, had put off having children for a few years in favor of their careers. This would become a trend by the eighties, and a problem by the nineties for career women due to fertility issues.

Women still had the primary responsibility for childcare, even with the increased number of wives in the workplace. Husbands/fathers did not alter their schedules and help more with household chores once a baby was born into the family. Due to this dismal reality, wives/mothers began to take on what would become known as the "second shift" of household responsibilities and parenting that followed a full day's work. No wonder the seventies wives were no longer feeling as romantic and that childcare became a premium.

Even though there was a longer wait between one's wedding day and conception, it did not yet alter the status quo for couples having children. Wives were not actively seeking abortions, but there was a heightened awareness of an available method for unwanted pregnancies. Most seventies wives believed that abortion was not in their cards, but identified strongly with the issue and were able to plan their families thanks to the Pill, combined with the philosophy that marriage was not only a means to raise families—that it was about partnership and careers, too. If wives viewed abortions as far from their realm, it remained an academic women's rights issue. The case of *Roe versus Wade* was decided on December 22, 1973, after two years of deliberation. The outcome of this case was that a woman's right to privacy was granted and a woman was allowed to have an abortion if she so desired. This was a huge victory for women and offered women of any social strata the chance to decide their own fate.

"Of course, I believed in abortion," admits Sally, who married in 1978 at the age of twenty-three. "I just didn't think it had anything to do with me. I knew all through college that it was an option if anything went wrong. I planned to have children and I saw it more as something my friends had to do when they were dating. I was the first of my friends to be married. Right after I married Hal, I found out I was pregnant. I had just been accepted to business school. We both came from poor Black families, and this was a big deal for me. My husband was a few years older and had already gotten a fairly good job. I knew that because he was working and was making good money he would want me to have the baby, so I didn't tell him and I had an abortion while he was out of town for three days on a business trip. I felt sorry for him, because he was ready, but not sorry for me. It was not an easy decision, but I feel I had to do it. I did get my degree and a good job and did well for three years at this accounting firm before we had our first child. This was better for me. I never told Hal, because I didn't think he would have understood. When I look at the world of choices for women, abortion is extremely important. I could have gone either way since I was married and we had the resources, but having my kids later worked for me and my career and my marriage."

In contrast to Sally's decision to have an abortion is Lisa's experience as a young mother:

"I was married in 1977 and I thought I was destined for an amazing career," begins Lisa. "I had gotten a job in a food company and was really happy. I thought my husband was everything I hoped he would be and that this was going to go so well. Then I became pregnant. It was a time when my friends were not only putting off babies, but putting off marriage. There was this feeling that women would work and do well and then have babies and husbands. So there I was, stuck in a life like my mother's or my grandmother's. Both of them convinced me to have the baby. And my husband was so excited, which made little sense since we had purposely decided to wait at least four years. I surprised everyone by going back to work right after my son was born. I found a wonderful part-time sitter, and my husband and I worked our hours out so that we were always covered. I just couldn't believe how young I was to be a mother and how anxious it made me. Work had never made me anxious and I was usually a relaxed person. Now I no longer felt invincible, I felt vulnerable and very, very responsible. That is what mothering is like. Then David, my husband, became very busy at work and got a promotion and began to travel. This was 1979, and our son was one. He began to make noise about my taking time out to care for our son and our marriage.

"I couldn't trust the woman who watched our baby full-time. So I decided to take time off, have another baby and stay in touch with my boss, doing consulting work for the firm. I finally found someone good with the children, and by the time my son was in kindergarten I went back to work and put our daughter in daycare at the company. I was relieved that this was available and I felt good about myself doing it. Taking care of the kids full-time had made me feel like life was passing me by even though I adored my little children. David adjusted and I learned not to listen to him but to listen to my own inner voice. It was my life, not his, that we were talking about."

The take-charge attitudes of both Sally and Lisa, in unique ways, are notable. By the end of the seventies, women were able to do this, because they had been exposed to a world outside the home, and the political climate for women had improved tremendously through endeavors by NOW. At the 1977 National Women's Conference in Houston, Texas, such illustrious women as Coretta Scott King, the widow of Martin Luther King, Rosalyn Carter, the wife of the President at the time, and former first ladies Betty Ford and Lady Bird Johnson attended. Their attendance signified the importance of women's rights and the ongoing battle to make it happen.

Daycare became an increasingly meaningful issue for wives in the 1970s. In 1975, the Comprehensive Child Development Act was passed by Congress, then vetoed. Earlier in the decade, in 1973, the New York City NOW chapter joined one thousand demonstrators at Health, Education and Welfare (HEW) headquarters to protest proposed federal regulations that would end daycare for many recipients. In 1978 the 95th Congress passed the Pregnancy Discrimination Bill, so that women would receive disability benefits for childbirth and recovery. It took two years of campaigning on the part of NOW and pro-choice groups for this to take effect. In brief, working wives with children began to advance themselves based on a social climate that was establishing new standards for women.

But there was no easy solution for working mothers, and what they did with their young children in order to be back at work full-time was unprecedented. While, in theory, mothers-in-law and mothers would have sufficed as caregivers, the seventies grandmother did not feel that the original trajectory of her life—to marry, have children, grandchildren, and die—was so appealing. Since she had been conventional about her marriage and her children in the fifties, she now realized her own power, too. Thus, many seventies wives, according to my research, found their mothers-in-law and mothers busy with their own lives, whether to play cards, work part-time or travel, and therefore not so inclined to care for their grandchildren. Meanwhile, their daughters were attempting to leave the house for twelve hours in order to put in a complete workday, including travel time and the time required at the office. As a result, the seventies wife had to be resourceful because no one was stepping up to the plate to help.

"I knew I could get part-time or full-time help," explains Charlotte, who was married in 1976 and had twin daughters in 1979. "But I saw some of my friends at home with their kids and others putting their kids in daycare and I didn't know what to do. I asked my husband what he thought and he said to try work first and if I couldn't abide it, to come home and be with the kids for a few years. Our daughters were six months old at this time. I worked for a family business and I asked my aunt, who was otherwise ahead of her time, if I could take off Fridays. She said no. She had no children and this business was her life. I couldn't believe there was no real support and I didn't ask my mother—I knew what she would say. She would say stay at home. But I felt deprived, denied my job, and I hated that feeling. My husband's support was fizzling once we had this instant family of two children. It didn't seem to matter to him what I wanted any more. I saw him as asking me to sacrifice and I didn't like it. I resented it. His life would be the same. All the messages about how women could have it all were missing. My closest friends told me outright that they weren't ready to have babies but they had husbands and jobs. I felt trapped, and in the end I made a deal with my aunt, after months of going back and forth. I did this for six years, until the girls went to school a full day in first grade. By then I was more comfortable with daycare, and the school bus dropped the girls off at an after school facility. I did not see my children on those days until six at night.

"I would work at home two days a week, and the other days I would put the girls in daycare and come to the office. The days at the office were much easier, which surprised me, because at home I had to be wife and mother, too. If a client called and I was trying to sound businesslike, I had my toddlers pulling on my legs and crying and getting into mischief. I felt like a fake. My husband would actually call wanting to know what was for dinner on the days I was at home. It was sheer determination that got me through and today I run the company and my daughters see me as an excellent example of a woman who can win."

For wives who were in part-time as well as full-time positions with small children, reliable childcare solutions were imperative. As the children became older, another kind of conflict presented itself for the working wife/mother. She had to attend soccer games and ballet recitals and chauffeur children to activities after school if they lived outside a city with no public transportation. In future decades, there would be wars between working mothers and those who chose to stay at home, and defectors from both sides. The zealousness of the seventies wife, frantically trying to create her place and get it right, pre-empted any schisms between the two factions of wives during this decade. As life became more expensive due to the cost of raising children, the husband's point of view changed. Husbands who might have resisted when the children were small, advocated that wives work at least part-time for the extra income as the children approached junior high school. This was expedient for the seventies wife, who found that having her own career was fulfilling. "If I have to let my husband believe it's purely financial, so be it," remarked one seventies wife who returned to work gleefully after a four-year stint of full-time mothering and wifing.

What set the seventies wife apart from wives of previous decades was her emotional awareness. As Dr. Ronnie Burak remarks, "The seventies wife was the one who had to feel her way through in order to decide to take care not only of her children and husband, but herself."

What is so striking about the seventies wife was her determination to make it work, despite the obstacles that could not be denied. There had not been much delving into the emotions of the nonworking fifties wife and the early-sixties wife. The late-sixties wife was vociferous about a future where women had choices, but she was not a part of the decade to experience it; instead she was the voice of the future for wives. Therefore, it was the seventies wife who became the leader, the trailblazer, working her way through the societal standards to rewrite them. In doing so, she would be aiding future wives in the decades to come.

Part Two:
Entering the Future

Chapter Five
The Eighties Wife:
A Variety of Power

I got married to Zackary in 1982 after a failed engage-ment to another man," begins Clarissa. "Because my first attempt at marriage failed before it began, I thought that I was being careful in choosing Zack for his ambition. This proved he would be a provider and he seemed to love me more than I loved him. I needed these things in a marriage, even though there was no question that I would work, because by the early eighties, this is what wives did. I was twenty-nine years old and ready to be married and my job as an interior designer was going really well.

"We had two children in the first three years of our marriage and moved to a nice neighborhood in the suburbs. I immediately had lots of business because all of the wives were obsessed with their houses and kitchens. That was when I realized that wives were very into status, whose husband did what, and where the children went to school. Even if a wife had a successful career of her own, she was supposed to be a society wife, with dinner parties and the right children who did the right things. Couples would show off and Zack began to pressure me to be a part of this scene. He wanted me to mix more with the other wives—he said it would further his career and mine. He kept telling me that together we made a great team. I didn't like that suddenly I was a commodity—there was this belief that what a wife did would help the husband because either she had a good job or she was socially adept."

Marriage continued to be a meaningful part of a woman's life in the 1980s. However, now a mixture of wife as an accomplished businesswoman and wife as a socialite was coming together as a blend of the seventies wife and the fifties wife. The eighties wife could enable her husband, and also be powerful on her own. The couple generated the accolades of two successful career people in one marriage. Social status mattered more than in the past. Being a wife only enhanced one's place in a world where the preoccupation with marriage as an entré into society was placed at a premium. The ticket for the eighties could be either success or family money, as long as there was plenty of money for the couple to boast about. Thus, the climate of the eighties was reflected in a rise to power through money that was no longer quiet but at times ostentatious, as corporate raiders and Wall Street demanded center stage. The wives of these successful men were unprecedented in their style and were distinctive from wives of successful men in the past. This, of course, did not apply to all wives. There were many working wives who were not a part of society. Still, the emphasis on society for those who could belong was a departure from the past two decades in the life of the wife.

For the eighties wife who took her job seriously and worked long hours in order to rush home to her husband and children, the decade began much as the previous decade had been for the seventies wife. However, now both wife and husband were afforded the opportunity to shine in unique and complementary ways. This flavor of the eighties wife in the first part of the decade was to be followed by irresolute wives and failed marriages. Although the option of divorce had been constant on the radar screen of the seventies wife, it was the eighties wife who put it into play. The combination of being independent by making one's own money, two decades of feminist treatises and a heightened self-awareness caused the eighties wife to realize that an unhappy marriage did not have to be her fate. It was the beliefs of the feminists and the commitment to the workplace, combined with mothering and wifing, that caused an eighties wife to be disenchanted to the point of seeking a divorce.

My research indicates that the idea of the career wife, who put her ambitions ahead of her personal life, became quite common by the mid-eighties. The early part of the eighties began with wives holding on to the myth of "having it all," much like their seventies predecessors. Yet B. Long's 1983 study showed that by the early eighties, women in the workforce were in search of career, and their desire "to raise a family" diminished from 77.8 percent to 64.48 percent by 1979. By the end of the decade, this kind of thinking would apply not only to college-educated women, but would also affect working class women as each recognized the deficiencies in marriage and at last sought something for themselves.

As with any decade, changes came in many ways, through both sadness and progress. In 1980, John Lennon was assassinated, and his wife, Yoko Ono, became a widow. In 1980, Ronald Reagan defeated Jimmy Carter in the presidential election, and in 1981 he appointed Sandra Day O'Connor as the first woman on the Supreme Court. In 1982, actor John Belushi died of a drug overdose, and in 1984, the singer Marvin Gaye was shot to death by his father while the two men were arguing. On July 29, 1981, Prince Charles and Diana Spencer were married at St. Paul's Cathedral to the tune of 52 million dollars in pomp and ceremony. On July 19, 1986, Caroline Kennedy married Edwin Schlossberg at a wedding in Centerville, Massachusetts. Three months earlier, on April 26, 1986, Caroline's cousin, Maria Shriver, married actor Arnold Schwarzenegger. Shriver, the niece of John F. Kennedy, stayed a Democrat while Schwarzenegger remained loyal to the Republican party. Actress Joan Collins was married for the fourth time, to Peter Holm, in 1985, in a marriage that lasted one year.

Working wives and mothers cheered for Christa McAuliffe, the first female astronaut, a married woman with young children, only to mourn her passing when the Challenger space shuttle crashed in January of 1986. In 1984, Geraldine Ferraro, a Democrat from New York who was both wife and mother, was chosen by Walter Mondale to be his running mate in the position of vice president. This was the first time in American history that a woman was chosen on a major party ticket. Ferraro was pro-choice and the women's groups that had fought hard for a woman to be considered on a presidential ticket were satisfied.

The Economic Boom and the Society Wife

The expectation that the eighties wife would aid her husband, not in the shadows as the fifties wife, but with her own weight added to the mix was enticing initially. In upper-echelon social circles, the power couple, with the husband a success in business and his wife a success in a variety of ways, became important. This was due to a new manner of wifing, the economic climate, certain social circles, and was a reflection of the first lady at the time, Nancy Reagan. While it seems unfair that author Kitty Kelly, in her *Unauthorized Biography of Nancy Reagan* attacked Mrs. Reagan for being a "social climber," it is true that Nancy Reagan devised a social White House. This lasted from 1980 until 1988, when President Reagan finished his second term.

The image of housewife was long gone, while the pressure to work existed for a multitude of eighties wives. Now it was coupled with an emphasis on society, since the booming economy did not require that both partners work. While plenty of working wives wanted to work, nonworking wives devoted themselves to causes and ran charity events. The latter gave birth to a climate of slick social scenes and ostentatious living. For those wives who did not work, their days were filled with committee and board meetings, often taking up as much time and energy as if they had "real" jobs with pay scales. This elite faction of nonworking charity wives was rising in cities and suburbs across the country. These eighties wives were sophisticated, determined and more materialistic than wives of decades past. Some worked but were able to put their energy into charity events and a social calendar all the same. This latest breed of wife wanted a good life for herself, her husband, and her children, as manifested in the form of a combined prestige; her own and her husband's accomplishments, as well as her children's, were each considered a reflection of her.

In 1980 the world was again changing for women. The nation's federal courts were mandated to offer equal labor opportunities to minorities and women. Women were 50 percent of the voting delegates at the Democratic Convention the year that Republican candidate Ronald Reagan was elected president. In December 1980 the post-election headlines of *NOW Times*, NOW's national newspaper, read "Women Vote Differently Than Men." But within a year, President Reagan had endorsed a proposed Human Life Bill that would refute the 1973 Supreme Court decision that legalized abortion. For all women, married and single, it seemed a brief time since their collective voice might have counted.

"I remember the day that President Reagan was elected," begins Susanna. "I had just gotten married the previous January and found out I was pregnant the day of the election. I prayed that Jimmy Carter would win, for all our sakes, but especially for the sake of women. My husband was not as sad as I was that night, although I think he shared my sentiments. By the time my son was born, there was a conservative White House and wives were social butterflies—not only friends of Nancy Reagan's, but women everywhere. I took maternity leave and joined a class for babies at the local Y. There I met all these women who were dressed to the nines to bring their infants to an hour-long class on Tuesday mornings. It was just the way things were turning. I remember that everyone asked where we lived and what I had done before Samuel, my baby, was born. It was as if all the wives were sizing up other wives. I came home and told my husband and he asked me who was there. I was appalled, but he told me that we lived in a city now and that this was how it was. My husband was an investment banker, which was a popular position in the eighties. He wanted to mingle with people like himself.

"I think that I resisted a bit, but ultimately I did befriend the women in my son's baby group. Most of them were not planning to return to work, which surprised me. They busied themselves with causes, luncheons and charities and the Christmas party for our little class. Two of the women clearly did not have the means that the other wives had and they were sort of ignored. This snobby attitude was very eighties; I had never seen it so apparent before. By the time that Samuel began preschool, two years later, the mothers were unfriendly except for an inner sanctum. They didn't have much tolerance if you worked or did anything but what they valued. They valued children and husbands as pawns in some kind of social game. I imagined that my husband would have found one of these wives more acceptable than me. I was back at work and not so interested in their way of doing things. It was funny that my husband knew two of their husbands, and in the end, I had to be a player. A bit player, as wife, mother and society dame."

Eighties wives were often known more for who they were married to than for their own accomplishments. The notion that women had power because of their husband's power, as much as in their own right in the workplace, infiltrated this decade. Legends were made of men on Wall Street during the early eighties, and vast amounts of money made in this industry set a trend for unprecedented greed and materialism. The branding of products and designer labels became the rage. Both working wives and nonworking wives of men who were in the world of finance were desirous of the goods that made a fashion statement, of the homes that indicated wealth and power. There was a clear dichotomy, not only between the haves and have nots, but between those wives who were a part of the workforce and those who took their role as social wife seriously, viewing it as a career of its own. As Claire Owen, psychologist, views it, "Money was important in the eighties, and women liked being wives of wealthy men. Middle- and upper-middle-class white women were dropping out of their roles as corporate wives and trying this out instead."

This applied even if these women had impressive careers of their own. What was interesting about any of these women, from those who fit the society pages to those who were working to change America, was how they were featured in the media. There were women who were known primarily as successful men's wives during this era, and for hosting lavish events. These women who were written up included Blaine Trump, Ivana Trump, and Gayfryd Steinberg. Women in the workplace during this era who also were immersed in society included Carolyne Roehm, fashion designer; Carolina Herrera, also a fashion designer; and Jacqueline Kennedy Onassis, who was a book editor during these years, and attended charity events as well. The backdrop of a strong economy played a large part in how society women were perceived. For working women, those who might have eschewed the role of corporate wife, there was always the chance in the eighties to be a corporate working woman. A handful of society wives decided to take this route.

"I had the jewels and my husband was definitely a player in the eighties," begins Greta, who was married in 1981 and worked at an investment banking firm through 1990. "I wanted to work, I wanted to use my degree. When Marc and I had met, in college, we both had the same ambition for the same job. The truth is, in the eighties, women could have careers, but not great careers. When Wall Street took off, it was clear to me that no women would be the movers and shakers; it wasn't going to happen. I did not like being just a Wall Streeter's wife; I wanted something for myself. Hal mistakenly thought I was a reflection of him but I was not. In my marriage I felt like a badly paid employee, but at my job I felt like someone who had talent and a future.

"Because of our circle of friends, I knew plenty of wives of wealthy men, and they seemed to feel important enough. There was an arrogant edge to the husbands because of their money, which translated into power. There was also an arrogant edge to some of the wives, who bought into it so totally. I wasn't one of those wives. I was the one who worked hard in her own industry and still played the game of the rich businessman's wife. I saw myself as straddling two fences, and it was better for me that way. As Marc's wife, I had little choice but to do the social thing, so it was up to me to hold on to something that was all mine, outside of his circle. And I did it. I like to think of myself as someone who worked toward a goal."

If the eighties wives who did not need to work were not frivolous because they had their causes, they could not be compared to the handful of eminent women, some of whom were wives, working to improve the world. Those women included Sandra Day O'Connor, the first woman to become a U.S. Supreme Court justice in 1981; Eleanor Smeal, the past president of NOW; Gloria Steinem, the publisher of *Ms.*; Barbara Walters, television journalist and reporter; and Barbara Jordan, known for winning a seat in the Texas State Senate twice in the sixties and in 1982 for being appointed to the LBJ Centennial Chair in National Policy at the University of Texas. Each of these women was highly visible and recognized for her achievements. With several exceptions, there was a dichotomy between those women who worked, even in high positions, and those who chose not to work but to focus on their influence without the workplace. The society wife of the eighties who did not work felt remarkably entitled. This type of wife had not existed in past decades of wifehood, and set a valuable new order of wife in motion.

Power Wives

When Tom Wolfe published his novel *The Bonfire of the Vanities* in 1987, the wife as "social x-ray" came to light. The novel, part satire, part cautionary tale, describes the plight of Sherman McCoy, a successful investment banker, and his "social x-ray" wife, Judy. Judy lunches with the other social x-ray wives and, on occasion, mothers her only daughter. Judy and her friends thrive on controlling the social scene and determining who belongs and who shall be ousted, but in truth they suffer a benign neglect as wives of Wall Street wizards. When Sherman and his mistress get into trouble by taking the wrong route back from the airport and accidentally kill a man, it is Judy's prerogative to divorce her once powerful husband. Judy exemplifies an eighties wife who stands by her man only until he fails and then becomes virtually worthless to her. Wives before the 1980s did not have to deal with these issues because avarice was not as flagrant and a social climate based on monetary success did not exist to the same degree.

"I definitely led the life," recalls Audrey, who divorced her husband in 1990, but stood by his side in the 1980s. "Tyler and I had this perfect marriage in the eighties. Tyler made buckets of money and I wore designer clothes and traveled in very chic circles. Our children were little versions of ourselves. It was sort of pathetic in retrospect, but it was what everyone did in the eighties. We had a country house and lived in the city during the week. Tyler had this big impressive job on Wall Street and our friends were all couples who were alike. The husbands worked as bond traders and the wives had gone to excellent colleges and had worked in good jobs in publishing or magazines, and then became full-time wives. We were busy running our husbands' and children's lives and planning school events. It took all of our time. We all wore velvet hair bands in the winter and tortoise shell or grosgrain hair bands in the spring and summer. We were busy decorating our homes and organizing our children, but we did not consider ourselves housewives or stay-at-home wives. We saw ourselves as women who worked for free because we could—at charities and at the private schools. We were very snobbish and didn't even know people whose husbands were in other fields. For instance, my son had a friend whose father was a surgeon, and we acted like that was somehow beneath us.

"I'm not proud of the way we were and I see it as a distinctly eighties mentality. When my husband got into trouble financially because the market crashed, I divorced him. It was purely a financial matter. He was no longer the same man and I didn't feel I could stand behind him. I suppose it was never true love, but a package that worked. I assessed my situation and thought I'd better get out while the going was still good for me, while I still looked good. I remarried within three years' time, and not to an investment banker. By then it was the nineties and there was little cachet to anyone from Wall Street. I'd say that the times were reflected in both of my marriages, but in the eighties I met so many women who wanted the whole deal, not romance and real affection."

The new brand of wife without work was extremely confident of her place in the world. She was not an unpaid laborer but a kind of royal person. If she was dependent upon her husband financially, she felt that the abundance of riches that he produced was hers for the asking. She did not do menial tasks but had household help for such matters. Husbands did not treat their wives as women who sat at home all day, a fifties version of a wife's work. When Rae Andre describes "the dissatisfied homemakers" in her book *Homemakers: The Forgotten Workers*, she addresses the typical stay-at-home wife, who was criticized for the way that she conducted her home life. Andre found that women who were homemakers were not appreciated; no dollar value was placed on their unending efforts as wives and mothers. This was not the case for the eighties society wife. This wife's stature resonated with her groups of friends, who devised a sharply honed position of wife as an enhancement.

Some women deliberately chose Wall Street men as their husbands. This was not only a conscious choice, but a kind of financial insurance. They had their own skills and didn't need to depend upon a man to provide for them. Yet, the mindset was that husbands were providers, regardless of the woman's personal success. These women saw their success and their capabilities as a kind of talent; that is, if necessary, they would use their talent for the practical purpose of making a living, but if there was a man who had amassed a tremendous amount of money and made an impressive sum, why not let him do the real job of working for a living?

This point of view of the eighties wife is a reaction to a culture that, despite the march toward equality of the sixties and seventies, interprets the wife as having less financial responsibility in the marriage. It was the unrelenting effort and optimism of the seventies wife that caused the eighties wife to be wary, to evaluate her capacity in the work world versus a life where she could command as she saw fit. The eighties wife considered it an option to utilize her work abilities for her home life, a lavish life at that. Although these women were in a category all their own, in cities and wealthy suburbs the profile of the powerful socialite wife appeared. "These wives in the eighties had so much wealth that nothing else mattered," comments Dr. Michele Kasson. "These women did not need to work even if they ended up divorced, and this set them apart from other wives. Work became irrelevant to them." What is curious is how deliberate women became about being social wives.

"I purposely interviewed every man I dated until I found the right partner," Katherine tells us. "I was married at twenty-eight in 1985, and I married a man who had gone to college and graduate school with me. I knew how ambitious he was and that he would make a lot of money. I knew that he wanted to live a certain lifestyle and so did I. The fact that I had the same degree as he had was beside the point. I worked until our first daughter was born, and then I stopped. But I was completely aware of what I brought to the table as an attractive wife who could go anywhere and be socially acceptable. We were living in a mid-size city by then and I knew that my husband wanted to move either to Los Angeles or to Washington for his work. My rationale for not working by then was that I was pregnant with our second daughter and it would complicate matters if I worked, too.

"Both Lance, my husband, and I viewed my not working as an investment in our social future. I became known in the community, because I met other wives like myself. There were plenty of us in the mid- to late eighties. Our husbands had the money but we all had achieved something before becoming wives. We had the schooling to do what our husbands did but we didn't have to work because our husbands were working for us. None of us ever stopped to consider that it would have furthered other women if we had worked and kept the inroads going for other women in our fields. We didn't look at it like that; instead, we saw this as a business opportunity too, these marriages. The husbands had to do the jobs they'd promised to do and we would be these amazing wives, unlike any who had come before us. Money and status were definitely a part of the marriage and in the eighties it didn't even seem cold-blooded; it seemed reasonable. From 1982 until 1987, money could be made everywhere, especially in finance and business."

It is interesting to note the shift in power that the eighties social wife viewed as belonging to her. These women recognized their worth and value, and therefore understood how necessary they were to the marriage. While the concept of peer marriage would evolve in the next decade, the concept of being important as a wife had seeped into the eighties wife's consciousness, rendering her influential and indispensable.

Still the Working Wife

By mid-decade, half the population at colleges and universities was female, earning undergraduate and master's degrees; over one-third were earning doctoral degrees. These educated women with graduate degrees were less likely to be wives and mothers, as researched by

S.D. McLaughlin in *The Changing Lives of American Women*. "Modern marriages" in which the husband still had more authority, while his wife had a career and more say than in "traditional marriages" of the past, were becoming popular. The husband was no longer the only earner in the marriage and the bride was no longer so young and innocent. More women married in their mid-twenties, rather than their early twenties, and had a solid education and skills in the workplace. In 1987, just over half of the mothers with children three years old or younger were in the workforce, according to the1990 U.S. Census. At this juncture, black women were more likely to work if they had children than were white or Hispanic women with children. It would require the entire decade before the working wife of the eighties developed an awareness of what her needs were in a marriage while she also had a career. The eighties wife's tolerance level was not that of her predecessors, but it had not yet evolved.

Wives who wanted a career and a marriage often chose less stressful and demanding jobs, whereas women without husbands would go for the position at the very top because they were unhindered and did not have the same obligations as their married counterparts. Married women were beginning to admit that they had forfeited the opportunity at work for their children, while unmarried women were admitting that they had forfeited the opportunity to have husbands and children for their careers. What a cruel blow it was that, with few exceptions, neither type of woman could, in theory, get to the top. It would take a good part of the decade for both single and married women with careers to absorb this hard truth. Meanwhile, the "having it all" mantra did not disappear.

For those single women who had careers and had not yet landed a husband, there was a popular belief that they would one day combine the two. Yet a wife's job at home was not diminished by her full-time commitment to the workplace, as we see repeatedly through the seventies and into the eighties. In March of 1982, *The Journal of the American Women's Association* reported that eighty-seven women doctors in Michigan felt "total responsibility for household tasks," according to Minton and Block's research in *What is a Wife Worth? The Leading Experts Place a High*

Dollar Value on Homemaking. The concept of a career as a luxury would dissolve by 1987 when the stock market crashed and wives, and husbands, realized that their jobs were a necessity. The burden of "having it all" hit home, now combined with the responsibility of supporting a family. So the liberated eighties wife made money in the workplace and continued the "non-work" at home, "cooking, cleaning, shopping, managing household finances, family correspondence and childcare," as Minton and Block remark.

"I always worked, and there is no question that I also ran the house," Dawn, who married for the first time in 1969 and the second time in 1988, tells us. "I expected to do this. I never wanted to run a company. I wanted a decent job where I could leave at five. Work was not the problem in my first marriage and by the second, the children were grown, so it was no issue at all. I did work part-time when the kids were small, and in those days, there weren't so many good jobs for women anyway. I had quit college to get married and in my second marriage I was able to finish my degree. It was much more important to do this by the eighties. That was when I began to think that I was finally living my life; what I cared about in this marriage was that we were equals. My husband had no children, and had no idea of what it takes to be working mother. But he always respected my choices. I have been an office manager in a physician's office for twenty years and it makes me happy. I was not torn about work and marriage in the eighties because I had what I wanted—a way to make money without it interrupting my life with my kids and my husband."

In the 1989 film *Working Girl*, Melanie Griffith portrays Tess, a working-class working girl, and Sigourney Weaver portrays Katherine, an elite, well-educated executive. Tess has higher ambitions than to be in a secretarial pool at an impressive brokerage house. When Tess rids herself of her boyfriend who lacks ambition, he soon marries another local girl, who has fewer aspirations than Griffith's character. In the environment that Tess decides to leave behind, marriage and work are a necessity, but career and marriage do not exist. Once Tess gets in the big leagues, she crosses the class lines and enters the privileged world of Wall Street. While Tess's honest character wins the heart of Jack Trainer, played by Harrison Ford, the man is only a part of her plan, and her career is equally riveting.

The dichotomy between classes and the decision to work at a career was apparent in the eighties, where many women of all classes wanted to prove themselves, wanted a place in the work world. One such wife was Abigail, who felt that her husband misrepresented what the marriage was to be in terms of her career.

"When I was married in 1980, I thought that Paul, my husband, respected my desire to have a career and to share responsibilities. I believe that he faked it, and that in fact he had little concern for my career or to help take care of the house. Once we had children, it became even worse. The bottom line was that they had little impact upon him. Our son and daughter might not have made a difference to Paul, but they certainly affected my schedule. I am ten years younger than Paul, and sometimes I think that generationally we were never on the same wavelength. If he ever acted as if he cared about my work or respected it, it was only because I was doing so well. I had an excellent job and he knew it. I don't know how I failed to see this coming—I had been someone who believed in equality and I ended up marrying a man who didn't feel this way at all. And it wasn't clear to me until we had children and this unending responsibility.

"In the end I wanted the career to work out and the children to be raised properly, but I lost interest in him because he wasn't fair to me. Paul must have sensed this and eventually he changed somewhat, but never enough for me. I have stayed in this marriage because I have had plenty of diversions with my kids and my job. But I would have done better with an equal partner, someone who really understood."

The working wives/mothers of the eighties suffered for being ahead in their thinking. The husbands/fathers were not up to speed, and the women were moving rapidly in the direction of choices and solutions. The solutions came in the form of daycare and private childcare, an issue that the seventies wife had attempted to sort out. Work combined with children was always the issue for working wives, from the time they marched forth in the previous decade through the birth of the twenty-first century.

The concerted effort of the eighties wife to achieve equality in her role as wife and mother is what set her apart from the seventies wife. It is not a question of the seventies wife not wanting this equality, but she was too callow to demand it. The eighties wife, on the other hand, thought she could demand it, and understood that she deserved it. After the seventies wife's call to arms, the eighties wife entered the decade slightly off kilter. In 1980, the Women's Committee of the Directors' Guild reported that 7,332 films were released between 1949 and 1979, and only fourteen of these films were directed by women. In television, the numbers were also bleak for women, with 65,000 hours of prime time television being shown between 1949 and 1979 and only one hundred and fifteen hours of it directed by women.

This kind of discrimination against women was not reserved for those in the entertainment industry. All of the fighting against sex discrimination and the plea for equal pay for equal work was supposed to have paid off. Instead, more confusion and disappointment was ahead for the eighties wife in her aspiration as wife, mother, and working woman.

Waking Up

The eighties wife expected that she would succeed in her goals as wife and mother. If women were led to believe that they were superior in their abilities to men, as they were taught by the feminists, they certainly were not treated that way. There was little advantage to being led in this direction, in any case, when the concept of equality, not superiority, would have sufficed. Martha Bayles describes the problem of academic feminists whose view was that women were superior to men morally in her essay, "Feminism and Abortion," in *The Atlantic Monthly*. In the workplace, there was still the ubiquitous glass ceiling that working wives in the seventies assumed would disappear with time and through proof of their talents. By the eighties it was becoming obvious to the seventies working wife, now in her second decade of commitment to work and wifing, that this was not the case. The eighties wives who were just starting out might have been more innocent and unaware, yet with time they would see the limitations placed on women. Certainly any ideas of superiority, when women were feeling inferior, seemed beside the point, almost counter-productive.

"My whole life I worked to become someone," begins Christine, who was married in 1981 at the age of twenty-eight. "My mother encouraged me and my sister to work in high school, to win scholarships to college, and we did. Then I knew I needed a business degree to get the kind of job I wanted. I felt that I was up against a world that was not only anti-women but anti-black. This was after the civil rights movement and the women's movement. It might have helped somewhat, but it certainly didn't make it smooth for me. I worked my way up the ranks in this corporation and I've never left. I went to business school at night and I didn't get married, on purpose, until this was behind me. My husband, Robert, was not as motivated as I was, and he became almost lazy after we had our first baby. It was as if he went to work because there was no choice and I went to work because I liked what I did. There was no way I was giving anything up that I'd worked for.

"Our weekends were so busy with the baby, and then I had another. I loved having these babies. Robert was not big on being a father and he wasn't big on my doing so well at work. I was the major breadwinner and if I hadn't taken care of the kids every free second that I wasn't at work, I would have thought I was a husband. I know that my fellow students in college and at business school all wanted the dream, a job and husband and kids, but I was getting tired of it. I expected so much more than I got. I had to adjust, had to give up what I thought it would be and get with the program, had to make do. I have taught myself to accept that I can't go much further at work, my husband is who he is, and children are time-consuming and ungrateful. My career has meant a great deal to me, it's been a big part of my life and I have done well. When I think of how my mother worked, I know I have gone far, even if it should be better than it is."

When the eighties wife began to recognize the deficiencies in husbands, their dissatisfaction in the face of glass ceilings at work, and the unrelenting nature of mothering, they were in for a rude awakening. Husbands had been on a pedestal for decades—if a wife of the past found her husband less than adequate, it was not something she flaunted. The 1988 film *Everybody's All-American*, starring Jessica Lange as Babs and Dennis Quaid as Gavin, epitomized the idea of husband as king and his wife as secondary. Although the love affair and marriage between Babs, as the Louisiana State homecoming queen, and Gavin, her college football star husband, begins in the 1950s, the movie is a journey through three decades of marriage. Gavin becomes a professional football player and eventually loses his fame as the years pass and his heroic feats on the field are no longer remembered or important. Babs, as the long-suffering wife who subjugates herself early on in the marriage to Gavin's fame, becomes stronger and more certain of herself and of her husband's inadequacies as the years pass. She remains with her husband, knowing he is a shadow of his former self, loving him for his weaknesses as well as his strengths. Our culture encourages husbands, let alone professional sportsmen, to be heroes, and wives to adorn them. This film shows us the flip side, that despite the posturing and sexist values, women have inner strength. Whether they defer to their husbands, if need be, is a personal choice.

When children were involved, wives had to face another set of issues. Someone had to be around to raise these children. As Rosanna Hertz points out in "A Typology of Approaches to Child Care: The Centerpiece of Organizing Family Life for Dual-Earning Couples," working mothers were still hoping for "quality time" in the eighties. "Husbands become sounding boards and only marginal participants in arranging the schedules of children. In this regard, women replace themselves, and in the process, the deskilling of tasks leaves mothers with changed relationships to their children, popularly dubbed "quality time" motherhood."

The idea of submitting to one's nurturing instincts was better received by wives in the eighties than those of the seventies or late sixties. Even if the eighties wife was overly invested in the dream of "having it all", she was able to be more honest about what a husband could or could not do.

Few men modified their work schedules so that they could share the responsibilities for childcare. For the most part, they did not change to the same extent as the wives, nor were they socially conditioned to do so. After all, what benefit was it to them? It was their wives who were attempting to create a new state of affairs.

These wives saw the fallacies and forged ahead anyway. They knew no other way to attempt success. A wife could not turn her back on her hard-earned career simply because she was a wife and mother. Or could she? This was the dilemma for many working wives. As Terri Apter points out in her book *Why Women Don't Have Wives*, the concept of being a mother is not the same as that of being a father. Women with careers who also are mothers are not putting the two responsibilities together in the same way that men do. A mother's issues are unlike a father's issues when it comes to parenting.

Rosalie's interview illustrates the feelings that working wives of the 1980s experienced.

"My son was born in 1982," Rosalie begins. "I worked as a television producer and commuted on top of everything else. I wanted a child and I wanted to work. There definitely was this school of thought at the time that women were special and that the problem was the men. I'm not sure if it helped to look at life this way; still, sometimes I did believe that all of my friends' husbands were jerks and that they knew nothing. In the end, I cared for my son, missed him when I was at work, worried about his schedule, spent more time on the weekends with him than his father did except for sports, where my husband chose to lead. I was the stronger parent; I was the mother. To say that I was exhausted and purposely did not have another child because of my job, my commute and my husband, is to say that I gave in. I suppose that I did but I knew no other way to get through."

There were wives who became mothers and recognized that there was a small window of time in which they would settle for domesticity and the consequences of that life. These wives and mothers were determined to return to the workforce, and to make a go of both work and mothering. This choice was almost out of a fear of becoming isolated and excluded, much as their fifties predecessors had been.

As reported by James P. Smith and Michael P. Ward in their paper, "Women's Wages and Work in the Twentieth Century," women's wages increased 20 percent more quickly than did men's in the years between 1920 and 1980. In the 1980s, two-thirds of wives with small children were working outside their homes. This was an enormous inroad for working wives/mothers, and it kept the unresolved issues on the front burner—those of childcare and of the perpetual second shift.

By the mid-eighties, the trend to keep one's maiden name in marriage was going strong. The tradition of taking the husband's surname had been dismissed by the feminist movement in the late sixties and early seventies. Yet the majority of women did not follow suit. Nevertheless, wedding announcements in *The New York Times* between the sixties and mid-nineties "showed a decided increase in the number of women who hyphenated or kept their maiden names," according to Rona Marech, in her article in *Horizons* of February 14, 1999, "With This Name...." Even so, Marech reports that only five percent of women in the United States have kept their maiden names or hyphenated their names. Given the tradition of taking their husband's surname as their own, husbands are disappointed if their wives are reluctant to do so. How can this be anything but a sexist tradition that connotes ownership?

As Carol Lloyd notes in her January 12, 2000, Salon.com article, "Why Should a Baby Get Her Father's Last Name?", "It seems that independent working wives of the eighties still conformed to the age-old tradition of using their husband's surname." A 1994 report in *American Demographics* magazine found that 90 percent of wives use their husband's last names. The ten percent who do not either hyphenate their maiden name and last name or use their maiden name as their middle name. Only two percent of wives use their maiden names alone, according to Lloyd's research. The explanation is that this is a patrilinear way of naming, which pleases both fathers and husbands. Yet women do choose, in some cases, to sustain their working last name and their family's last name, having had separate names for two roles. If, in fact, the answer is tradition and stability for the family, the small population of wives who have resisted have felt justified.

"Being an eighties working wife, I wanted to keep my name, no matter what my husband and his parents thought," explains Marcie, who is a full-time flutist with a symphony. "The question for me was, why was my father's name more important to me than my husband's name. Both names belonged to men, not to women. The truth was, because it had been mine for thirty-two years before I married Steve. I could not justify changing my identity for a man I might or might not have a child with. I might or might not be with for the rest of my life. I was a realist, because I was not a young bride, so I kept my maiden name. There was pressure from Steven's family, and then there was my career and name notoriety. That was what won out in the end. I was somewhat known with the surname I had since birth, and I cared about my career. I also cared deeply about my husband and my marriage. But I decided to keep my name.

"Then in 1988 we had a child and I wanted it to be easy for her at school. So we gave her my last name as her middle name and my husband's last name as her last name. For work I still use my last name, but for school purposes and family functions, I use both. Is it a compromise? Absolutely. Does it work? Yes, I suppose it does. The truth is, I have two men's last names, my father's and my husband's."

Another issue facing the eighties working wife and mother was the decade's dictum on fashion. If the women's movement evoked the braless look, the conservative dress that settled in during the seventies and became a uniform for working women during the eighties was beginning to bore many women. They were earning more money for their endeavors than in the past and feeling satisfied, although it certainly was not a case of parity in the workplace. This seemed the right time for them to discard their "dress for success" look in favor of shorter skirts and sheer blouses. For many it was about self-expression; these working wives felt they had conformed for years as a way to be taken seriously.

"I wore the uniform to work on a daily basis," recalls Audra, who worked in an accounting firm from 1983 until 1995. "I wanted to blend in with the crowd, although the crowd was thin—few women, and I was the token minority female. I wore these drippy navy blue jackets and skirts, sometimes brown, sometimes beige. To be elegant, I wore all black, with lots of shoulder pads and covered legs. But I wanted to be feminine and I wanted to express myself a bit through my clothing. Since most of my hours were spent at work, it would have to happen there. My husband made a fuss when I went to work in a sexy blouse and shorter skirt, but I felt good about myself. My daughters liked it, but my husband insisted that it was inappropriate. I didn't want to dress like a man anymore. And I'd done well enough at this company that I was not dispensable based on my shirt and the length of my skirt.

"I know this is no big deal, but after all those years of repressing my individuality, I liked wearing something stylish. It made work fun. The thing about work when you are married with kids is that it fills your day. When you get home, dog-tired, all you want to do is put on sweats and curl up on a couch. There were so many things I had to do to stay in that job that I was thrilled when in the late eighties I could dress to my liking, within reason. This gave me confidence in a way. I think this was a bigger deal for working women than people realize. I've been doing it ever since."

Thus, the working wife closed the decade feeling more secure about her job and, in some cases, her marriage. While we cannot dismiss the amount of stress that a career inflicts upon a marriage with children, the eighties working wife was proud of her accomplishments while tuning in to her sacrifices. As Dr. Ronnie Burak remarks, "The original eighties wife needed to prove that she was independent. The idea of being superwoman still mattered to her." The working wife's response to her husband's failure to step up to the plate in terms of household responsibilities was cumulative. There were times when she simply basked in her progress, proud of how far she had brought herself; at other times her frustration was acute.

Divorce Arrives

Marriages started to suffer as wives exhibited signs of defeat in their undertakings. There was a population of eighties working wives who were becoming disillusioned with their marriages and the unrelenting challenge of balancing their lives. These working wives were joined by those society wives and stay-at-home wives who also found their marriages lacking and were willing to pursue a divorce. The fact that divorce was becoming not only more commonplace, but more acceptable, was appealing to many wives and husbands alike. This wave of acceptance would forever alter the complexion of divorce in America. The National Center for Health Statistics reports that in 1990 the average time for first marriages to end was after eleven years, and one-third of divorces occurred within the first four years of a marriage.

Among the privileged wives married to eighties tycoon-type husbands, some asked for a divorce once their husbands had fallen from grace, such as Seema Boesky, who divorced her husband, Ivan, after he was found guilty of making one hundred million dollars from insider trading in 1986, and Cristina Ferrare, former model, who divorced her husband, John Z. DeLorean, the auto baron, after he was arrested for and accused of trafficking cocaine and money laundering, in an attempt to save his car company. Other wives, with and without careers, chose to stand by their husbands despite notorious scandals, including Lori Milken, who remained married to Michael Milken, the famed junk bond trader at Drexel Burnham, who served two years of his ten-year sentence.

Then there were those wives married to powerful men whose marriages did not last although no scandal was involved. Ivana Trump is an example of a quintessential eighties wife, who was married to real estate mogul Donald Trump until 1989 when he asked for a divorce to marry Marla Maples. Although Ivana Trump's divorce was fodder for the gossip columns, as an eighties wife and mother, Ivana represented the working rich and impressed the media with her style and flair. In 1985 Claudia Cohen, a television journalist, became the wife of Ron Perlman, known for his unfriendly takeover of Revlon, at a wedding at the Palladium for four hundred and fifty people. The couple subsequently divorced in 1994. Carolyne Roehm, the dress designer, and wife of Henry Kravis of KKR, who was a leverage buyout mogul and major philanthropist in the eighties, would be divorced in 1989. Although these women led luxurious lives, many of their marriages were ill-fated.

Famous marriages and divorces in the 1980s included Madonna, who had a glamorous wedding in 1984 when she married actor Sean Penn. The couple divorced four years later. Actress Cybill Shepherd divorced her husband of four years, David Ford, in 1982, and in 1980, Harrison Ford's first wife, Mary Marquardt, his college sweetheart, found herself divorced after Ford met screenwriter Melissa Mathison on the set of *Apocalypse Now*. The marriage to Mathison took place in 1984 and lasted until 2000. Both women and men were finding divorce easier to implement than they had anticipated. However, by 1990, the U.S. Census reported that three out of four divorces were filed by women, not men, each year. From 1970 to 1981 the number of single mother families grew from 956,000 to 2,700,000, according to research conducted by *Feminists Chronicles*.

While not all wives in the eighties who found marriage to be disillusioning were confident enough to act accordingly, more women were able to consider divorce than ever before. Lawrence A. Kurdek's 1989 study, "Relationship Quality for Newly Married Husbands and Wives: Marital History, Stepchildren, and Individual-Difference Predictors," reports that wives who suffered in marriages were those in low income marriages who had a low educational level, stepchildren, financial issues and unrealistic expectations. By the 1980s, women in this predicament were willing to divorce. In 1989, Teresa Castro Martin and Larry Bumpass found in their study, "Trends in Marital Disruption," that one-third to one-half of all marriages ended in divorce.

"If I had been less conscious of how wives were supposed to be, it would have been easier," Marina, who was married in 1982, tells us. "I was an awful wife. I tried to follow the conventional standards but instead I followed the rules of the eighties—have children, get good help, and go back to work as soon as possible. This was what women were doing, and it seemed right for me. What was wrong with my marriage was that I was so busy taking care of the children's schedules, running the house, and keeping up at my job at a big company that I could not be the kind of wife my husband needed. We wanted very different things from our marriage. I looked at my husband and I saw that he worked hard at his job, and expected me and the kids to fall into place. But he simply wasn't there for me. My husband never helped with the kids and he never saw us as a unit. To him, it was a choice—either I took a child or both children somewhere or he took a child or both of them somewhere. It was never the idea that we all would go together. It wasn't how he saw us. I never felt that he was trying or that he loved me. It was lonely and unhappy. Finally I decided it was time to go. I contemplated divorcing my husband in 1982 and didn't have the guts to do it until 1989. I had my career and my kids but I no longer had this pretense of a marriage. It was a relief."

For many working wives in the eighties, the tremendous disappointment of having husbands who were not as willing to share the responsibilities of children and household as they purported they would, was enough incentive to file for divorce. While the fifties wife had no expectations of her husband sharing home and child care, and the sixties wife had one foot in a traditional marriage with her ears open for the promise of equality for women, the seventies wife was the guinea pig of women in the workforce, and the eighties wife continued her work, only to face the harsh light of day. Still, most husbands simply did not live up to their promises of pitching in. This had serious ramifications for wives and the divorce rate soared.

"I was so busy running around as a good wife," recalls Angelina, "that I didn't notice my marriage from 1984, when we married, until 1989, when I knew we should be divorced. My husband, Craig, and I had both come from poor working-class families. We both had decent jobs and worked long days. Craig wanted me to be completely at his service when he came home at night and I couldn't do that. I was too worn out.

"Then he was given a promotion and he traveled for work. He wanted me to stay at home, he never asked me to come. I wanted to be invited but I couldn't have gone because of work, and I really didn't want to go. But I wanted to be asked; I wanted to count enough to be asked. Instead, he said nothing and when he got home, he wanted me to wait on him, like our mothers had waited on our fathers, without question. It was a part of our culture, but I refused. My mother had not had the kind of job I had or the guts I had to say no. I wanted something back, too. Craig started to become critical of me, and if I fought him on this, it got worse. His view was that he worked hard, and I didn't work as hard. My mother warned me that marriage can survive if the women give more than they receive. I wasn't buying into it, so I asked for a divorce."

There were wives who felt misled by their husbands, and expected some kind of understanding about their ambition but did not find it. Lourdes, unlike Angelina, had an explicit discussion of how she would carry out her career plans once she and her husband had married.

"I felt like I did it all alone, and I really came to resent him," begins Lourdes, who married in 1981 and divorced in 1988. "I didn't want to be with him sexually or socially, or to even share my thoughts. I don't know why I waited so long to face the fact that Scott and I did not operate on the same level. He was sexist and demanding as a husband, and not giving. How I had missed that before we were married is a great mystery to me. I guess he was on good behavior and I didn't know him as well as I thought I knew him. I kept thinking it was better to be a wife with children than to be a single mother. And in the eighties, the divorce level was rising, but there was a stigma to being divorced. In l987 I decided I had to do it anyway, no matter what the consequences were. I became a single working mom, and I knew then, once I was on my own, that Scott had never been right for me. I doubt that in the seventies I could have done this, and in the nineties I would not have felt so outrageous asking for a divorce. But I had to do it when I did it, and thankfully I had a solid job and the guts to go it alone. Changing one's status from wife to single mom is not easy, even when it's necessary."

A factor in the eighties wife's divorce correlates to her level of education. According to research conducted in l984 by Allen and Kalish and reported in "Professional Women and Marriage," if a woman has had six or more years of education, she will find herself at a higher risk of divorce. In addition, this group of educated women was more likely to postpone marriage and children, and be less involved in both roles. If a woman had married later in life, or had established her career first, she was not as dependent upon her husband as a provider, or upon her marriage to provide stability or status. These women were unlike the earlier eighties wives, who had hung in for almost a decade, working, mothering, but then finally faced the idea that their marriages were less than optimal, but sensing that they had invested too much to readily walk away. Only a trigger point—such as the children leaving the house, or perhaps a parent or adult sibling becoming ill, or even the wife/mother herself facing a brush with a serious illness—could cause her to contemplate divorce.

According to the 1998 National Center for Health Statistics, between 1960 and 1970 the divorce rate rose from 9.2 divorces to 22.8 per one thousand married women older than fifteen years of age. In his article on July 22, 2000, in *The New York Times*, "New Look at the Realities of Divorce," John Tierney reports that two-thirds of divorces are filed by women. Tierney cites the reasons why women divorce: because of domestic violence, because husbands are not as successful as their wives, and because wives are not afraid of losing their children through custody arrangements. The last reason is the one that separates women from men, who fear that they will lose their children in a divorce. Since children are the largest consideration in any divorce, with finances second, divorce is one situation where women often have the upper hand.

Divorce in the eighties provided a way for women to cope with the disillusionment in their lives. This not to say that divorce was recommended or that it was for everyone, but it became a viable option. Despite how arduous divorce and its aftermath can be, and how devastating it often is for children, by this time in the history of women's lives, wives were willing to take the risk and instigate divorce. When all of the coping mechanisms from overshopping, to trading confidences with other unhappy women, to the use of antidepressant drugs, had been tried unsuccessfully, and women took a hard look at themselves, divorce was the choice that many of them made.

The attitude of the eighties wife who divorced her husband was one of authority. She felt justified in her plan. This view of divorce was adopted not only by middle- and upper-middle-class women, but by their working-class sisters as well. Each had withstood challenges in the workplace and disappointing marriages. Many felt they were alone anyway—raising their children and working for a living—so why not cut loose and find some personal happiness?

"I was willing to take a chance," Anna tells us. "After trying every way I could think of to hold this marriage together, I simply let go. I served Terrence with papers and it made me feel in charge of my life. Then I had to figure out our finances, how our children would react. It isn't that I hadn't considered all of this, but I had put myself first, for once in my life. I have always been devoted to my daughters, but I have had an excellent career track as well. As a result, my personal life had been a rocky road and I had been unhappy with my husband, not with myself or my mothering. I became exhausted in the marriage, in every way, about money, about love, about cleaning the house. At first I had a corporate job and it made me sick. It was too much stress, and Terrence could have cared less that it bothered me so. Then I took a job at a small company, again in marketing, and it's been much better. It is still a big job but without the corporate garbage that made me so crazy.

"Part of why I work so hard is so give my daughters what I believe they should have. I saw there was no way to win by getting divorced, but at least it would lessen the pressure and tension in our home. I also wanted the chance to have a happier life, to take the risk of meeting the right partner—to have a romantic and sexy relationship with a man, just for myself. I am convinced that a mother who stays at home doesn't help her daughters, doesn't set the right example. But a mother who can leave a bad marriage is showing her daughters the world as it should be."

As women stopped being pleasers and felt more justified in their actions, they began to consider life after divorce. Would they find another partner, would they remarry, and would they be able to decipher what had been wrong in their first marriages so that it could be avoided in the second? According to the 1990 U.S. Census, 75 percent of the divorced population remarries within three to four years of their divorce. For the eighties wives who entered the dating arena, it was no longer the free and easy dating scene of pre-AIDS America. Although scientists believe that AIDS developed in the sixties and seventies in Africa, it was first recognized in the United States, in New York City and Los Angeles, in 1980. It was coined AIDS in 1982, and initially affected primarily homosexual men. When the famous actor Rock Hudson died of AIDS in 1985, he surprised his fans and forever affected the public's perception of his leading man image.

AIDS soon began to spread to heterosexual men and women. By the end of the eighties, there was an acute awareness of the disease in the heterosexual community. The promiscuous single world of the sixties and seventies was brought to a screeching halt. Women who had been married from the start of the eighties expressed relief at not being single in a universe where a mainly sexually transmitted disease could prove fatal. Divorced women had to consider protecting themselves from sexually transmitted diseases, including AIDS.

"Maybe I chose the wrong time to be divorced when I filed in 1987," begins Liz, who has not remarried. "But I couldn't stand being married another second because my husband, Josh, took too much for granted. He didn't help with our son, and he didn't take the marriage seriously enough for me. It's a shame that it ended this way. Something happened to me, and I wanted to have another experience altogether. I wasn't only unhappy that I was married, I felt like I was drowning. I purposely chose a younger man, but I worried that he had been around and that he would break my heart. I promised myself not to fall for him and required that he wear a condom. I think that my children wondered about this relationship, but this one was about me, not them. It lasted for five years, beginning once I was divorced. I have no regrets and I have dated many men since.

"I look back on my marriage and I truly believe that the decade we were married in contributed to the failure in the marriage. I liked being Josh's wife at first, it was important to me. I wanted to be his wife for a long time. We would go in and out of phases, but I saw him as a good provider and I saw that he was open to my career. I always had the option that if I didn't want to work, I didn't have to and he left that up to me completely. It's hard to explain, but even with all of our efforts, the marriage couldn't survive. And I'd been raised to be married. My mother had told me how important it was, from the time I was small.

She was proud of my career, but more proud of the fact that I had children and a husband.

"Under these circumstances, it was difficult for me to get divorced. It sounds like I was cavalier about it, but I knew I had the rest of my life ahead of me and I wanted it to be better. In the end, my marriage didn't work and I wanted out. I worried about my children in the divorce, but I wanted the divorce anyway. In the eighties, women were starting to do this."

When a woman divorced, she recognized that the illusion of a successful life as wife, mother and career woman had failed. The marriage was not working, even if the other parts were. "The eighties wives were very disillusioned and depleted," remarks Claire Owen, psychologist. "They were tired of corporate life, trying to climb the ladder at work and even more tired of their husbands. These men had not pitched in and had not lived up to their part of the bargain." Research indicates that marriages where the husband did not take responsibility for household chores and children as he promised his working wife he would, had a greater rate of failure. As social scientists, including Jessie Bernard, have observed, marriage is usually a better deal for the men than the women. Married men are happier than are married women, and men live longer when they are married rather than single. These men had not evolved; they weren't trained or prepared to help their wives. Some of these wives held important jobs, and resented their husband's lack of commitment to these tasks. So while the superwoman ideal died hard for the eighties wife, once it did, it often manifested, in many cases, in divorce. The wives, who instigated a divorce, felt courageous, which was a departure from the past decades.

This change in attitude on the wife's part was due to the social policies that made it challenging for women to do anything beyond motherhood and wifing. In the eighties, women as wives and mothers were struggling to create a better world for themselves. Whatever social strata the eighties wife belonged to, she was far removed from the prototype of the fifties wife, dissimilar from the late-sixties model, and out of synchrony with the ardent seventies model. If the eighties wife made any blunder, it was when she conformed to the beliefs of the seventies working wife.

Eventually, this role seemed both overwhelming and deficient. By the end of this period, the eighties wives, some devastated by their realities, others resolved, decided to improve their lives.

Chapter Six:
The Nineties Wife: Desperation and Isolation

I was married in 1991 and I had not a clue what to expect when I did it," begins Agnetta, who at forty had her first child four years earlier. "I had known George, my husband, for a long time. We had been neighbors since we were in fifth grade. Then we were high school sweethearts, and finally we lived together for one year before we married. But in my mind, living together doesn't prepare anyone for marriage.

"Marriage is a deeper commitment and also involves more responsibility. I was not in a hurry to be married because I think I knew it would be more demanding than a live-in situation. At first we didn't want children and chose to pursue our careers and to be fancy-free. When I hit thirty-five I began to panic and wasn't so sure I'd become pregnant right away. By then I wanted a baby, and so did George. It took a full year to become pregnant and we did see a specialist. In retrospect, now that we have our daughter, I can't imagine what was so important that we put off beginning a family. I suppose we moved slowly to savor our life without children.

"I worked until our daughter was born and then I gave up my job because I'd been at it since college, and there was little left to prove. I had seen it all, and the women at work who were baby boomer wives were miserable. These women had been so diligent about their careers that their children and their marriages suffered. They taught me what not to do. George and I had plenty of time for travel and

fun before our baby was born. Most of my friends put
themselves in the same position. So when they had their
babies, their marriages were not so new, nor were their
careers. They were ready to be stay-at-home moms. I never
expected to be at home with my baby. I guess I looked
around at other women and decided this is the best route
to take."

The legacy of the eighties wife led to later marriages,
and consequently, more infertile women yearning to be
mothers. Some of these wives regretted the years spent
building a career while postponing marriage. For those
wives who had worked until their mid- or late thirties, time
off to raise a family and to concentrate on the life of the
wife was a welcome relief. In a classic switch from the fifties
wife, who had no intentions of building a career and felt
she was unanchored without children, the nineties wife
might or might not choose to work. The nineties wife
recognized that the seventies and eighties wives had paved
a road as best they could in the work world for women.
The hopelessness that had enveloped the baby boomer wife
in the eighties was not lost on the nineties wife. In fact,
much of the nineties wife's decisions and behavior was in
reaction to the wives of the previous decade.

The concept of marrying one's best friend was appealing
to the nineties wife, as she intended to put the
disappointments of the divorced eighties wife to rest. To
this end, she would not necessarily remain on a career track
once she had children, nor would she commit to giving up
her career for motherhood. Rather, she warned her
husband, her best friend and confidant, that she would
have to play it by ear. Many husbands were supportive, if
baffled, by this shift of gears. Husbands were not prepared
for the nineties wife, whose underlying theme was one of
loneliness and despair, even if they appeared to be
thoughtful about the complexities of wife, mother and
career woman. These wives had witnessed the exhausted
prototype of the eighties wife, and enough eighties divorces,
to feel self-protective. However, they could not determine
how to improve their station as a wife, and their prolonged
road to marriage and parenting had its own consequences.

The political climate of the 1990s began on a conservative
note with George Bush as president. In 1990 the president

signed legislation requiring the federal government to collect hate crime statistics, as reported by Carabillo, Meuli and Csida in the *Feminist Chronicles*. Hate crimes were based on race, ethnicity, religion and sexual orientation, but they did not include any crime that was predicated on gender. It was as if gender had been removed from the litany of biases that existed, which in reality simply was not the case. When President Bush vetoed the Civil Rights Act of 1990, thus denying women and minorities the right to be protected from discrimination in the workplace, it became apparent women were still considered "others," but not seen as a minority.

The nineties were a time of both progress and difficulties for a handful of illustrious women. Elizabeth Dole, wife of Robert Dole, Republican presidential candidate in 1996, resigned as Secretary of Labor to become the president of the American Red Cross. At that time, she was the highest-ranking woman in Bush's administration. In 1991, Dr. Frances Conley, one of the first female neurosurgeons in the country, left her position as a tenured professor at Stanford Medical School, due to sexual harassment. In 1992, Muriel Siebert, the first woman who had bought a seat on the New York Stock Exchange in 1967, was honored as the Veuve Clicquot Business Woman of the Year for her efforts on behalf of women on Wall Street.

The news of the nineties included reports on some famous wives and husbands. The divorce of Princess Diana and Prince Charles was finalized in 1996, after a much-publicized failed marriage. Around the world, the public became aware of Charles' liaison with Camilla Parker Bowles, who was divorced from her husband in 1995, and of Diana's affair with James Hewlett, which lasted from 1987 to 1992. Leona Helmsley, married to real estate mogul Harry Helmsley, was sent to prison on April 15, 1992, for tax evasion. In 1998 President Clinton's involvement with Monica Lewinsky became front-page news, mesmerizing wives and husbands alike across America.

Impressive unions included Trudie Styler's marriage to Sting in 1992, when she was thirty-eight and Sting was forty. The couple married after having been together for ten years, and after the birth of three children. The same year, Iman married David Bowie, and Jane Fonda married Ted Turner.

Celine Dion married her manager Rene Angelil in 1994, and in 1996 Sarah Jessica Parker married Matthew Broderick, creating a powerful acting couple. In 1997, Karenna Gore married Andrew Schiff at the National Cathedral in Washington, while her father was Vice-President. The same year Jada Pinkett married Will Smith. In 1998, Barbra Streisand married James Brolin and Sharon Stone married Phil Bronstein. A meaningful wedding for Americans was when our "prince," John F. Kennedy, Jr. married Carolyn Bessette on September 21, 1996, at a secret ceremony on Cumberland Island, off the Georgia coast. This marriage came to a tragic end in 1999 when the couple died while John F. Kennedy, Jr. was piloting a private plane.

While marriage continued to be a goal for the majority of women, from 1970 to 1994 the number of Americans aged eighteen and over who never married more than doubled from 21.4 million to 44.2 million, according to the 2000 U.S. Census. The projections for the future show an increase in never-married women under the age of fifty-five. And so the trend toward an unmarried population of Americans had arrived. According to John Gottman in his book, *Why Marriages Succeed or Fail*, marriage was not as compelling for single women who had experienced several sexual relationships already, and were no longer in their twenties. By the late nineties, interracial marriages were on the rise, with the U.S. Census reporting that the amount of interracial couples had doubled from two and one-half million in 1980 to five million.

Infertile Wives

As evidenced by the first batch of baby boomer wives, raising children, working and wifing proved all-consuming. It was this way of thinking that led to the nineties working woman's decision, whether conscious or subconscious, to extend her time as a single working woman. For the multitude of wives who married late in life, having put their careers ahead of interpersonal relationships, marriage and mothering occurred after the age of thirty-five, forty or forty-five. By 1990, as reported by the U.S. Census Bureau, the average age of first-time wives was twenty-four and one-half years, as compared to twenty years of age for the fifties wife. According to the U.S. Statistics on Marital Status, women between the ages of thirty and thirty-four who were not married had risen from 9.4 percent in 1970 to 22.1 percent in 1999, and women between the ages of thirty-five and thirty-nine who were not married had risen from 7.2 percent in 1970 to 15.2 percent in 1999. By the time that many of these women did marry and were ready to have children, their fertility had peaked. One third of women over thirty-five are infertile, as the 1990 U.S. Department of Health and Human Services/Office of Women's Health has documented, with age being the primary factor.

Women delayed marriage for several reasons, with the workplace and career being one of the main considerations. These women who worked outside the home were less financially dependent upon men, and not so confident that marriage was the end all and be all. Another factor was the steady rise in the number of divorces, and the amount of unhappy marriages in their midst only added to the unmarried nineties woman's speculation. According to research conducted by Allen and Kalish, delayed childbearing occurs more often in women who are well educated, including those with graduate degrees. These women have become more invested in their careers than in becoming wives and mothers. These women wanted to have children immediately after marrying, only to realize that a biological clock was real and consequential. Infertility clinics began to spring up across the country as in vitro fertilization, surrogacy and gestational carriers all became options for women with infertility problems.

"I put off having children until 1990, although I was married in 1982," begins Amber, who is a graphic designer and has her own company. "I was very young when I married and I didn't even want children at first. I wanted to experience travel and work, career, then children. I had my first child without any problem, but the second one was a huge problem. I never actually blamed myself but I do know that what I went through could have been avoided had I started earlier. The truth is, I was ambivalent about having kids and I was very certain about my career and my marriage. I realized something early on that women don't usually know: kids kill the romance.

"In the end I wanted children and I wanted a family. I have made this marriage into one where the kids come first. What I went through to have my son is something I try not to think about. We did four in vitros until it took and I was on too many hormones. I was very absorbed in the outcome so I could deal with the process. In retrospect, I am happy I had those years alone with my husband, but I paid the price with the second pregnancy and what it took to get there. I see my marriage as divided into two marriages— the one we had before we had our children, including the hell I went through to get pregnant, and the one afterward, which is totally about the kids. I think when it is so hard to have kids, you end up acting differently about them once they're here. They take over even more than in young marriages with younger mothers."

The nineties wives suffered through the agony of infertility with the emotional and physical toll of failed in vitros and other options. It was not until the year 2002 that the mental state of the infertile woman would be considered. *The New York Times* ran an article, "Fertility Clinics Begin to Address Mental Health," on October 8, 2002, written by Laurie Tarkan. Tarkan noted that while fertility experts had made great strides in terms of technology in the previous ten years, the "emotional health" of the women had been neglected.

Another important issue in the world of the infertile that surfaced somewhat late in the game was the concept of men as part of the problem. If the nineties wives, immersed in the high-tech procedures at fertility clinics, were aware that their husbands could be a part of the problem, they still seemed to blame themselves and the path they had taken in their lives. This was echoed by those outside the hellish world of the infertile, who assumed it was a woman's problem. On April 1, 2003, *The Wall Street Journal* ran an article entitled "Guys, Your Clock Is Ticking Too," written by Amy Docker Marcus, announcing that male sperm lost its power as men grew older. Marcus reports that the most recent studies reveal that the quality, speed of travel toward the egg, and the amount of semen produced by a male all diminish with age. According to this article, male fertility can diminish by the time a man is thirty-five.

It is ironic that while a growing number of wives found themselves infertile, the Institute of Medicine declared that 750,000 abortions were performed per year in the United States due to ineffective contraception. This seemed especially unfair and haunting to those women who years before had opted for an abortion only to find out later that it is not always so easy to become pregnant, and that age is an important factor. Several of my interviewees remarked that because they felt young, and looked young, they had the wrong idea that their eggs were also young and would defy nature somehow.

Gretchen definitely believed that she could have a baby whenever she decided to settle down, without considering her biological clock. Today she has a daughter as the result of a donor egg and a sperm donor, after much angst over having a child.

"I married in 1994 and even then I wasn't certain that I wanted a child," Gretchen begins. "I was forty-two at the time and I should have paid more attention to the situation. A few of my closest friends had children who were in middle school by then. My friends loved having children and they hinted that I ought to do it. I thought that because I had a young body and looked young that my eggs were young. I learned after ten months of failed attempts to get pregnant, that it wasn't the deal at all. That was when I became upset about this and felt I had to do it. Our marriage really suffered because I couldn't stand not having a child. I don't know what I'd been thinking, but I suddenly had to have this. I would go to the clinic before work to get shots and I was so upset, looking at the other women, all of us losers. It began to be more important to me than being a wife.

"My mother warned me to find a way to make this happen and to stop carrying on about it. My husband, James, wasn't so certain we had to have a child. He has a son from his first marriage, who was in college at the time, and he thought maybe we were both too old to start with diapers. But he also respected my wishes, so we did this work-up, both of us. It turned out that he was also having a problem and that we needed to find donor sperm as well as a donor egg. Once we made this decision, rather than to adopt, which James thought was crazy, I settled down. I began to concentrate on the marriage more than I had been. I realize how easy it is for women with careers to get off track and to lose sight of what life is really about. Or maybe we hesitate because of what other women have gone through. I watched my older sister have kids, a job as a nurse and a husband who worked long hours. It was so hard for her. So I skipped doing it when I should have. Instead I worked hard as a hotel manager. In the end, I wanted what she wanted but the window of opportunity was closing. It is technology that saved me. It wasn't easy convincing James to go along with this. But we have a darling daughter and that is the miracle. I have worked full-time since Elissa was born because I have always worked."

Enough of the nineties wives who began having children later embraced motherhood, often because they had come close to being denied the opportunity. In their quest, they somehow forgot that they had been the ones who had avoided the role initially. Many of these wives had an almost naïve sense that marriage was timeless, and so was pregnancy. They had put off the responsibilities of a family in order to have the freedom that single-hood provided. Unlike their seventies and eighties counterparts, many of these wives had put all their eggs in one basket, the basket of the workplace. But one day they woke up and decided that getting married and having a child was imperative. As Dr. Ronnie Burak views it, women became obsessed with having the children they had never had. Husbands were not as interested, however. "Maternal love is stronger than paternal love," Dr. Burak remarks. "Women are so emotionally involved in their infertility they feel they cannot live without a baby. They blame themselves, and they regret having waited so long."

"I did not marry until I was forty," begins Layla, a scientist, who at forty-five has undergone two unsuccessful in vitros and is now pregnant with a donor egg. "I was beginning to give up on marriage, let alone having a child. Once or twice in my late thirties I considered preserving my eggs, but I never did anything about it. And at twenty-one I had an abortion because I couldn't even think of having a child at that point.

"When I met my husband and I knew he was the one, we decided to marry quickly, hoping to have a baby. I was tested in 1999 and began to understand the consequences of putting off having children. I had worked so hard in my career and had never met the right guy. Once I met Alan, I regretted my past; I regretted that we had not met sooner. Alan cared much less about having a child than I did. For me, once the problems began, it became an obsession. I was determined not to pay the price for my ignorance. I was going to have a baby, no matter what. We did all of these elaborate work-ups and paid quite a bit of money to the fertility clinic. In the end, we had no choice but to use a donor egg. I was okay with it because I became pregnant right away, and did not have to take the hormones for long. This is what happens to women, and I don't understand why we all ignore the truth, that women can only have babies for a short period of their lives."

The nineties wives were the first to hit the infertility wall and recoil, partly in surprise, partly because they now had to face another demanding task. After the constant rigors of work came the nagging question of when and how they would marry. The real issue was not when to marry, but when the biological clock would kick in, and what was required to turn back time and become pregnant. The problems inherent in having a baby in one's forties, along with the infertility issues for women, rose to the surface during the nineties and continued in the twenty-first century.

Playwright Wendy Wasserstein had her first child at the age of forty-eight in 1999, along with other celebrities who also had children later in life. These women include Susan Sarandon, who had her third child at the age of forty-five; Mimi Rogers, who was pregnant at forty-five; and Jane Seymour, who gave birth to twins at the age of forty-five in 1996. As Salyyn Boyles notes in her article "Preserving Fertility" for the *WebMD Medical News*, published on September 13, 2001, some celebrities admit to having fertility treatments, including Seymour and Wasserstein; others do not. Boyles refers to Dr. Michael Doules, president of the American Society of Reproductive Medicine, who questioned how celebrity status could impede any aging of a woman's ovaries. He indicated that some celebrity women might have used assisted reproduction without telling the media.

Sylvia Ann Hewlett's book, *Creating a Life: Professional Women and the Quest for Children*, released in 2002, addressed what had happened to the nineties wives and baby boomers. Her book was a cautionary tale for young women, and not surprisingly, met with controversy and resistance on the part of the women who had placed the work world ahead of their personal lives. These women were not pleased to hear what Hewlett had to say. As *Publisher's Weekly* (October 7, 2002) noted, her advice is that women should marry young, have a baby before the age of thirty-five and work at a company that understands the demands of motherhood and work. Yet the questions raised by Hewlett could not be ignored by women who had chosen careers over having children.

The dilemma was very real without an easy solution. According to an article written by Rita Rubin in *USA Today*, "Older Moms Add a Wrinkle on Motherhood," working class women do not put off having children and the cost of fertility treatments are prohibitive for them. "Virtually all middle-age new moms have had to rely on donor eggs, surrogate mothers or adoption. This group includes prominent artists and politicians whose careers may have diverted them from motherhood early on but provided financial resources necessary to become mothers at a late age," writes Rubin.

Thus, those well-to-do women who married in the nineties and wanted children but had missed their fertile years had more options than did working-class wives. The financial costs of fertility clinics were steep without the emotional and physical stress. While fertility clinics catered to this group of women who could put money down for a result, the success rate was still grim.

"Our marriage really suffered because I couldn't stand not having a child," says Roye. "I don't know what I was thinking all those years, but when I married Jan in 1997, it had to be. Both of us were surprised when it became so important to me, unexpectedly, out of the blue. It was like I'd been pretending it didn't matter and suddenly I had to have it. I was forty-five at the time, and after some lousy episodes with in vitro, we opted for a donor egg. I calmed down once I was pregnant and actually became a better wife. I realize how easy it is for women to lose track of time and to have this belief that it will work out eventually. I know that technology saved me and we put a lot of our money into procedures. Jan refused to adopt, which I would have done. So this was our solution. We have a daughter who is half ours biologically, and we are older parents, doing what we should have done years ago. But I do have my child, and it wasn't easy making it happen."

For some women who entered the arena of wife over thirty-five or forty, fertility clinics provided a last-ditch effort. Adoption was a more familiar concept and another option. Yet the arrival of technology and sophisticated procedures proved more appealing to certain couples. What the nineties wives wanted was what the seventies and eighties wives had struggled with on a timely basis: children and marriages while attempting to sustain their careers. Baby boomer and post-baby boomer females viewed life with a kind of resolve that the fifties wife was missing and the sixties wife had only begun to believe was possible. But even if these women were able to move mountains at work, the attitude of catering to one's personal needs was revolutionary; the nineties wives were not always equipped to do so. When it came to husbands and children, these women were more than willing, however, even to the point of having children with modern science as their only hope.

Domestic Abuse and Marital Rape

In 1990, Governor Richard F. Celeste of Ohio gave clemency to twenty-five women prisoners who he believed had committed crimes because they were victims of battering or other kinds of emotional or physical abuse. In March of 1990, the Ohio supreme court and state legislature declared "battered woman syndrome" a defense against murder and other crimes. On June 12, 1994, Nicole Simpson, the wife of former famed football player O. J. Simpson, was found murdered outside her home in Brentwood, California. At long last, the concept of battered wives came to the forefront. Despite Nicole Simpson's repeated phone calls to 911, she became a victim of domestic abuse. This much-publicized atrocity occurred even though measures had been taken by the Feminist Majority in 1992 to create domestic violence coalitions and to fight the growing amount of violence against women. On Christmas Eve, 2002, another haunting tale of wife murder would occur with the disappearance of Laci Peterson, a twenty-seven-year-old wife who was eight months pregnant. On April 18, 2003, Scott Peterson, her husband, was arrested with murder charges pending after the remains of a woman and her fetus had been found in the eastern San Francisco Bay.

Wife abuse has existed for centuries. According to Marilyn Yalom in her book, *A History of the Wife*, marriage as sacramental began in the eighth century, with a wife being expected to treat her husband as "lord and master." Yalom writes that women were allowed to be beaten, by law, and that husbands had authority, not the wives. Even if the husband-as-revered aspect of marriage became replaced with a more modern view of the institution over hundreds of years, wives continued to be mistreated physically as well as emotionally by their husbands. In fact, it was not until the 1980s that women were partially able to come to terms with such a practice being exercised by husbands, and not until the 1990s that the issue received full coverage. The question of whether marital abuse increased in the nineties or if it was a woman's ability to finally speak out is difficult to answer.

"I had a long-standing boyfriend, Fred, who then became my husband," begins Georgia, who married in 1990 and divorced in 1997. "I had no idea that he was the way he was. I guess he was able to cover it up when we were dating and first married. Then he became really cruel to me. One night he tried to push me down the stairs. I had this vision of my friends hearing about how I fell down a flight of stairs to my death and how my husband was playing a heartbroken widower. The truth was, he could have killed me that night, which would have been murder. He was very scary and had been drinking. I think if Nicole Simpson had not been brutally killed by her husband, I never would have had the courage to leave my marriage.

"The worst part wasn't when Fred would throw me across the room. The worst part was the things he said to me, the names he called me and when he said I was useless. That was how horrible my marriage was. I used to say to myself, this can't be my life. Then I left and put it behind me, or sort of behind me. You never really forget being treated like that."

Emotional abuse, which has existed always in marriages, was finally being recognized in the nineties. Women seemed less reluctant to hide their problem, but still uncertain of how to fix it, if it was, indeed, fixable. As author Susan Forward notes in her book, *Men Who Hate Women and the Women Who Love Them*, women lose their self-esteem when they are in a psychologically abusive relationship. Forward describes how these men attack their wives with behavior that ranges from threats to critical attacks to cruel treatment, which, over time, destroys the women. Not only did these husbands not act responsibly for their actions, but they often assigned blame to their wives for every mishap. Wives were ill prepared for their husbands' behavior and did not know how to react.

A common way of dealing with an abusive husband is found in Cheryll's interview.

"I wasn't aware that other wives had my problem," begins Cheryll, who divorced her husband in 1996 after fifteen years of emotional anguish. "I felt so alone in the world and I doubted myself. I remember thinking that it had to be me. Paul, my husband, would tell me what I did wrong and why I was a bad person, an inadequate person. But he also told me that I was terrific and pretty and that he loved me. And he bought me things. It was very confusing, because I never knew which side of Paul I'd get or what I had done to deserve the wrong side, his mean side. I was always on edge and frightened. He had a violent temper and that really frightened me. He would lose his temper in front of our boys and he would tell me I was no good. This was so demoralizing. I would pretend it wasn't happening to me. I would make excuses for him all the time. Then one day I couldn't do it anymore, I had enough."

A wife who is emotionally abused and feels trapped becomes fearful and insecure. Forward tells us that these women might become forgetful or withdraw and become distant in order to cope. In some instances the marriage can be renegotiated. In other situations wives hit a threshold and there is no turning back. These women gather the courage to leave the marriage.

Another chronic and much-ignored problem that most women kept a secret until the nineties was marital rape. While date rape garnered some attention in the eighties, the subject came more fully to the attention of the public in the early nineties. In 1992, heavyweight-boxing champion Mike Tyson was convicted of rape, and women gained some credibility in the realm of date rape. The fact that Tyson was found guilty gave victims of date rape the hope that if they were willing to press charges, there is a system that could help women after all.

The 2000 U.S. Census reports that more cases of marital abuse go unreported even today than any other crime in America per year. As noted by David G. Curtis, Ph.D., in his essay, "Perspectives on Acquaintance Rape, "the awareness has been slow. Although the early and mid 1970s saw the emergence of education and mobilization to combat rape, it was not until the early 1980s that acquaintance rape began to assume a more distinct form in the public consciousness." In 1987, Mary P. Koss's study of rape was published in *Ms.* magazine, explaining that if a woman did not want sex with her date, and intercourse occurred, it was indeed rape. It was not until the nineties, after date rape was acknowledged, that wives began to talk about marital rape. The pervasive sense of shame, that it was somehow the woman's fault, was not easy to shake. But women were now able to face the fact that this could happen, across socioeconomic boundaries, with men they knew—with husbands—and without any real support system for them. They had to admit that they were indeed victims.

"I did not know that I was being mistreated until I read some magazine articles on date rape," begins Ghia, who married her college sweetheart in 1993. "I didn't know that Cole's forcing me to have sex, as his wife, was considered a kind of rape. I knew that it was wrong. I knew it made me sick. But he told me that he could divorce me for refusing to have sex; that made me think I had no choice. In the end, I went to see a social worker who helped me. I was getting rashes from being near my husband. The doctor gave me cortisone cream and antihistamines, but the social worker told me it was because I couldn't deal with this problem. It took me years to admit this was happening to me, that my own husband was acting this way.

"I did not leave my marriage but I told Cole he had to see someone to get help. I told him that I felt like I was being forced to have sex and that I was becoming ill. He laughed at me at first but after some time, he began to think about it. We had to rework this entire marriage, and we did. I had to make him see it my way, which wasn't easy. It has been hard for me to forgive him, but I didn't want to be divorced from him. We have a long history together. Today, after much counselling, we are working it out. But I know in my heart that I was a victim of Cole's and that it should never have happened."

"Date rape and marital rape are forms of abuse," comments Dr. Michele Kasson. "Women are in a position for this to happen because they are victims. Date rape sometimes happens because women are being drugged, which is a different scenario than in a marital rape. This is truly a rape. In marital rape, a wife says no, but she is being abused by her partner. It is difficult for women to get away from this. She is caught and trapped in a number of circumstances." What is notable is how often the women describe a feeling of helplessness. This is different from a self-esteem issue, which is often seen in wives at various points in their lives, and manifests when the husband is emotionally abusive. The hope with marital rape is that things will change over time in the marriage, with counseling, if the women want to remain in the marriages and save the relationships.

K.A. Lonsway writes that marital rape is not included in a definition of acquaintance rape in her essay "Preventing Acquaintance Rape Through Education: What Do We Know?". Acquaintance rape is when a woman is forced to have sex with someone she knows. Marital rape, as defined by Elizabeth Rider in *Our Voices: Psychology of Women*, is a "forced sexual assault in an established relationship, such as husband-wife or partners living together." What used to be considered husbandly rights, a husband being entitled to his sexual due with his wife, historically, could not have been considered an assault. The reason that women are reluctant to report incidents of marital rape, relationship rape and other physical abuse, is that they are ashamed and can no longer trust their partner. What is hopeful is that women can overcome their hesitancy to report such acts. In some cases, wives do not press charges but divorce their husbands. The nineties wife was the first of modern wives to feel confident enough of herself to take these measures.

"I had no idea that Andrew would become the kind of husband he became," recalls Shelley, who married in 1990 and divorced in 1999. "He had a temper when he drank, but that was not too often. It took me a long time to understand what was going on. In 1993, after we'd been married for three years, he forced me to have sex one night. I was crying and saying no and he ignored me. He acted like this was what he was supposed to have. Then he bought me flowers the next day and a bracelet. I was confused, was it me, or him who was crazy? After that night, there were a few incidents where he forced himself on me. And one night he actually hit me.

"We both came from nice families, and were of the same religion. Our fathers had similar jobs, one was a carpenter and one was an electrician. Our mothers were traditional wives, although they both held part-time jobs. Once I told my mother about Andrew, and she said it was because he drank but assured me that he was a good husband. It wasn't until I read an article on date rape that I realized I was being raped by my husband, forced to have sex. I told my best friend, Lucinda, and she urged me to seek help. That was when I had to admit it to myself. By then, Andrew was talking about having a baby and saying that we were finally ready. I think he was shocked when I told him I wanted a divorce. I moved in with Lucinda, who was single, and I pulled myself together, but it took years to get over what happened. I never forgave him for how he had treated me and I couldn't stand being his wife."

A famous marital rape scene that occurred in nineteenth century England is found in *The Forsythe Saga* by John Galsworthy. When Irene, the unhappy wife of Soames Forsythe, is forced to have sex with her husband, she feels used and sordid. That Irene never wanted the marriage but married out of economic necessity makes Soames feel all the more entitled to have sex with her, and be justified in his actions. Marital rape was not confined to the pages of novels, however, but often a part of a woman's wedding night, as documented by Juanita H. Williams. For those women who became wives during the Victorian era, wedding nights were more like a rape than "romantic dreams of sanctioned closeness," Williams remarks in her essay, "Sexuality in Marriage."

As Susan Brownmiller notes in her book *Against Our Will*, it is important that both parties agree to have sex before each encounter. The act of sex should not be required of the wife, but based on longing. "All rape is an exercise in power.... In the cool judgment of right-thinking women, compulsory sexual intercourse is not a husband's right in marriage, for such a 'right' gives the lie to any concept of equality and human dignity," writes Brownmiller.

"My husband, Rex, whom I married in 1995, did not understand me, especially when it came to sex," explains Delia, who divorced in 1999. "We did not last long. The sex was mandatory. I did feel like I was being raped, but when I told my best friend about it, she thought I was wrong. That is how marriage is, she told me, and you can't do much about it. But I thought I'd die if he made me do anything more. I wasn't prepared for forced sex. I wasn't sure how it got that way. Rex kept telling me that I wasn't a good wife. He wanted sex every night. Wild sex. I didn't like it and withdrew. He was furious. Another problem was that he had been around before we were married. When we were dating, he always used a condom. Neither of us wanted kids, so I assumed the condom would remain after we were married. But he stopped using it. I became petrified that I would get AIDS from my own my husband having sex I didn't even want."

Although scientists believe that AIDS developed in the sixties and seventies in Africa, it was not recognized in the United States in New York City and Los Angeles until 1980. The syndrome was named AIDS in 1982 and recognized at the time as a disease that infected homosexual and bisexual men. However, by the end of the eighties and into the nineties, the disease had spread to heterosexual women and men. By the nineties, the promiscuous lifestyles of the late sixties, seventies and early eighties were brought to a screeching halt. Women who were married in the nineties were relieved to be out of the single world, where a mainly sexually transmitted disease could prove fatal. Some nineties wives, however, lived with the lingering fear that their husbands had been promiscuous in their single lives.

The major problem with marital rape was the fact that it had not been acknowledged by wives or the culture at large. The nineties wife was the first to be strong enough to be willing to discuss the matter and, in some cases, to leave the marriage as a result. Yet the lingering sense of failure due to how they were treated sexually by their husbands troubled these women. The idealism of marriage was cruelly shattered by marital rape.

Affairs and the Nineties Wife

When Jane Champion's film *The Piano* was released in 1993, it was a cautionary tale for the nineties wife. The film takes place in New Zealand in 1851, with Holly Hunter playing the part of a mail-order bride. Her awakening from sexual repression and her decision to leave her husband for her half-Aborigine lover, played by Harvey Kietel, struck a chord with the nineties wife. The idea of risking it all for a lover, for one's own contentment, for endless love, was not about marriage per se but about romance, sex and communication. Holly Hunter's character was mute, but her communication with her lover was complete.

If wives had not impressed upon their husbands how valuable communication was to their contentment in marriage in previous decades, it became a mantra of the nineties wife. This is especially true because her take on her immediate predecessor, the eighties wife, was that she had failed at this aspect of marriage. Thus the nineties wife required both passion and friendship in her marriage, an ongoing dialogue on the mundane and the extraordinary. In short, these wives were in search of the one man who had it all—who could be sexy, romantic and accountable in the daily grind of life. For those wives who could not satisfy these demands in their marriages and who were not willing to simply confide in female friends what they could not confide in husbands, there was the option of taking a lover.

The majority of wives hesitated to give up the security and status of marriage by seeking a divorce, and were reluctant to rock the boat with their children. Instead some chose to have extramarital affairs in a unique and unmitigated fashion. These women felt neither guilty nor remorseful about their extra-marital trysts. Rather, they felt entitled to better their lives through the relationships with their lovers. This was revolutionary, even if infidelity itself was not.

"I was not ready to leave my marriage when I began an affair with our contractor," begins Rosa, a wife of ten years in 1992, when this took place. "I suppose I was a typical eighties wife, who worked, had kids and lost track of the marriage. I would not have admitted this in the eighties because I was trying too hard to hold it all together. My affair coincided with my leaving my job. We had just moved three thousand miles away and my husband, Bob, wanted me to be at home. He discouraged me from getting work in a new city. The more he talked about it, the more I hated him. Not that I didn't see some wisdom in what he said, but I couldn't stand him by then. That is the truth. I agreed because our youngest son was only two at the time. And I really tried. But I felt so isolated. Here I was in a strange place, in a strange role of stay-at-home mom. I had no close female friends, they were all far away, and I was lonely.

"I never wanted to break our family up but I loved how my contractor, Jake, would listen to me every day. He seemed to care how I felt, which Bob clearly did not. I felt like my marriage was about all the right things, children, our home, career moves on both our parts, his, and mine to a lesser extent. But there was no energy for the marriage. Maybe we both messed up, but it felt to me like it was Bob who had made the mistakes. I was so neglected by him that I came to dislike him. I was at home every day with this young, kind contractor and his crew. In the end, I sort of fell into his arms and he nourished me. There was no future, but it got me through a tough spot. In the end, I let it go, after a year. The house was finished and I had to move on, I had to work on the marriage. I doubt I'd be in the marriage today if it hadn't been for Jake. The affair helped me through an awful time."

If a woman wants to use an affair to better assess her marriage, to even improve her marriage, she can do so. The weight of the marriage, the responsibility to the marriage, cannot be ignored even in the most passionate of affairs. What a wife eventually chooses to do is reflective of how beholden she feels to her husband and children and the degree of misery she is experiencing in her marriage. What is notable is that the nineties wife had affairs and was willing to take the risk for the experience. The affairs existed outside the marriage, while the marriage existed in all of its usual forms.

In *The Bridges of Madison County*, the 1992 novel and subsequent film starring Meryl Streep and Clint Eastwood, we see the role of wife versus lover, with the role of wife winning out. Streep's character, Caroline, is a wife living in the middle of nowhere, who meets a perfect stranger, a photographer who arrives on location in her hometown while her husband is away at a fair with their two children. Even in this brief interlude, Caroline is taken with her lover in a way she never had been with her husband. He embodies the romantic spirit, a sexual awakening and true love. However, the practical side of Caroline's personality wins out, and she refuses to leave her marriage. Instead, she pines for her lover for the rest of her days.

There are stories like Caroline's in real life with variations on the theme. An example is the love affair and subsequent marriage of Melanie Griffith and Antonio Banderas, who met in 1994 on the set of the romantic comedy *Too Much*. At the time, Banderas was married to the Spanish actress Ana Leeza and Melanie Griffith was married (twice) to Don Johnson. The couple left their spouses, according to an article in the *Calgary Sun* on October 17, 1999, by Louis B. Hobson, "Feed the Fire: Antonio Banderas and Melanie Griffith Reveal Secret of Their Love," to marry each other in 1996. Similarly, in 1999 Meg Ryan and Russell Crowe shared a secret tryst while on location for the film *Proof of Life*. Ryan filed for a divorce from her husband of ten years, Dennis Quaid, but did not end up with Crowe. In each of these instances, whether based on real life or fiction, the power of an extramarital affair is very real and a crucial factor in a woman's life.

For Natasha, who fell for her lover completely, her decision to leave the marriage for the lover brought her happiness, even if it dismantled her entire family. "I was married and had two small sons when I met Joshua, my lover," begins Natasha. "This was in 1991 when I was on a business trip. I had no intentions of leaving my husband, or of having an affair, but it happened anyway. I believe that if my marriage had been satisfactory, no one could have turned my head. It is because I was unhappy, whether I was willing to admit it or not, that I fell for someone else. What began as a sort of fun and unpredictable affair ended up as a staid marriage in a small town in the Midwest. My parents and my in-laws were appalled and my husband, Stephen, begged me not to leave. I left because once I had the affair, I knew there was no going back. I would not have ever tolerated my life as it was after having met Joshua. Our sons were at the center of the maelstrom of course, and that was the hard part. I didn't care about money or about anything else from my previous life. I wanted my boys to be with me. Joshua, who began as a lover with not a care in the world, a never married man, ten years younger than I was, ended up being my support system through my divorce and an excellent stepfather.

"I cannot say that I believe that having an affair is the right thing to do, but it saved me in the end and I found a life I never thought was possible. If I had been married at another time, even ten years earlier with two small kids and a job as a teacher, I would not have taken the risks I took in the nineties. The nineties, to me, were a time when women were willing to spread their wings. I ended up better off."

Not all nineties wives were as willing as Natasha to rock the status quo for a life with their lover, or even a life apart from their husbands without attaching to their lover. In my research for *A Passion for More: Wives Reveal the Affairs That Make or Break Their Marriages*, I learned that while 60 percent of wives believe that their lover is a wake-up call, only 25 percent of married women who conduct extra-marital affairs end up with their lover. The lover is the catalyst to leave a poor marriage in 33 percent of the cases, yet 45 percent of the wives remain in their marriage after the affair. What I found most striking is that 90 percent of the women feel entitled to have the affair. This attitude is an indicator of how women perceived themselves as wives and mothers, and what part of their lives was about their own fulfillment. If the wife felt neglected in the marriage, one option was to find a lover. Divorce was not a first choice, but a lover might do the trick, even if it was a temporary solution.

A wife who becomes entwined with her lover is pulling away from her husband, whether it is subconscious or deliberate. Feeling neglected and unappreciated, she looks elsewhere. The nineties wife who chose a lover did not find sufficient comfort in her marriage or with her close female friends to feel fulfilled. She had come to the conclusion that her husband had let her down. The irony here is that the lover can open up the wife's eyes to what her marriage is about. It might occur to this wife later, once her husband began to show his feelings or once she saw life through the eyes of her lover, and as a lover, that her husband actually was connected to her. If only the husband was able to show his wife that side of himself, if only the nineties wife was not so needy herself, so invested in the marriage yet so disappointed by the results. Unlike the eighties wife, who was immersed in holding it all together, keeping all the balls in the air, the nineties wife had some time for reflection. She noticed her own isolation and acted on it. That is when the lover stepped in, since the nineties wife hesitated before initiating a divorce and was willing to risk an affair instead, in some cases. The lover provided what the husband could not, be it companionship, communication, affirmation or sex.

"Why should I have divorced in 1996, when I could have a lover and be married?"asks Sharon, who had been married for five years before she had an extramarital affair. "I loved my husband then; I love him now. But there wasn't enough sex in our marriage and he wasn't a very sexual person. I am, and I was even more sexual in the nineties, in my late thirties. I'd always been sexual, and Duane, my husband, stopped being sexy after a few years of marriage. We had no children and I was still very into it. So I met a man who became the perfect lover. He wanted little besides sex, while Duane wanted everything else. It was a perfect setup. Sometimes I even think that Duane knew about it on some level. This went on for three years, until my lover and his girlfriend moved to Mexico. I'll never regret this affair. It really helped me at the time."

Sex was one of the reasons for women to engage in an extramarital affair. As early as 1976 when Shere Hite first published *The Hite Report*, sex mattered to women and wives often found themselves frustrated by their sex lives. While in 1976 this news was shocking, and women might have been reticent to act on their desires, by the 1990s women were willing to have affairs if that would provide the sex life they sought. For wives willing to cross the line for sex, the lover offered little else, nor was the wife interested in companionship or romance, merely sex. In other words, women were operating much as men have throughout history.

Ariel, like Sharon, found her affair helpful to her marriage. "I had an affair with a twenty-six-year-old when I was forty because of what I was missing with my husband. My lover was young and sexy, not lumpy and older like my husband. He was a free spirit and this came out in the sex. I was willing to do things with him that I had never considered with Peter. I found it all so refreshing, so sensual, that I didn't worry about jeopardizing my marriage. I didn't worry about getting caught. I only told my sister and my best friend, and I trusted both of them. They knew why I did what I did.

"My lover helped me more than anyone had, even if it was mostly about sex. I wish that Peter had asked me the questions that my lover asked me in bed. I wish this had happened before we were even married. We had been married for seven years before I had a lover. I guess it took me a while to realize what was missing. I stayed in my marriage because I felt that sex alone could not sustain a relationship, but I stopped pretending that I didn't care about sex. I saw this lover for years, on and off. It saved my marriage, and somehow made me feel less lonely. The affair saved me from a messy divorce."

The National Center for Health Statistics in 2000 recorded that divorce declined between 1991 and 1995, due to social and financial factors. The theory is that with more states becoming proponents of joint physical custody, there was less economic incentive for women to divorce. This has been researched by Richard Kuhn and John Guidubaldi in their paper "Child Custody Policies and Divorce Rates in the United States." If, in fact, wives looked at divorce in this light, it might have caused an increase in infidelity, in a deliberate method of getting what was missing from the marriage without jeopardizing the entire entity. After all, nineties wives had more freedom than any of their predecessors. Many of these wives worked part- or full-time, but extramarital affairs were often sparked by the workplace. However, extramarital affairs during this decade were by no means confined to the workplace and could occur in any way at any time in a wife's life, from meeting a fellow parent at daycare, to meeting a man at a health club, to meeting a man randomly at an airport, train station or bus depot. The idea that it could happen anywhere, under any circumstances, was thrilling, daring and plausible to the nineties wife.

The wife of the 1990s carefully weighed her role as an upstanding wife. In many cases, she chose to posture as this type of wife, while searching for free expression of emotions or sex, or both, with another man. The lover sufficed where the husband had failed. The nineties wife became conscious of her needs in pursuing an illicit affair. The nineties wife was exceptional and unique in her attitude, and she created a new norm that would be noted, if not followed, by the twenty-first-century wife. The nineties wife felt free to have the life she yearned for with her lover and was willing to take the risk for the reward.

If the nineties wife was one to recognize her own sexual desires, it had been a long journey to this knowledge. Our ever puritanical, sexist and hypocritical society of the late twentieth century was able to view women as sexual objects but wives as sexless. The leftover nineteenth-century Victorian mores seemed unshakable. So what existed in the eighteenth and nineteenth centuries as the romantic movement, which broke from tradition, as Juanita H. Williams reminds us in her essay, "Sexuality in Marriage," and emphasized romance as the opposite of middle-class marriage, was replaced with the Victorian concept of sexless wives. Despite the sexual revolution of the sixties, this view returned in the late seventies and eighties. Wives were too tired from their complex lives to fuss much with sex in their marriages. But the nineties wife took exception to this way of thinking. She felt that sex was necessary, and if she could not have the experience with her husband, she found it elsewhere, if she so chose.

Egalitarian Marriages/Competition Between Spouses

Egalitarian marriages where two partners were equals did not enter into the equations of the modern wife until the 1990s. The previous twenty years had been building up to this concept whether or not it was apparent within each decade. For example, wives of the seventies might not have considered equality in marriage because they were so preoccupied with finding their place in the work world. If the eighties wives dared to dream of shared power and communication in their marriages, they did little about it. How could there be equality between husband and wives in dual-working families of the seventies when husbands were bailing on the household and parenting responsibilities? These eighties wives were too perplexed, then too let down to stay, contributing significantly to the rising divorce rate. By the nineties, the divorce rate had peaked and wives were sticking it out, all the while considering how to make it an equal playing field.

These women knew that their responsibilities were double and were determined to do something about it. The nineties wife reflected a society still struggling with the balance of working, wifing and mothering. The false starts of the previous two decades only worsened the situation. Yet, it was the nineties wife who understood that peer marriages were imperative. After twenty years of trudging along, the nineties wife saw that she deserved to be appreciated as a person. In fact, the nineties wife was not so sanguine that she wanted to work, instead expecting equal power in the marriage, whether she had a career or not. Being just a housewife was not only an offensive phrase, it was not up for discussion. Wives were free to choose, and they wanted to be equals with their husbands because they deserved it. They had the option to be or not to be working wives/mothers.

Husbands remained a problem, however, because in order to facilitate this change and make egalitarian marriages the norm, husbands had to share equally as parents and in the home life. They had to be communicative and helpful. Men were not conditioned for this role, not even the best of them, who subscribed to the rhetoric. According to Robert M. Jackson, in his book, *Destined for Equality: The Inevitable Rise of Women's Status*, women have not gained total equality, even though there is no longer anything holding them back, for the most part. So while Jackson believes in progress and in a future where women are equal, he does not believe that women have arrived yet. According to my pool of interviewees, there is wisdom in Jackson's view, but the nineties wife's agenda cannot be discounted. As psychologist Claire Owen sees it, "The major disillusionment of the nineties wife was partly because husbands were improving only slightly on the home front and careers were stalled at middle management for women. These women felt hopeless although they certainly had tried their best."

"There was no way that Joe could be the man he promised to be," sighs Beth, who married in 1991. "We had so many conversations about how he would help with the kids, be supportive of my career, before we got married. In 1993 we had our son, and we decided that we could manage our marriage with just one kid. The reality is that Joe didn't know how to be my best friend once the going got tough. Children take time and he worked long hours and is an avid sports fan. He couldn't pour the kind of energy and attention into the marriage that I wanted. He was always there for me emotionally, if I was upset about something at work or if I had a fight with my sister. He knew too well how my boss treated me. I wanted something beyond that, something that was deep and safe at the same time. I look back now and realize it probably could never have been, even with our great plans for the marriage. We worked hard to support our little family, came home tired and began again the next day. I think we should have stood side by side doing dishes or something. We should have taken turns cooking dinners. Who knows? We're still married and I've stopped wondering why it was so important to me ten years ago that we weren't close enough, that we weren't really equal. I say to myself, it was what it was and we survived."

By this time in modern American history, many families depended on dual incomes. This only made a nineties wife more aware that her efforts counted, even if they fell short of her goal. With working wives having been at it for two decades by now, the structure of the family and of the marriage was undeniably changed. From 1970, when 41 percent of married women were in the labor force, to 1990, when 58 percent of married women were in the labor force, membership in children's school-related activities such as the PTA diminished by 25 percent, according to Janet Z. Giele's research. There were few husbands who took the place of wives in these instances and working wives/mothers could not always stretch that far, and became conspicuously absent at children's school events. This dichotomy between working and nonworking mothers was being staked out. It would be the twenty-first-century wife who cared about such matters, who drew the line in the sand between those wives/mothers who worked and those who did not.

"There I was: a wife who worked and mothered," begins Charlene. "My husband, Dan, seemed to lack the ability to multitask. By 1998, I realized I had a busy work life, a busy mothering role that exhausted me, and an odd kind of equality in my marriage. We made joint decisions for our two children. I had some close women friends, but most of us worked and didn't have too much time to get together. Still, I considered them a support system. I was tired of the workplace by the mid-nineties but I knew I had to keep going financially, there was no choice. I felt saturated. I was becoming impatient with younger women at work who had no little children at home. I only identified with women who had the same situation as I did. I really began to think I was having a meltdown. Dan was very understanding and he tried to help because my hours were so long. He would get home early those years when the kids were little. He let the sitter go home and took charge until I returned at about eight-thirty or nine at night. I married a great guy, but true equality about work and mothering doesn't seem to exist. We are partners in parenting, life decisions and sex. Sex had gotten quite low on the totem pole with all the ordinary tugs and pulls. But we stuck it out. We made the effort."

Home offices became an option for the nineties wife. While it was an option for some nineties husbands as well, more wives than husbands jumped at the chance to establish a work setup in the house. The nineties wife was willing to try a home office life even if she enjoyed the workplace environment because she felt it would help her to balance work and children. The pitfalls of being a full-time working mother and wife are what caused these women to take a serious look at home offices as an alternative. In theory, it was a tremendous solution, but in reality, it was stressful. Young children were plopped in front of television sets for hours while mothers as working women tried to negotiate deals from their ersatz office space carved out from a crowded family room, to be able to watch the children while working. It was not always easy to choreograph work versus home versus children, in equal parts.

The flexibility that these women anticipated in creating a home office did not often surface until their children were in kindergarten or all-day preschool programs. The discipline required to work at home without being sidetracked was significant as well, something that not many women had factored into the equation. According to Ellen Golden, senior program officer for the Women's Business Center of Coastal Enterprises, the number of women-owned businesses has increased by 89 percent in the past fifteen years and the number of self-employed women has grown 77 percent since 1983. This is proof of the eventual success of working mothers who established home offices and small businesses in the 1990s and would bear the fruit of their labors in the twenty-first century.

"In the end I decided to work at home for the sake of my daughter and my husband," begins Rene. "This was in 1996, after having juggled work and a pregnancy, daycare and my mother-in-law as baby-sitter and fill-in person. I was so happy at first, but it definitely cost me my independence and many work hours. Somehow, I didn't have the skills to get it all in order for about a year. I was not as exhausted as when I had to be at work by nine each day, but I was also not as much my own person. I felt like a stay-at-home mother who worked when she could pull it off, not a working mother and equal to my husband.

"I think that wives who think there should be equality in their marriages have to understand that children and finances change all that. Becoming practical kind of ruins the idea of a marriage based on equals—it's more like we each have a job to do. And it isn't in equal parts."

In my research I found that the majority of nineties wives who opted for home offices reported that the adjustment was more demanding than they expected. They missed the workplace, the sterile, crisp, uninterrupted, adult environment without the onslaught of children and the demands of running a home. According to the U.S. Bureau of Labor Statistics in 1995, 60 percent of all marriages in the United States are two career marriages and these couples constitute 45 percent of the workplace. Research conducted by Catalyst, the nonprofit advisory organization for women's issues, suggests that despite this high percentage, the workplace remains unsympathetic to a woman's needs in terms of her family and a pliant schedule. Notwithstanding this treatment of working mothers, women continue to seek work outside the home. The emergence of the home office was an option for women who felt the emotional tugs of being with their children and the commitment to the work world. This was a trade-off that gave young wives/mothers a clear conscience and husbands a way to feel excused when their long hours kept them away from home. Toward the end of the decade, men began to work at home, in tandem with their wives or on their own. There was a population of wives who remained in the workplace while their husbands were immersed in home offices and childcare.

Ideally, the couple had the opportunity to carve out flexible schedules that enabled either parent to be at home with the children on a part-time basis. As Epstein, Seron, Oglensky and Saute found in their study, *The Part-time Paradox: Time Norms, Professional Life, Family and Gender*, these decisions are made based on which spouse brings in more income. In this way, it becomes a decision based on the conventional roles in a marriage. If the husband brings in more money and is the major breadwinner, then his work is more valued and the marriage caters to his schedule.

Practically speaking, although the results are often sexist, a couple with children needs the larger income and this way of thinking is indicative of this fact.

When it comes to the working-class mother, she and her husband both contribute to the family's financial standing. There is rarely a dispute or consideration about who will take the children to daycare, if not to a mother's or mother-in-law's home, while the wife is at work. A wife knows that this is a part of her day. In this social sphere, childcare is still the responsibility of the wife/mother, and the father/husband is not expected to have any specific chores around the house or with the children. That both the wife and husband work is often mandatory, but mothering remains the wife's job. Working class couples do not have the luxury of private childcare or a nanny in order to exist as a dual-career couple. Since the couple needs money, the wife has little choice about working or not working. It becomes a necessity.

Maria, who has been a common-law wife for nine years, knows that housekeeping and childcare are her territories, while her husband works long hours as a day janitor and then a night janitor. "We both work but he works more because he is the man," explains Maria. "He says I count as much as he does about things, but I also know my place. If I have trouble with my schedule and the kids, maybe my mother will help or I'll do another daycare that I've heard about. But he does not consider this his problem. I am happy with him, and I want to keep things the way they are.

"I don't think of my work as anything special, but something I have to do. And my husband feels the same about his work. He has no choice and he cares about doing it right. I have pride because I work and I am proud of him because he works. We both have these jobs, mine includes the house and kids. His work is outside the house, and he knows he has to make enough money. We work as a team in order to survive."

The life of the nineties wife was filled with contradictions and obstacles, lessons to be honed along a slow progress toward equality. She saw that marriages based on equal regard for the wife's and the husband's needs are idealistic and challenging to achieve. With this realization, the nineties wife danced around many issues in order to remain married. If their marriages were less than satisfactory, some nineties wives were willing to go beyond the marriage in order to suit themselves. In other areas of her life, including mothering and work, the nineties wife proved to be an acrobat, bending and twisting in order to satisfy her husband and children. What set her apart from her predecessors was her level of awareness of her actions and her unrelenting hope for improvement.

Chapter Seven:
The Millennium Arrives:
The Backlash and New Accolades

I was really looking for a family unit; the person who will be with me for the rest of my life," begins Emma, who at twenty-four became a bride in 2000. "Both Scott's parents and mine are happily married and that has been an example for us. I see my husband as the right person to take the journey with, to be there with me for all that life offers. That is not to say that it is perfect, because we are not the same religion and not from the same background. Our decision to get married and to make a life together is about finding solutions. We know how difficult it can be and we have discussed all the scenarios so that we are not surprised. We are taking steps in how to handle our careers, having kids, where we will live. Since I work for the government and Scott is a physician, we are moving to the city where I need to be. Scott has made this decision to move there for me. He is three years older than I am and is just beginning his medical practice. Both of us are making lots of adjustments. And there is so much stress. We've already bought a house because we know we are going to be located in one place for quite a while.

"I suspect there will be hurdles ahead, but we are a team, and we can work it out. We plan to have a child by the time I am thirty. I don't want to put it off beyond that. All of this has been discussed and agreed to. Scott will support whatever I do about my career, but I already know that I will not hold out, like my mother and her friends have done. I will make the changes and stop working such long hours because I know it will help the marriage. I believe in romantic love and true love. I know Scott is the one for me."

In the desire to get it right, to be successful wives, Generation Y women, born between 1980 and the present, often view their mothers with skepticism. This generation of young women deliberately decided to worry less about high-powered careers and more about having true love and partnership. Their courage to emphasize the personal over the professional came from a determination to be good wives and a sense of the world as uncertain. This attitude was reinforced in the wake of 9/11 and Operation Iraqi Freedom. The idea of coupling represented a safe haven for these young women. They had witnessed Generation X, born between 1961 and 1980, holding on to the behaviors of preceding decades of working wives, all the while sorting out how the nineties could be a departure, in the midst of confusion and doubt.

The optimism of the young wife of the twenty-first century is refreshing, if a culmination of wifely experiences. The agenda of these young women who believe in creating their own destiny in marriage is unlike that of any modern wife to go before them, and a reflection of all that has been successful and unsuccessful in the role of the wife over the decades. While young women today seem ready to be married earlier, the statistics are not yet clear on this. What is evident is a backlash at the style of the nineties wives, combined with an impressive sense of self. The twenty-first-century wife has taken a good look at the errors of her predecessors, especially her mother's generation, and has decided to revamp the role. If the fairy-tale life of the wife is being reinvented, it is performed in a fashion that offers young women a chance to get it right— the balance of wifing, romance, mothering and career.

In the 2002 release of the film *Sweet Home Alabama*, Reese Witherspoon plays a young woman who married her local sweetheart and left for greener pastures. In deciding to shed a conventional life in her small town in Alabama, she ditches her husband and goes to New York City to reinvent herself. She becomes a single working woman and a chic young woman about town. Her engagement to a quintessential New Yorker, the opposite of her childhood sweetheart, and the son of a female mayor of New York City, causes her to reflect upon her life, her future, and the value of true love. There is little question that the nineties wife, or even the eighties wife, would have gone for the sophisticated New Yorker and never looked back. Witherspoon's character has a purity that causes her to be reflective and to choose based on her heart.

The political climate changed drastically in 2000, when George W. Bush became president and Laura Bush became our first lady. The styles of Hillary Clinton, wife of former president William Jefferson Clinton, and Laura Bush could not be more disparate. At the same time President Clinton stepped down, Hillary was elected the junior Senator from New York state. The November 2002 elections resulted in nine female Democrats and four female Republicans elected to the Senate. In the House of Representatives, sixty women were elected as Representatives and three as delegates. After the November 2000 election, four female Democrats and two female Republicans were elected as governors. In this way, the decade reflected a steady increase in the number of women in politics, including those who had husbands and children.

The famous wives who married in the twenty-first century include Gloria Steinem, feminist and cofounder of *Ms.* magazine, who married David Bale in 2000. It was Steinem's first marriage, at the age of sixty-six. On June ll, 2002, Heather Mills married former Beatle Paul McCartney at a wedding ceremony and reception that cost over three million dollars in an Irish castle. A wife of five years became a bona fide queen on the eve of the millennium when the Queen of Jordan, Rania Al-Abdullah, was crowned and her husband, the son of King Hussein, was named the king's successor in 1998. Liza Minnelli entered a short-lived marriage with David Gest, an event producer eight years her junior, in March of 2002. Debra Messing, star of *Will & Grace*, married screenwriter Daniel Zelman on September 3, 2000. On July 4, 2002, Julia Roberts married cameraman Danny Moder. The couple had met on the set of *The Mexican* in 2000. Jennifer Aniston and Brad Pitt married on July 29, 2000. On April l3, 2002, Benjamin Bratt married

Talisa Soto. George Stephanopoulos, the adviser to former President Clinton, married Alexandra Wentworth at a wedding ceremony held at the Cathedral of the Holy Trinity in New York City on November 20, 2001.

Those who divorced include Jane Fonda and Ted Turner, whose divorce was finalized in 2001; Tom Cruise and Nicole Kidman; and the former mayor of New York City, Rudolph Giuliani and Donna Hanover. Although Giuliani was praised for his leadership after 9/ll, his divorce the following year did not garner the same sentiment from the public. Many were offended by how he and his future ex-wife conducted their divorce war. However, by the following year, Donna Hanover announced her engagement to a former beau, and on May 24, 2003, Rudolph W. Giuliani married Judith Nathan, his third wife. The couple was married at Gracie Mansion, with Mayor Michael Bloomberg presiding over the wedding ceremony.

The Search for Husbands

In the past thirty years, women have exhibited independence in several categories; as never-married women, divorced women, and as women who married late in life after establishing themselves in their careers. Nonetheless, the quest for the right partner, who equals the right husband, looms large for women in the twenty-first century. The choices of the past five decades of wifing have made it obvious to these women that marriage is a priority, even if the rules have changed and can still be improved. *The New York Times* Sunday wedding announcements remain a popular first read for married and single women of all ages, proof of the allure and value of marriage. The legacy of the divorced baby boomer wife has resonated in the choices that these young wives-to-be have made. They are hell-bent on avoiding divorce and succeeding the first time around.

Along with the continuing significance of finding the right partner, the frustration of not finding a partner has manifested in a new form of book that depicts the plight of the single girl. From *Bridget Jones' Diary*, by Helen Fielding, to *Hers*, by Laura Zigman, to *The Single Girl's Guide To Fishing and Hunting*, by Melissa Bank, the essential message is that singlehood is hell and it's a rat race to get the guy and seal the deal. Of course, true love wins out, but this group of poignant and humorous renditions of a single woman's life only proves to young women that while they might be eligible, the right man can be elusive. "Being in a relationship, like being a parent, counts more for women than for men," explains Antoinette Michaels, relationship expert. "Women go about it differently and getting married remains a big part of their self definition."

The fact is that marriage has retained its intrigue and exists as a priority on many a woman's wish list in the new century. This sentiment was evident in the unduplicated success of the film *My Big Fat Greek Wedding*, released in 2002. The film earned more than two hundred million dollars, making it the most prosperous independent feature film ever released. The story line is appealing—that a family with a strong ethnic style and religious commitment expects its offspring to follow the same traditions, but instead true love enters the daughter's life in the form of a man from outside the realm. Both obstacles and joys are presented, and the daughter ends up the winner.

Another universal theme is found in the December 2002 blockbuster film *Maid in Manhattan*, starring Jennifer Lopez as Marisa Ventura, a single mother who lives in the Bronx but works as a maid in an elegant Manhattan hotel. Ralph Fiennes stars as Christopher Marshall, a senatorial candidate. When the two meet, Fiennes' character mistakes Lopez's character for a wealthy woman and the two fall in love. After some initial hesitancy once he discovers that she is a maid at the hotel, he realizes it does not matter to him, she is the woman of his dreams. The audience is satisfied because our society is deeply invested in the Cinderella story of rags to riches, and living happily ever after as husband and wife.

The marriage gradient, discussed earlier, prevails for the twenty-first-century woman who hopes to be married as well as for wives of this decade. Lamanna and Riedmann's research in their book, *Marriages and Families: Making Choices in a Diverse Society*, indicates that "while the marriage gradient does exist, the practice sets the stage for greater marital power for husbands than wives, because husbands have greater educational and/or financial resources." If this theory has been applicable in past decades, by the first decade of the twenty-first century we realize that it is not necessarily true. Rather, the most current wife feels warranted in choosing whomever she wants as her husband, regardless of any disparity in backgrounds.

"I was not intimidated by James' family or the way he was raised," Lauren begins. "I came from a much simpler life, and my parents were working class. I wanted to marry James, wanted to be his wife. This was 2001, and the world was changing. My grandma warned me that James and I came from different worlds and that it was hard enough to survive in a world where the husband and wife were from similar backgrounds. She said this would be too difficult, and I should give it up. I wouldn't dream of such a thing; it made no sense. We wanted to be together; we deserved each other. I wasn't marrying him because of his family but because of him. I was sophisticated, if not wealthy, and I felt like I could have any life I wanted. I wanted to be married to James and I wanted to be his wife. Should he have married someone who came from his exact kind of family? Maybe, but not because it was better for him, only if he liked someone better than he loved me. Not because they were from the same background. That wasn't enough of an incentive. Not anymore. I'm the one he's chosen. We'll both benefit from this marriage."

Further proof of the value of finding the right partner and being a wife can be seen in a phenomenally popular reality series on the subject. The February 2003 television show *Joe Millionaire* attracted thirty-six million viewers who knew that Evan Marriott, a construction worker, was only posing as a young man worth fifty million dollars. For the twenty young single women who were waiting to be chosen to be "the one", it might have been a grueling few days. In this ersatz world of love by numbers, the producers of *Joe Millionaire* even provided a two-carat diamond ring, worth twenty-five thousand dollars, according to the March 3, 2003 issue of *People* magazine.

The craze to find one's soulmate on television included a show that aired in April 2002 called *The Bachelor*. This rendition starred a Harvard graduate, class of 1992, thirty-one-year-old Alex Michael, who was selected from a nationwide search. Michael was to choose from twenty-five women until he found his perfect match. The response from the nineteen million viewers who watched this series at its height, was sympathy for Trista Rehn who was not chosen by Michael, but made it as far as runner-up. ABC then decided to air *The Bachelorette*. In a gender switch, Trista was granted the chance to choose from twenty-five single men to find her mate, in the best-case scenario, or at least the pretense of a knight in shining armor, at worst.

The belief that love equals marriage may be uniquely American at this point in time. There is a European trend toward partners not marrying in order to have long-term commitments and children, and to purposely not take vows. In an article published in *The New York Times* on March 24, 2002 titled "For Europeans, Love, Yes; Marriage, Maybe," Sarah Lyall describes "a profound shift that has changed the notion of what constitutes a family in many countries, more and more children are being born out of wedlock into a new social order in which, it seems, few of the old stigmas apply." This mode of thinking is predominant in the Nordic countries, England, and France, Lyall tells us. According to her article, 49 percent of all births in Norway in 1999 were to unmarried couples as were 62 percent in Iceland. *The London Times Magazine*, in July 2001, echoed these sentiments with an article entitled "Bride and Gloom," by John Cornwell. He reports that according to the Office of National Statistics in Britain, fewer than 300,000 people are getting married per year since the 1990s, which is 25 percent fewer marriages in one decade. "Nowadays," writes Cornwell, "more than 70 percent of women cohabit before marriage, compared with two percent in the 1950s."

In Canada, *The Globe and Mail* reported on July 12, 2002, that more Canadian couples lived together than married, as reported by the latest Statistics Canada data, up twenty percent between 1995 and 2001. According to Krista Foss in "Living Together: A Popular First Step, Data Show," "young Quebeckers...choose out-of-wedlock relationships as a happy substitute for marital bliss." The American view of marriage is not quite like the European and Canadian style, even for those U.S. couples who co-habit. Love, marriage, and remarriage are sought after and encouraged in the United States. In America, according to Costello et al, while the divorce rate is over 50 percent as reported by the 1990 U.S. Census, and the rate of remarriage is at 75 percent.

"I have lived with Roger for fourteen years," begins Lutecia, who at forty-five would hesitate to marry today. "I wanted very much to be his wife in the beginning but he had a son from his first marriage and a very visible ex-wife. I don't think he would have been able to make the commitment. So he made the same commitment to me without any vows and by the year 2003, I can handle it. I see that we did not have to be married to be devoted to each other. I sure believed we needed it for a long time, and it came between us. I resented Roger's position on marriage for years and I found it unfair to me. It made him too involved with his former family and it kept me from a rightful status of wife. That is how we were raised and only recently has this feeling lessened for me.

"What I get in this relationship is companionship and love, and I know that Roger admires me and is crazy about me. I'm the stable one; he's the underachiever. By now I've realized what I cannot get, and that is a husband. I doubt I will become his wife and I know I will never have a child. I can't deny that I would feel more secure if we were married, but I also see our commitment is for the long term. It isn't how I was raised, and my sisters have been married for years, with kids, which makes it harder for me. I am finally working this out, finally seeing that marriage is not the answer, it's about the couple."

Unlike Lutecia's take on living together in mid-life is Andrea's experience, at the age of twenty-four.

"I married my husband this year, right out of graduate school," notes Andrea. "I knew that I didn't want to wait and my parents and friends never even suggested that. He is my match, we are in the same field—both of us are medical researchers—and I didn't want to just live with him. I know that some of my friends are living with their fiancés and boyfriends, but I didn't want to be in that position. Peter, my husband, understood. I'm not sure he would have liked it either. We wanted a big wedding and to go on a honeymoon right after. In some ways, this was not much different from how my mother and her sister and brother got married in the late seventies. The difference is that I have landed a good job, as good as Peter's, and we do not want to have kids right away, like my parents did. We definitely wanted to be married, though. It made a difference to us in the level of commitment. Also, there is this part of me that knew not to let Peter go. I have seen so many divorces with my mother's friends and how miserable women are once they are not with someone, and I wanted to protect myself."

In the mind of a young twenty-first-century wife there is the belief that finding and holding on to the right partner is of utmost importance. The recent past has shown that career advancement was a hindrance to marriage and vice versa. The backlash arrived in the form of young wives of the twenty-first century who decided not to pay the price for the complications of marriage, children and career. This group may be convinced that marriage is the solution, yet the U.S. Census reports that there are over two million single women living in New York City today. Granted, this entire population is not comprised of young, hip twenty-first-century women with great confidence and the mind-set to not make their mothers' mistakes, but reflects a large population of all ages.

Even if the sixties taught women to consider themselves first, and Gloria Steinem was credited with having said, "A woman needs a man like a fish needs a bicycle," (a statement which was actually attributed to several others, including Irina Dunn, an Australian journalist in 1970), the swing back toward the theory of nabbing that guy before someone else does has definitely taken hold in the recent past and applies strongly to the present. Perhaps the social conditioning of centuries cannot be erased by one revolutionary decade like the sixties. While a woman's consciousnesses could be raised when it came to the workplace and to the idea of peer marriages, which were so significant to the nineties wives, the fundamental premise of putting the marriage first and getting this part of a woman's life right resurfaced by the new century. "What we have today," remarks Dr. Michele Kasson, "is still the dream of having a husband because women still feel deficient without one." These women who are not married begin to feel hopeless even if they are attractive and have much to offer. The conditioning that creates the Cinderella complex, that someone will take care of us, exists with a new component—that of the twenty-first-century wife who views it as required. Her understanding is that she is perfectly capable of taking care of herself, but it is nice to know this is not imperative. A man can definitely be the provider; she has no shame about this, she has nothing to prove. The dichotomy between capacity and practice does not daunt this new type of wife.

The lead section in *Newsweek* on March 3, 2003, "From Schools to Jobs, Black Women are Rising Much Faster Than Black Men. What It Means for Work, Family and Race Relations," included an article on "The Black Gender Gap" and "Time To Tell It Like It Is," by Allison Samuels. The salient point is that compared to the number of black women who might be "crashing through the double ceiling of race and gender," their black male potential partners are "educationally, economically, professionally" behind. The point raised is whether these successful women will lower themselves to find a black husband. "In bars, colleges and other gathering spots across America, the question is much the same: where are the decent, desirable black men?" The 2000 U.S. Census reports that 47 percent of black women between the ages of thirty and thirty-four have never been married. For white women of the same age, the rate is ten percent. If these black women do not marry outside of their race, according to the article, they may end up marrying down, resulting in an "interclass romance."

"I have saved enough money to get my nursing degree," begins Audrey, who at thirty-four has been an aide to the elderly for the past nine years. "I begin school in the fall and my husband, Jimmy, doesn't want any part of it. He is a construction worker and he isn't going to change for me. He isn't interested in school; he never pretended to want to do better. When I say that I will work in a hospital after I get this degree, he doesn't say much. But I have a few friends who have done it and the men don't like it. I don't want to give up my dreams but I don't want to upset Jimmy. He feels like he's less than I am, but he also doesn't want to improve. I do. I always have wanted to. I was a great student in high school and then I got married and had children. Now they are bigger and it is time for me to get on with my plans. I see other black women want to do better and I'm right there, I'm part of this.

"If my becoming a nurse comes between us, that is the way it goes. I doubt I'd ever meet someone else, and I love Jimmy. But he can't stop me and he won't stop me. I need to do this for myself. My mother tells me I'll end up alone. I say why, because Jimmy can't do better? I should stick to this job because he can't give his up? I don't think so."

The outstanding African-American activists such as Sojourner Truth and Ida Wells Barnett were all too aware of what Patricia Hills Collins notes in her essay "The Social Construction of Black Feminist Thought." Collins writes: "Black women cannot afford to be fools of any type, and their devalued status denies them the protections that white skin, maleness and wealth confer."

Black women in the twenty-first century are in a unique position, because black college-educated, achieving women are causing "a monumental shifting of the sands" according to the *Time* magazine piece. The article asks "...is she leaping into treacherous waters that will leave her stranded, unfulfilled, childless and alone?" These questions arise because the black woman's achievements have been unduplicated and the prototype is now being set.

It is curious to note that while the majority of unmarried nineties women often put their ambition ahead of having a husband and children, and later complain that they had neither, the twenty-first-century wife is not as willing to do so. The focus is on the goal of partner/husband, resonant of a concept that is deeply etched in our culture; regardless of class or race, it exists as a timeless status. Thus, the opportunity to get ahead for black women and their willingness to take risks is notable.

For a large population of women of all social strata, we cannot negate the draw that marriage is for women today. The twenty-first-century wife, of any age, understands that gender goals have been split, shared and analyzed in the past four decades, from the sixties onward. In the end, marriage appears the winner, and a goal for enough women that the twenty-first-century wife has reconsidered her position. The baby boomer's daughter asks herself what modelling her mother has offered her. This generation is somewhat cynical as well as skeptical that her mother's ambition, combined with her endless fatigue, is not the answer. These young women see that their mothers defined themselves mostly by what they do in the world, and it is not attractive to the daughters. They are purposely choosing a different route, one that avoids their mothers' experience.

Another factor for the young women of the twenty-first century was their mothers' divorces, which discouraged them greatly. It occurred to these daughters that the right partner might not only be imperative but could save them from the hellish divorces that their mothers had endured. In researching for my book, *Women of Divorce: Mothers, Daughters, Stepmothers - The New Triangle*, I learned that 60 percent of these daughters were determined to succeed in marriage because of their mothers' experiences and wanted very much to be married. These young women were confident that their marriages would work in the face of failure. This group had the courage to leave a failed marriage and begin again, based on the examples set before them. Either way, marriage remained their destination. As Elizabeth A. Rider writes in her book *Our Voices: Psychology of Women*, marriage remains the "typical pattern of adult life" for women. Since our society expects women to marry, when a woman is not married, she feels that she is less than her married counterparts. The 1998 U.S. Census Bureau found that 80 percent of white American women and 60 percent of black American women had been or are presently married, proving the significance of marriage in a woman's life.

Military Wives and Wives in the Military

Military wives are unlike any other type of wife in America, whether they are married to men who serve in the military or are enlisted in the Armed Forces themselves. According to iVillage.com's website on women in the military, these wives are expected to be patriotic, flexible and committed to the specific requirements of military marriages. Research indicates that 45 percent of military wives are not a part of the workforce but are stay-at-home wives. These women complain most often about feeling isolated and the length of time that their husbands are away from home. In addition, these women and their families move frequently, with an average of 2.4 times over a five-year period.

Another problem for these wives is that they are expected to meet regulations that would not affect a civilian marriage. As documented by Weinstein and White, editors of the book *Wives and Warriors: Women and the Military in the United States and Canada*, the military views the wife as someone who not only is supportive of her husband's career, but she is expected to do his share at home when he is unable to be there, due to his commitment to the military.

"Maybe I wasn't warned or something," begins Talia. "My mother and father are civilians and we really didn't know anyone in the military. I married Stewart because I thought he would serve for a short time and then we'd get on with our lives. I believed that was the plan. Instead we are going on seven years in our marriage with him serving and I don't see any end in sight. I had a child from my first marriage and he adopted her. Then we had two more together. I would say that my life is about taking care of the kids and the house, inside and out, because Stewart is never around. If the yard needs mowing, I do it; if the toilet breaks, I've learned what to do. Sometimes I'm not even able to reach my husband, let alone get him to do these simple things.

"Trust is a big issue in this marriage because we are separated so much of the time. We have to know that the other person is there and that we are each doing our job. I used to work at a department store but I can't manage that any more because of the kids. So I'm basically a full-time military wife, which is not like being a normal wife. I have become friends with other women in my shoes and that has helped me. And I plan to work once Stewart does leave the Armed Forces."

Talia's interview brings up two common themes in the life of the military wife; the first is that a support system of other wives in the same situation can be imperative for one's well-being; and the second is that two-thirds of military wives, according to iVillage.com's report, will pursue their careers once their husbands have left or retired from the military. For the military wives who seek support groups, there is the realization that their husbands are more connected to their careers than men who are not in the military and also to each other. The wives seek each other out to understand their identity as military wives and to assuage the isolation and sense of despair that often comes with their role. *The New York Times* ran a piece on March 10, 2002, by David W. Chen, "Two Wives Become Comrades in Anxiety." Two military wives, Deirdre Adams and Amy Worthan, both young wives married to officers, met and became friends while their husbands were stationed in Afghanistan. Chen reports that the women have become inseparable at Fort Drumm, located near Watertown, New York, and "comfort one another whenever someone wobbles emotionally, or something goes awry."

What is unique about the military wife in the twenty-first century is that she is positioned to subjugate herself to her husband's needs, especially if she is a military wife not in the military herself. As we have seen through interviews with wives married to civilians, who constitute the majority of this book, and through data on nonmilitary marriages, this way of thinking applies specifically to women married to men in the military. The civilian wife of a military man is put into a situation that is the direct result of being married to a member of the military.

The status of both married women in the military and military wives has been shadowed by the sad events at Fort Bragg in the summer of 2002. As reported by Fox Butterfield in *The New York Times* on July 28, 2002, within weeks, four women died at the hands of soldiers stationed at Fort Bragg, all wives of military men. Although the soldiers did not know one another, the explanation offered by their fellow military men was that these men were affected by the separation from their wives and concerns over their wives being unfaithful. However, this explanation was disputed by Deborah D. Tucker, the chairwoman of the Defense Department's Taskforce on Domestic Violence. She is quoted in Butterfield's article as saying that these marriages were troubled to begin with and had a history of violence. These husbands wanted to control their wives and regretted they might lose that control while they were deployed to Afghanistan, Tucker believes.

The first murdered military wife was Jennifer Wright, dead in June of 2002 at the age of thirty-two. Her husband, Sergeant William Wright, hit her with a baseball bat and then strangled her because she wanted a divorce. She had three young sons. The second death occurred when Delta Force Sergeant First Class Brandon Floyd and his wife, Andrea, who had three children, were found in a murder-suicide. As reported by Maureen Orth in a December 2002 *Vanity Fair* article, "Fort Bragg's Deadly Summer," on June 11, 2002 Green Beret Sergeant Rigoberto Wives came back from Afghanistan and shot his wife, Teresa, and then himself, orphaning their six-year-old daughter. On July 9, Sergeant Cedric Griffin, an Army cook, "was accused of stabbing his wife, Marilyn, more than 70 times before setting her body on fire." The last military death in Fort Bragg that summer occurred on July 23 when Joan Shannon, a military wife married to an Army major, murdered her husband, ostensibly to obtain insurance benefits.

Military culture is foreign to many of us and there seems to be a different creed by which these husbands live. Yet it is chilling to learn wives have died violent death at the hands of their husbands, men who have made a commitment to serve our country. With one exception, that of Joan Shannon, these women have been murdered because they are wives. In the twenty-first century, a time when wives are more in charge of their lives than ever before, these deaths signify a step backward, to ancient civilizations when husbands were at liberty to kill their wives for any action they interpreted as a misdemeanor.

The bright side is that there are also wives who are married to military men who are comfortable in their marriages. These women do not seem to mind moving about frequently and accept being separated from their husbands for long periods of time. The feelings that many military wives often experience are documented in a web site called Military Women.org, where a common problem seems to be hiring childcare for their children. Expenses are also an issue for these young, non-working wives. Nonetheless, there is an acceptance, for the most part, of the lifestyle dictated by their husbands' commitment to the military. The movie *The Deep End*, starring Tilda Swinton, deals with a military wife who has to confront her son's homosexuality and the death of his lover on her own. Swinton's character lives in Lake Tahoe with her three children and father-in-law, in a place where life appears simple and uneventful. After she fends off blackmail with no access to her husband or his funds, she unravels, realizing her own strength and how isolated she has been as a mother and military wife.

"I have adjusted to life as a wife of a man in the military," begins Anita, who at twenty-eight has been a military wife for six years. "We are left alone when our husbands are on active duty and my group of friends all have little children. I think that it's such a different world from being married to a civilian that you just have to hand yourself over. I married a man who had been married before but had no children. He really wanted to marry me and he was worried that I wouldn't adjust well to life on the base. At first I hated it and felt alone with my two little boys. But eventually I met other wives and that helped me.

"I do wonder if I would be working part-time if I hadn't become a military wife. Jeb doesn't want me to work and there aren't many options—it isn't expected of someone married to a military man, unless she works in the military, too. I know a few wives like that, but they mostly stick together. If my husband is on base, his hours are long, in twelve-hour shifts, and that is something else that I had to get used to. I remember how my dad was home from work by five every night when I was growing up. I know I can't compare it, but being a wife to a man in the service is harder than being married to a man who is a civilian. I talk to my friends who are married to civilians and it's much looser, much easier."

Some wives who are married to military men are in the military themselves. Twenty percent of the Armed Forces is comprised of women today, which purports a steady increase. In 1990, as reported by Questia Media America, Inc., eight percent of women served in the military in the Persian Gulf War. In these marriages, where the wives also serve, there seems to be more equality and the wives feel satisfied, if challenged, with their positions. This adds a healthy dimension to any marriage, military or otherwise. An anonymous sergeant in the Air Force married to a man who is also a sergeant in the Air Force posted "The Life of a Military Mother" on MilitaryWomen.org, expressing her satisfaction. She described her night shift duty, which occurs every two weeks, as an adjustment in terms of her children's schedules, but manageable. Her overall feeling is that she and her husband work together as a team and that while it is a disciplined life, they are content as a couple, as parents and in their positions in the Armed Forces.

Another take on a military couple is when the wife is in the military and her husband is a civilian. As described by Raleigh, a twenty-six-year-old wife who works in intelligence, the combination has its challenges.

"I am in the military and my husband is not. We are different races and have had very different childhoods. It was important to me that we have a military wedding and my husband understood. I wanted the saber bearers and the swords and the ceremony to reflect military life. Because I am a second lieutenant and work on the base, as well as travel, I feel this is a huge part of my life. My husband made a commitment to move his business to where my base is because it is the only way that it could work for me. I see that this was a huge act of faith on his part and I am very appreciative. I know that I want to remain in the military once we have children but I want to travel less than now. I am away over one hundred days of the year in my present position and that will have to change. Also, the military is very sexist and it has bothered me more since I got married than before.

"Because of my unusual job, we have had to plan out our lives ahead of time. We had to talk about where to live and how to live and whose career comes first because the military takes so much of one's life. I already anticipate a struggle once we have children and I will have to make choices based on my feelings about my husband and family. I remember how my mother always had a part-time job and put her children and her marriage first. I know that I was raised to do the same, but it isn't easy when you are the spouse in the military. Being an intelligence officer is high stress and that too will undoubtedly have to change as the marriage grows, as we grow as a couple."

The challenges that face wives who are in the military are virtually unprecedented. The sexism that women have perceived in the military has been documented as early as

1980 with the release of the comedic film, *Private Benjamin*, starring Goldie Hawn. The macho attitude of military men cannot be overlooked, despite the growing numbers of women in the Armed Forces. These women exhibit physical and emotional courage as well as the desire to be immersed in a life that is extremely structured and disciplined. From this point of view, it is a great step forward for women. However, with this opportunity women face sexism, as wives and/or as women in the military, and the timeworn tugs that apply to all wives everywhere who wish to balance their lives as wives, mothers and career women.

Self Esteem and Sexual Confidence

The attitude of wives of assorted ages by the twenty-first century is that the world is their oyster. Whether a wife is a veteran or in the middle of her career as wife or newly wed, she resists falling prey to any past pattern in marriage that was less than optimal. This positive way of thinking pertains to young wives in particular and apparently exists in other parts of the world. An October 7, 2002 forecast in *Publishers Weekly*, the trade magazine for publishers, described a new novel, *For Matrimonial Purposes*, by Kavita Daswani as "Husband Hunting, Indian Style." Daswani left India and chose an American husband over her family's objections. When Heather Mills was quoted in an article in *Vanity Fair* the same month and year, she intimated that if there is no romance, women do not need men, since women are self-sufficient in today's world. Clearly, in both cases, these women believe that being a wife is a woman's choice, not a privilege that a man offers.

If the fifties wife was a case study in emotional and sexual repression, the sixties wife all about the sexual revolution, the seventies and eighties about infiltrating the workplace while being a wife and mother, the nineties about affairs and disappointments, the twenty-first-century wife is about having survived these machinations. The seasoned wife is as responsible to herself by the twenty-first century as is her Generation Y counterpart. Notwithstanding this recent and impressive attitude of wives in America, as recently as

1999 the *Journal of the American Medical Association* found that 43 percent of wives were not satisfied sexually.

"I have never been more confident in my marriage than I am today," begins Michelle, who at fifty has raised two daughters and has returned to work full time as an occupational therapist. "The first years of my marriage I was trying so hard to be the good wife. This was in the late seventies when some women, including me, still didn't want to rock the boat. I would work in my husband's office if he needed me to, but mostly I was at home with the girls. As soon as they were in high school, I decided to go back to school part time and once the youngest was a sophomore, I began to work full time. I felt I had put my years in as a traditional wife and mother and it was my turn.

"Everything in the marriage improved once I was happy in my life. The sex was better, my sense of myself was better and I had this feeling that I'd raised the kids and done a nice job. Then I had to pay attention to being a wife, because I felt like I could just take care of myself full-time, get sex when I wanted, and it would do. I think that is what happens to women once they feel they've accomplished something. I suppose that my marriage has worked because my husband and I respect one another."

Respect is an issue for the twenty-first-century wife, who recognizes this is a necessity in marriage. John Gottman's book, *The Seven Principles for Making Marriage Work*, indicates that couples who are critical or defensive in their exchanges suffer. If the marriage is longstanding, and the disrespect has been played out over time, the damage is there. These couples might need counseling and/or a renegotiating of the marriage. It is up to both partners in a marriage to demand respect. Yet when we look at the history of how women have been treated, it is not always easy for a woman to ask for this. As Carol Tavris explains it in her book, *The Mismeasure of Woman*, women have been made to suffer "low self-esteem, passivity, depression, dependency on others, an exaggerated sense of responsibility to other people." In addition, because they suffer from these afflictions, they are unable to choose the right partners or to stop pleasing others, Tavris tells us. While this certainly has been a condition for countless women for the past five decades, it has only been addressed openly in the past twenty years. With the newly found self-esteem of Generation Y and the changed attitudes of wives of previous decades in the new century, the paradigm shifts. The respect that a wife and husband share is at the heart of the matter in many marriages and from this starting point, the marriage is one of sharing and confidence.

"For me, being a wife is about love, closeness, sex, work and family," explains Briana, who was married in 2000 at the age of thirty-eight. "I come from an unusual family. My mother has always been the breadwinner and she has held down two jobs. I was raised to view marriage as a challenge, but a worthy one. The one thing that I saw in my parents was their mutual respect. I married the man I wanted to marry, someone I had known in college and did not date until we were both back in our hometown. He is very handsome and I had to ask myself if I could live up to this, was I pretty and sexy enough? In the end I do have the confidence on every level.

"It was implicit since I was small that I would be a wife and that I would have a career as well. I was taught that I would be good at both, and so I am. I am responsible for keeping in touch with my in-laws and for making family dinners. At first I thought that wasn't fair because my husband and I both work long hours. I didn't understand that it was being put upon me because my husband hasn't the skills, and he cares about his family. I feel that he is grateful that I do this, so I feel appreciated and good about myself as his wife for doing it. I feel that I entered this marriage with my eyes wide open and with my sense of my own abilities""

Sexual confidence in marriage is tied to the confidence that wives report in the day-to-day responsibilities of being a wife. We see women in the public eye with their partners, exuding sexual confidence and a general sense of self-esteem. These women are more visible and this kind of confidence more apparent than in the past. Photographs of well known women such as Catherine Zeta Jones, Susan Sarandon, Julianne Moore, Jessica Lange, and Jennifer Aniston, all show us women who with self-assurance lead exemplary personal lives and careers. Film stars of the fifties and sixties, such as Marilyn Monroe and Liz Taylor, were reported to have struggled with their personal lives and did not exude the overall health of these stars of the twenty-first century. The good news is that ordinary women report the same sense of accomplishment as some of the major stars. The chance to feel good about every aspect of a woman's life is a new and refreshing experience for women.

A departure from this sexually confident wife of the twenty-first century is the sexually deprived wife who has recently come to the media's attention. In March of 2003, for example, *The Wall Street Journal* reporter Sue Shellenbarger noted the latest malady, called "DINS"— dual-income no-sex couples. Shellenbarger describes the problem as stemming from a woman's gain as a wage-earner, which upsets marriages because it alters the balance. She notes that research conducted by Denise Donnelly of Georgia State University found that 16 percent of couples have sex less than once a month. According to Shellenbarger, for women it is exhaustion more than work that causes them to not want sex. Interestingly, even though the couples are described as dual-income working couples, research indicates that wives who work and wives who stay at home are both exhausted by the end of the day.

"The truth is, I am too tired for sex," explains Kathleen, who has been married for seventeen years and is a full time working mother and wife. "Maybe I am a low energy person, maybe I am someone who doesn't prioritize sex, but it has seemed overrated and extraneous to me since my third wedding anniversary, which was some time ago. By then we had twins and I was already back at work. I've been tired ever since and I can't make that extra effort; I just can't make it happen. My husband, Max, and I have spoken about this, off and on, but now we don't even bother. I once told him if it was so important, he should go out and find someone. I didn't mean to have an affair, but a high-class prostitute or something. I can't come through on this, and yet I do love Max, I love my husband.

"When we go on vacation, which is not so often, but sometimes, without the kids, it is better. But it isn't what it should be and I'm aware of this. I think that sex was always less than optimal for me and that I was looking for other qualities in a marriage, such as companionship, accountability, commitment. And I got those. Still, I sometimes wonder if I hadn't been so busy at work if the sex would have been more important to me. Now I'm older, so who can judge? It's almost like that part of my life, the sexy young married role, slipped away. The working mother part took over."

In February of 2003, *Reader's Digest* ran an article, "Your Marriage: Getting Better All the Time," by Joan Declaire, along with an accompanying survey of 1,000 couples. The couples were divided by ages and labeled accordingly. Couples between the ages of thirty-one and forty-three were placed in "The Partnership Phase," where women found that their husbands were unemotional and the couple was too busy taking care of the children to focus on the marriage. At this juncture, the couple was in jeopardy of becoming distant from one another, and sex had to be emphasized in order for it not to become lost in the shuffle.

In what was labeled "The Affirmation Phase," for couples who were forty-four to fifty-six, wives genuinely enjoy sex and appreciate that the children are older and more independent. Declaire suggests that at this age women might also desire sex as an affirmation that they are sexually desirable. In marriages where the women were between the ages of fifty-seven and sixty-five, "The Crossover Stage," men seemed to genuinely appreciate their wives and sex becomes very important to the marriage, but, Declaire tells us, as husbands retire, wives become more interested in a world beyond wifing and mothering; at last they are free. Unfortunately this is at a time when the husband is looking for more closeness and time spent together.

After the age of sixty-six, "The So In-Love" phase, where "years of knowing and loving each other yield a comfort level and compatibility that trump even the newlywed glow." While sex may diminish, there are ways to be physically close at this stage. This positive view of sex in marriage feels modern and revolutionary in its findings and approach. The honesty of these couples shows us not only the value of sex in marriage but also how fragile it is in comparison to the machinations of daily life.

"My marriage began as a lusty, sexy event over fifty years ago," recalls Judy, who is seventy today. "We have been through so many stages together and, without question, the sex was more important as the years went on. It was not until recently that my husband, Bert, and I stopped sex and traded it in for lots of holding and companionship. I have always considered my husband very attractive and sexy. He has aged well but so did I. I do remember worrying about sex right after menopause. I was no longer so sexual, and I doubted that I was as sexy. I pushed for sex in those years because I was afraid that since we were the same age, my husband would want sex for longer than I did. I never told him my fear, or my worst fear, was that he would find a younger woman more attractive. I just made a special effort to please him and to feel good about myself.

"Our marriage has lasted long past that, and I now see that sex moves in waves in a marriage. But when I look at my husband today, I see a man who is virile and young, and I see myself as his young wife. To the outside world we are a pair of grey-haired older spouses, but not to me, not for the years we have shared. I am more confident of myself in this marriage today than ever before. I think I finally understand both my needs and Bert's needs. That is why I feel so good. Plus women today are allowed to demand things, make decisions. I like that."

In contrast to Judy's experience with sex in marriage over five decades is that of Antonia's, a young wife of two years, who just gave birth to a daughter five months ago.

"Sex was so important at the beginning of my marriage and toned down once I found out I was pregnant. I did not feel lumpy and unattractive during my pregnancy like I remember my mother felt with my little brother, years ago. I felt good about how I looked, I felt sexy but in a sort of 'next-stage part of my marriage' way. I never doubted that I would be sexy again or that the marriage would resume its course once Clara was born. But it isn't quite the same and she wakes up a lot in the middle of the night. I still care so much about sex with Keith, my husband. Even though I am preoccupied with having a baby and with adjusting to all of it, moving into a house and being on leave from work, I have those feelings for him. I never want that to change and I am convinced I can keep it going.

"My fantasy is that Keith will always want me as his beautiful wife and I will always be able to have that hold on him. I imagine it can be this way, but I admit, having a baby threw me for a loop. I see the world as not just about sex and being in love, but about that plus raising a family and being there for the rest of it. I understand now that sex is deeper than attraction. I only hope that at forty or forty-five, we'll desire each other and life won't wipe away these good feelings."

Sex remains at the top of the list for couples, Lynn Schnurnberger wrote in her article "Our Weekend at Sex Camp" in *More* magazine in April 2003. Apparently there are sex workshops across the country for couples who suffer from a lack of interest in sex with their partners, sexual problems, and missing their grown children. Schnurnberger found that married couples in their forties and fifties attend these seminars, as a method of improving their sex life.

"My husband guaranteed great sex when we were married in 2000," begins Margo, who is forty and works as a nurse practitioner. "But things have waned since then. My problem is that sex has to be a part of the deal. And I am very attached to Hal sexually. It is important to me that we don't lose this part of our relationship. I am certain that his response to this would be that sex is always better and more exciting at the beginning of a relationship. But I don't feel this way, I am still quite desirous of sex with him."

When Kim Cattrall, who plays Samantha on *Sex and the City*, and her husband, Mark Levinson, decided to write a book on sexual satisfaction, *The Art of the Female Orgasm*, published in January of 2002, it was not meant to reflect the character Samantha's attitude about sex. The publication was to represent the point of view of Cattrall and Levinson. Nevertheless, *The New York Times* Sunday Styles section ran an article on January 27, 2002, "Good Sex Tips from Samantha." Described by Cattrall as a solid guidebook, the philosophy behind the project is that one has to be fortunate enough to find the right partner and to make sex a priority. According to Dr. Jennifer Berman, who with her sister, Dr. Laura Berman, has written the guide *For Women Only: A Revolutionary Guide to Reclaiming Your Sex Life*, more women than men are unhappy in their sex lives. This is not surprising news, since women, including wives, have not been encouraged historically to enjoy sex or to seek it out. My pool of interviewees advocate sex in their marriages and a desire to make it effective, if necessary.

The new millennium raised familiar, if thus far unaddressed, issues for wives and brought a raised consciousness and strong sense of self to the table. The past decades offered enough evidence of progress and obstacles for the twenty-first-century wife to feel justified in her actions. As a result, husbands became more accepting of their wives' attitudes and opinions with the knowledge that they no longer rule. The exception is the military wife, who has a separate experience from other twenty-first-century wives, and is enmeshed in a society dictated by military standards.

The search for the right husband continued, this time with the certainty that marriage would not infringe on women's potential. Rather, these women believe that they are justified in their quest for a sexual, emotional and financial equation that pleases them in their role as wife. Young wives today are in search of true love and partnership.

Chapter Eight:
The Twenty-First-Century Wife:
Enlightened At Last

I have looked closely at my mother and grandmother and I've come to the conclusion that I would do it differently as a wife," begins May, who at thirty-two is just married. "I see that my grandmother always catered to my grandfather and that my mother half-catered to my father, half-catered to us, with the rest of her energy worked at her part-time job as best she could. I was raised to be a wife, and it is something that I always wanted. I knew I'd be married one day and my mother was a good model for that, for becoming a wife and holding onto it.

"My husband, Darren, is definitely the right one for me, and there have been no compromises in any way to become his wife. I have an older sister who got married in the nineties and she hasn't been as sure of herself as I am. She married because we were raised to be wives, and we were supposed to do it sooner than later. The only reason that my mother sort of let me off the hook on being a young bride is because she knew that my older sister was feeling trapped and down about being a wife and mother. I waited and ended up pleasing my mother because Darren is the same religion and we are both first-generation Americans. We are the same age and grew up in the same town. This really works for us. Neither of us was in a hurry to be married. For me, one of the most important parts of our marriage is that we treat each other as equals. I didn't want to role-play the subservient wife, and I wanted an equal voice in terms of my career, my interests. I made this point clear from the beginning. I wasn't going to compromise on that."

Generation X wives, in the last decade of the twentieth century, were boastful when it came to their husbands as supportive and willing to share the responsibilities of home and children. But eventually, these wives discovered that their husbands fell short and attempted as best they could to compensate for their husbands' deficiencies. In response, the twenty-first-century wife has no such intention, preferring to create her own reality. If husbands have not stood up to the plate, despite the elaborate efforts and acrobatic moves of their wives, they will now. These women command such behaviour, both young new wives who are just starting out and wives who have been at it for long enough to see the beguiling aspects of marriage. The ambition of being a wife is not reduced but replenished with a new twist. In addition, young wives today are in search of achieving husbands, regardless of their own talents, and view this deliberation as a means of having options. More seasoned wives recognize this new pattern and mindfulness of the younger wife and support it.

By the twenty-first century, being a wife has become a more popular objective than ever before. The role of wife is not only meaningful, it is coveted. Diverse media outlets have run pieces on a variety of takes on the role of wife and the latest trends in marriage. Whereas the magazine articles and television shows of the fifties and sixties were based on a specific image of marriage and it was expected for women to be wives, the media today presents marriage and wifing as something to maneuver, something to win at. Wifing today is an achievement, along with a career, children, travel—a separate and significant venture in a woman's life. This final chapter concentrates on the cusp of the new century, where trends are reflected through the news. The media informs the public about marriage in this decade as it has never done before, partly because the media's power is great today, partly because marriage is a motivation for so many women.

In a March 2003 article in *Marie Claire* by Samantha Altea, "How Long Should You Wait to Get Married," she interviews six couples on the time between meeting and marriage. One couple out of six, Soo and Nick, decided not to get married, believing that marriage bred complacency. This couple preferred the freshness of their monogamous relationship that they feared would be lost in a prescribed marriage. Another twenty-first-century movement is that of celibacy in marriage, which means marriage without sex or a kind of second virginity. In a *New York Times* article on August 4, 2002, "It's Never Too Late to Be a Virgin," Elizabeth Hyatt interviewed couples who had decided to abstain from sex close to their wedding day. According to a new bride who subscribed to this theory, Hyatt writes that it will "ensure that the sparks fly during her honeymoon."

Apparently some women on the verge of marriage feel guilty about not being virgins on their wedding night, even though our society is one in which cohabitation is quite common and often precedes marriage. The "born-again virgin" is partly in reaction to failed marriages, and a way of pulling back in order to start fresh, should the opportunity present itself. Yet another article on marriage, which ran on February 6, 2003 in *The Wall Street Journal*, "Ready to Pop the Question? Hold Off Until You've Done the Interrogation," warns couples of full disclosure. In anticipation of Valentine's Day, Jeffrey Zaslow, in this article, suggested that couples beware before committing to marriage in the twenty-first century. The "crucial questions" to ask these days include ones such as: will your spouse keep in touch with former lovers?; will one's mother's advice be more important than a husband's?; who uses the newer car if there are two cars in the marriage? All these questions are asked in order to avoid divorce.

Zaslow reports that in 1988 of two hundred brides polled by Diamond Cutters International, 46 percent said they would consider exchanging their engagement ring for a "bigger, better diamond." In 2003, 81 percent of those women who were willing to trade up their diamonds are no longer married, indicating that there is a correlation between wanting to upgrade one's diamond ring, one's home, one's car, and ultimately one's husband. It is this latest version of the new wife who sticks to her marriage, not the one who begins again with a new ring and new man, which so fascinates us in the new millennium. In the early years of the new century, the new wife gathers wisdom by observing the misfortunes of her predecessors in order to march toward contentment in her role as wife.

Achieving Wives

Recognition of a woman's achievement has always been a complicated matter for our society. An achieving wife can cause a stir, amassing respect and speculation at once. Our society has looked closely at these couples because the baby boomer wife who has achieved wears a badge of both suffering and heroism. While there are those daughters/young wives who resist taking advantage of their mothers' inroads, ambition is not alien to young wives in America. Ironically, this ambition and sense of achievement may manifest in having the right husband, among other successes reminiscent of the fifties and early sixties wives.

An article in *Marie Claire* magazine in the March 2003 issue focuses on how women today are not looking for love in their marriages but for men with money. "Wanted: $mart $ingle $uccessful Men," by Melissa de la Cruz, offers the hard facts on why some women today believe that "love is highly overrated." The premise of the article states that single women between the ages of twenty-five and thirty-four will only accept a very successful husband for several reasons. According to the handful of women with whom de la Cruz spoke, the desire to not be equal to a man in every way so that he can be the successful one, even though she has an impressive career, is one path to take. One woman uses a written test on her potential mates to weed out the riffraff. Another wants a man as successful and loving as her father; yet another is in search of a man who is "wealthy, successful and confident," and appreciates the challenge of appealing to this kind of man, and beating the competition.

In a sense, these young single wives-to-be are both reminiscent of the fifties when women deliberately chose a provider, while at the same time more confident than any of their predecessors in their audacious claim to want a man with money. These women are convinced of which man is not the right husband for them, which catapults them into a category of knowing their own needs. Their independence in the workplace strengthens their convictions, but does not influence their decision to find a wealthy husband.

A role model for young wives today does not exist, and the definition of a twenty-first-century wife is unlike past wives because her voice is so audible and her requirements so specific. This applies not only to young first-time wives but also to divorcees who are ready to marry again and have become aware of their mistakes from the first time around. There is not much left of the good girl, the complacent female, in this group of women. And while coupling might continue to be riveting for women of every age in any stage of their lives, the twenty-first-century wife offers the option of being in a marriage where the wife is calling the shots and not pretending anything. Not only do young wives adhere to this, but wives of decades past adopt it as their motto in the twenty-first century.

"I married late, at thirty-nine, and one of my prerequisites was that my husband have a successful career," begins Leslie, who became a twenty-first-century wife in 2001. "I had been at it in the workplace for so long that there was no way I wanted to keep it up. I decided upon a man who had a son because I thought that his track record was good. He'd given his ex-wife the condo and their boat and that meant he had money. I wasn't going to put up with a struggling artist for a husband; I would have preferred not to be married. The amount of money I had made as an executive did not enter into it, and my money is kept separate. I did this on purpose because I didn't want to provide for him, I want to achieve in the workplace and be married to someone who pays. I know it sounds very calculating but when you've been in the work world a while and you've been single a while, you see how things go. Plus I watched my friends who married early divorce or lose interest in their husbands because there wasn't enough money coming in. If I waited so long, why would I do it to end up like that? My husband likes that I have a career; it makes him think he is important. He likes us to be a couple where we both work in a real business. I like that, too, but

I was achieving in my career before I met him , so he really has nothing to do with my success."

Achieving couples have existed since the modern wife left her home and hearth in the seventies and began her journey into the world. Each decade since has brought more achieving wives and women. Achieving wives over time who have caught the eye of the media include Joanne Woodward, married to Paul Newman, Hillary Rodham Clinton, wife of former President Bill Clinton, Jennifer Aniston, married to Brad Pitt, and Madonna, married to Guy Ritchie, Elizabeth Dole, married to Bob Dole, Teresa Heinz, wife of Senator Robert Kerry, Jill Clayburgh, wife of David Rabe, Lynne Cheney, wife of Vice President Richard Cheney, and Michelle Pfeifer, married to David Kelley. This is not to say that the stereotyping of wives and husbands has disappeared altogether. In our culture, we continue to make note of those wives who are in the spotlight, as more step forward and set a new standard.

Michael S. Kimmel reminds us in *The Gendered Society* that a gendered marriage has not by any means disappeared. In this kind of marriage, the woman "traps" a man, and her female friends laud her for it. Meanwhile, the man is giving up his autonomy and he "mourns", according to Kimmel, at his traditional bachelor party. Considered the "last night of freedom," men become inebriated and have "lap dancers or prostitutes" to document this rite of passage into the role of husband. Notwithstanding these customs, both males and females are consenting adults in the choice of marriage. This custom of bachelor parties, much like that of a bridal shower, only shows us how the division of the sexes has dictated the roles of wives and husbands, and continues to do so today.

The downside of marriage for an achieving wife can be loneliness. This loneliness affects couples who are deeply rooted in their achievements, since the marriage almost becomes a relationship based on parallel play. There is no arguing because both wife and husband are too preoccupied with their work. There is a mutuality, based on their commitment to work, travel for work, a crash and burn syndrome after an intense week of work, and an ongoing recognition of each other's ambitions. With all of this, the marriage, in its essence, has not been nurtured but assumed to be status quo, when in fact, it is running on empty. In Allison Pearson's 2002 novel, *I Don't Know How She Does It: The Life of Kate Reddy, Working Mother*, it becomes painfully obvious that once the achieving wife has children, she is torn between children and work, and the marriage is placed on the back burner. While we know this syndrome had surfaced by the end of the seventies, and was quite troubling to the eighties wife, the fact that it has not been resolved, and makes for the stuff of novels today, is concerning. The reality is that this issue remains a conflict in a woman's life. If anything, the issue is periodically readdressed, as it applies to women of various economic brackets in a number of different kinds of jobs. The dilemma for working wives/mothers is acknowledged now, more than ever before, but persists without any real solution.

For Marguerita, who at fifty has been driving a taxi in a small town for the past ten years, her twenty-eight-year-old marriage is about her commitment to work and her husband's lack thereof. Only in the past three years has she re-evaluated her marriage and her own aspirations.

"Our culture believes that you have to be married, and it doesn't matter if the man is selfish; he's allowed to be selfish. I was taught that this is what you get. So my husband is like all the others, he's fifty percent a good husband and fifty percent lousy. The men are raised to be pampered and spoiled. He wants a submissive wife and he wants me to stay home and wash dishes. But he doesn't work hard enough to do that and I want things for myself and for our children. I drive the cab because it helps out and I know it is my nature to be independent. He would like me to be a subservient and poor wife. I won't do that.

"As things turned bad with money, I stopped wondering if I loved my husband. If I did, I don't any more. My sisters come to me and tell me to tone it down. Two of them still live in South America and they are traditional wives. We raised all our kids the same way, but then I saw that my kids needed more. Money was not falling from the sky and I had to make something on my own. I stay in this marriage because of our religion and because of the children, but I work for myself, for my feeling that I do something good and that helps people and that I make money. If I hadn't begun to work ten years ago, if I'd stayed like my sisters, I'd be miserable. Instead I made a life for myself and that has helped. Only in the past few years have I felt like it is one hundred percent that I'm doing the right thing. In the beginning I was scrounging for a baby sitter for my youngest and had to make my own hours. That is one reason I chose driving a cab."

If the achieving wife has been at it for thirty years, the twenty-first-century wife who seeks flex-time jobs that still have benefits and quality childcare has slowly but not satisfactorily evolved. The conundrum for women is that part-time work rarely offers medical benefits, nor does it always make it worth the working mother's efforts in terms of compensation. As Karen Kornbluth writes in her *Atlantic Monthly* January/February 2003 article, "The Parent Trap," the only way that part-time work could have real value that would help working mothers would be if there was a fresh view, if the government would provide grants that were determined on the person's financial status, not whether she worked a full-time, part-time or flex-time job.

Another issue for achieving wives was how their husbands perceived their wives' success and how this affected the marriage. Not all husbands were prepared by the twenty-first century for wives who earned more than they did and who had more prestige in the workplace, despite the decades that had built up to this occurrence. However, the fact is, these wives were on the rise and their accomplishments could not be denied, no matter how the husband dealt with it. For wives who out-earn their husbands there can be tension in the marriage, and if the husbands are convention bound, they might feel threatened. Others are unscathed by this gender bender, while some husbands are ambivalent. An article in *The New York Times* published on February 3, 2002, "His Thoughts About Her Earning Their Keep," by Ellyn Spragins addresses this issue. Spragins quotes an anonymous working wife who found it bothersome that her husband did not have the same kind of ambition as she. Other couples are more pragmatic and pleased with the outcome, whether it is the wife or the husband who produces the healthier income.

Glenda's experience is indicative of the baby boomer wife and her husband who may feel more threatened by an achieving wife than does a Generation X husband. Glenda has been in the position of being the major breadwinner and simultaneously lived with a traditional husband's view of her success.

"I've been disappointed but I've hung in," begins Glenda, forty-four, who until recently was an executive who earned four times what her husband earns as a consultant. "When it gets to the point when I openly resent his lack of money making and the rollercoaster he subjects me to, he tries harder. Before finances became trying for us, Andy made his work seem more important than the marriage. He both wanted me to do well and resented me for it in this sexist way. I have learned to stay in an imperfect relationship. Money was always the issue and I have put up with it because I have always been successful. I was the one with a terrific job and money was coming in because of me.

"When our daughter was born ten years ago, I wanted to stay home from work or go back to nursing, which was my first career, so that I could be with her more. That was when Andy really had a fit. He knows he has to take better care of me in this relationship and still he pushed me. That lasted about three years, and then I quit my big job because I got tired of holding him up and tired of leaving my daughter when my husband could have done better. So we'll never live in a great house, we'll live in this split level forever. I refuse to be the only one bringing in money.

"I stopped listening to Andy and I went back to nursing and I took a big pay cut. I decided to raise our daughter, not be at meetings morning, noon and night, and to follow my own interests, just like Andy has done. I do not make him the center anymore. Sometimes I ask myself, if Andy had made more money, would I love him more? I don't know about love, but I'd resent him less. I didn't know myself until we had a baby and then I learned who I really am. My job didn't mean that much to me, as an executive in a large company. It was Andy who pushed me, who wanted the money and the lifestyle it provided. I had to work hard to get back what I needed. I married a strong personality and then I became my own strong personality. This feels right. I know what I can do in the workplace and I know what I choose to do in the workplace."

Another aspect of the achieving twenty-first-century wife is how honest she is about being on overload. While this speaks to the fact, as in the seventies and eighties, there are no remedies for the overworked wife/mother. Instead, these wives are willing to bare their souls. The cover-up is over, the reality disclosed. The raised consciousness of the sixties wife, funneled by Betty Friedan, experienced a lull in the seventies with the progress of working women. The pretense, as we know, was in full swing. If feminist treatises and essays, works published in college texts, were available to women in the eighties, this decade of wives chose to ignore the problem and sustain the effort to keep it going. The nineties wife considered few resources, rather she looked to peer marriages as a kind of dreamy solution. Now, in the twenty-first century, the women's magazines have made room for women to express their feelings. What ran in both *Glamour* magazine in September 2002 as an excerpt and was published as *The Bitch in the House*, offers us a view of Kristin Van Ogtrop's "Angel at Work, Devil at Home" experience as a working wife and mother of two young sons. Van Ogtrop is the executive editor of *Glamour* where she is never moody and never ruffled. She honestly describes herself as "a better mom at work than I am at home." In addition, her manner, which is so effective at work, has caused her sons to talk back to her, and her husband to remind her that he is not a person who needs supervision. She writes of her accomplishments and satisfaction at work combined with her concern that her children will be harmed by her dedication to her profession.

Younger marriages, including those of women under thirty, do not address the gender divide, but respect the achievement of a wife in tandem with the achievement of a husband. The Generation X wife, in her early thirties today, is often in a healthy marriage where the partners are supportive of one another in terms of their achievements and where roles are not dictated by gender. The wife feels she is well suited to her husband and her ambition has been laid out early on in the game. Perhaps this couple even attended college and/or graduate school together and has been aware of each other's plans for years. As Dr. Michele Kasson sees it, the couples are compatible and comfortable enough with each other, and sexism does not come into play in the marriage. "These couples are well matched," remarks Dr. Kasson. "Whether this includes their income levels or not, their intelligence and world view are similar enough and the husbands are not threatened by their wives who can achieve."

"Tony and I work at the same facility, which is an old-age home," begins Trina, who became a wife in 2003 at the age of twenty-nine. "We met at work and I had the better job and made more money. We laughed about it in the beginning, but it will not change and we know it, at least if we stay where we are. I also have more schooling than Tony has had, but he can definitely get a business degree at night, if he decides to. This is completely up to him. My mother keeps asking me why I don't push him to get that MBA. It's not my choice; it is up to him. I don't feel like he is less because I have my degree or my job; it all seems perfectly natural to me. I believe that Tony and I are equals and that we are both capable people. If he gets ahead of me, that is okay and if I get ahead of him, that will work, too. Or if we are side by side, it's yet another option. I do not ever intend to be a stay-at-home wife and that has been clear since we started dating. As long as it is all understood and no one feels hurt or deceived, my success should be welcome in this marriage, just like his should be."

With the working woman's dilemma still in full kilter, it is clear that a dependency on private childcare remains an issue in the twenty-first century. The working wife/mother may be at her very best at the workplace, but nothing causes a meltdown as quickly as a crisis in childcare. If achieving women assume that because their working lives are in order the rest of their lives will fall into place, their lives have not evolved to this degree, and the uphill battle persists. In theory, homes ought to be run as tight ships and husbands ought to be trained to do the right thing, but it isn't always the case. The magnitude of the issue of childcare and working wives was visited in an article in *The New York Times* on March 10, 2002, entitled " A Death In the Family," by Lynn Berger. Berger describes a "breakup with the nanny" as a "trial of city life," filled with repercussions for mother and children alike.

My sense, based on my interviewees, is that this is not an issue only for working women in cities, but for those who live in suburbs and small towns as well. The interesting point is that the achieving wife remains so determined. Despite the obstacles, she continues her dance of perfection with the desire for a life rich in choices. This most modern of wives will look at her predecessors with a kind of healthy narcissism that buoys her up to tackle the next task. Her progress is most apparent, even to herself, and she is reluctant to compare herself to working wives of previous decades. By the twenty-first century, the achieving wife feels equipped and confident to come out the winner.

New and Old Traditions

One cannot discount the amount of energy and consistency that is required in a marriage. While compromises are specific to each marriage, we are aware of the general issues for couples—tugs of time for one's partner, the challenges and values of raising children, the ups and downs for the wife and/or husband in the work force. One necessary ingredient that was lacking in unsatisfactory marriages of the recent past, according to the wife, was communication and support. This requirement is as meaningful for the twenty-first-century wife as it has been for a wife of any previous decade. How the wife today deals with these issues is what sets her apart.

Over the past fifty years, wives seem to have made the repeated mistake of expecting their husbands to take the lead once the marriage is established when it comes to romance and sex. Since the relationship suffices as a support system even when it operates at a less than ideal level, husbands often take their wives for granted over time. Many husbands suffer from the misconception that the sustenance they offer their wives in the early days continues to flow without any replenishment. This recurring problem upset the eighties wife, in particular. She became disillusioned as romance evaporated, and lacked the skills or modelling to know how to recapture the early feelings in the midst of her frenzied life as working wife/mother.

It was not until the nineties that wives were willing to show their hurt, face their unhappiness and let go of the posturing. While this did not improve the condition or men's typical reaction to marriage, at least the wives could come clean with their emotions. As Claire Owen, psychologist, tells us, "Men will do whatever it takes to get the woman there, but once they get the wife, they abdicate responsibility. This is not conscious behavior but a typical male response. The implicit message of the husband to his wife is, 'Of course I love you—I'm here, aren't I?' Meanwhile, if a wife wants sex and romance, as the majority of wives do, she will have to make it happen; the energy will be generated by her."

"I thought it would be different, I thought it would be better," begins Nancy, who at fifty has been married twice. "My mother was widowed and remarried and I watched her please my stepfather. I had the chance to really see her as a wife, not married to my father, but just as someone's wife. She always tried to please him, but she also had her own money and her own life, and she worked. What I learned from her is how to demand what you want instead of trying so hard. Her message to me was to have something that was all mine and that a husband is an asset, too. Being a wife is a goal. It has to be in place and it is part of how women should live their lives. You try to get it right, but you also have to face how lousy it can be.

"I am of a different generation, but how I act with my husband has to do with how my mother played out her role as wife with my stepfather. Even if she preferred me and my sisters, she acted like her husband was number one. That was because she had to have a husband in those days. The common thought was that while widowhood was embarrassing, remarriage equalled being a wife with a family and was a healthy thing to do. No one faced the tugs, the problems, how hard marriage can be, either the first time around or the second time. There is no question that what I saw in my mother's charade taught me to care less about being a wife, to try less than she did. Other times, I admit that I thought I'd be happier than I am. I tell my husband, Peter, all the time that it's supposed to be better, more romantic, more caring."

Unlike Nancy's experience, Valerie has evolved in her twenty-five year marriage with a defined sense of what improvements were necessary.

"When I got married, I couldn't wait to share everything," sighs Valerie. "That's how naïve I was. I saw fairly quickly that everything changes and that I was not as carefree as I wanted to be. We had children fairly soon and then someone had to be the adult, and it wasn't going to be Danny, my husband. I found it hard to be a wife when I was so busy being a mother to two young children. I found Danny had become very self-centered, and I tried to remember how my mother had handled her seven children, but it wasn't even a comparison. My husband did not understand that I was still working and that we had these little children. I was no longer his full-time wife and somehow he couldn't grasp that. I began to lose faith in the idea of women's equality because I knew there was no equality in my home. If I'd ever imagined that Danny was going to be a modern husband, I was fooling myself. He traveled during the week for work and came home on weekends. During the week I arranged for sitters because I worked a night shift and often found myself walking out the door as he was coming in from a week away. We had no time for the marriage, and those years were really tough.

"The reason that I stayed and worked to change this marriage is because I felt serious enough about it. I had these young kids, four of them, and I learned that I was at fault, too. I had to learn how to be a wife again. My husband felt so neglected and I could barely function as a wife and a mother. I thought of the role of the traditional wife and what I had to do to get back there. But times were changing and I didn't want to be 'just a wife.' Those were the worst years of my life, and I think that it would have been easier to have divorced and to have started again. My husband told me I was a bad wife. I'd run out of tricks, I couldn't remember what I'd been shown by my mother, by other women. I couldn't do it all. Then it was a miracle, and my children finally began to grow up and be less dependent on me. From rock bottom I climbed back up, as if from a dark pit. I see all the phases of our marriage and I know the closeness we once had. I have made the decision to stay and to rebuild. I like being Danny's wife and I have always loved him, even in the worst times. So I've readjusted my skills and tried to let the disappointment and anger—

directed at Danny—that ruled my life all those years, go. I am working on becoming a new wife."

When a wife of long standing is in the situation Valerie describes, there are many layers to her discontent. There is also her investment she has in the relationship, which has its own merits. As Helene Drusine writes in her essay "Just A Housewife," the "new man" of the twenty-first century is not merely helping his wife with the home and children, but "sharing" these responsibilities. This, of course, is the goal, and something that we see younger wives able to implement in their marriages. Nonetheless, the value of stay-at-home mothering and society's persistently negative view of mothering as a lesser profession than others has not dissipated, according to Drusine. My research indicates that wives do continue to battle these issues, but less so today than ever before, with the latest breed of wife feeling that she is well aware of what can go wrong and how to avoid it.

There are young wives and wives-to-be for whom the concept of ambition is quite arbitrary. This latest brand of wife views a traditional wife's role with the same amount of cynicism as she does a working wife's role. That is to say, either can be had; the option belongs to the woman herself. These women believe in equality and have a keen sense of privilege in their role as wife.

For Caddie, who became a wife in 2003 at the age of twenty-nine, there are few hindrances and many challenges.

"My husband, Raoul, is full Puerto Rican and I am American, of French and English descent," begins Caddie. "We met at work, where Raoul is a supervisor and I work at desktop publishing. It isn't that he makes so much more than I do but he has more responsibilities and works harder. Already we have planned our future and he understands that I only want to work part-time once we have children. I am discouraged by the baby boomers who are mothers and wives because I was a nanny for several years, to three different families, and I watched these women closely. In one family, the wife worked full-time and she never saw her child except on weekends. She was definitely missing out. The part-time working mother had the best deal because she didn't feel isolated like the non-working mother and she had one foot in the work world. The one who was a stay-at-home mother and wife seemed trapped to me; she was isolated. Even if her husband could afford help, she was powerless because she did not make her own money.

"I remember how my mother stayed at home for us, and she always seemed trapped. This taught me what I had to do for myself. So even if my husband comes from a culture where the women do the domestic work and often they are at home while the man is out at work, he understands my plans. Not that he can cook or clean but he is trying because he respects my need to have a partner who views me as an equal. I will go back to school in a year to become a lawyer and Raoul will stay at home and write novels, eventually, and watch our kids. This works for both of us and we support each other's dreams. I have no illusions about how difficult it will be once we have children or about what children do to a marriage. But we are madly in love and my being a wife today is not like it used to be. I have dated a lot and I have looked around carefully. I am sure that I have made the right decision in this marriage."

Caddie's great optimism is refreshing and promising for the future. That is not to say that women are so facile about becoming a wife that they all wake up in Caddie's shoes. The rate of divorce has doubled since 1965 in the United States as reported by the 1998 U.S. Census. This Census also reports that 4.3 divorces occurred per 1000 people and of the divorced population, 75 percent remarries. The median age for remarriage after divorce is 34.2 years for women and 37.4 years for men, according to the 1990 Centers for Disease Control and Prevention.

While divorce and remarriage are common, the idea of everlasting love is one that dies hard in our society. If it was not so arduous a task, film and books would not continue to focus on the topic to the extent that they do. The 2003 major film release *How to Lose a Guy in 10 Days*, starring Kate Hudson and Matthew McConaughey, provides comic relief regarding the unrelenting fate of the single urban woman in search of a suitable mate. The humor is all about the game of getting the man, with the ultimate message being that true love wins the day. For those women of all ages whose luck fails them and who are not living the outcome of Kate Hudson's character, there are other options these days. For example, *The Wall Street Journal* ran a piece in February of 2003 by Lauren Lipton entitled "Note to Self: Be My Valentine." Lipton cited a single woman who purchased a "Valentine's Day Packet" at an inn that she would enjoy solo.

The concept of buying into a single life was queried when Barbara Dafoe Whitehead's book, *Why There Are No Good Men Left*, hit the stands at approximately the same time. Whitehead's cautionary tale focuses on how ill-equipped women are to find a suitable mate in today's world. She believes that dating is no longer popular during college and that a courtship is missing as part of the process, thus putting women at a disadvantage. The worst decision a woman can make, accordingly, is to live with a partner, which places the man in a better position than the woman when it comes to commitment. The man who leaves a relationship in our patriarchal society is not in as direof straits as the woman he leaves. She worries about how she will meet the next man and how fast her biological clock is ticking.

To complicate a woman's perception further, there is the glossy, glamorized version of motherhood that emanates from the pages of fashion magazines. The message here is both cheerful and superficial, as a magnificent model postures as wife and mother, holding a baby much as she might hold a bag. She smiles at her ersatz husband, a handsome model, and their appearance together signifies wifedom and motherhood being as easy as pie. We are led to believe that wives today are fashionistas throughout, beautiful, brilliant, and deserving, and that marriage is facile. The good news is that for every woman in everyday life, there are varying degrees of successful wifing.

Tanzea, who was married in 1977, has evolved with each decade.

"If I had been more aware of what it entails to be a wife, I would have done it better at the beginning," remarks Tanzea, who at forty-four believes she has figured it out. "I wanted loyalty and to feel protected. I didn't understand that it wasn't my fault I couldn't get these things. I kept waiting for it to get better, and then we had a child. That was when I learned that children can actually harm a marriage. I was still working in the eighties and I took our daughter to daycare. I was doing it just like I was supposed to. In the nineties I saw what was lacking in my marriage and I had an affair. A few of my friends were doing the same thing because they had the same frustrations in their marriages. But it was no real solution. Finally, I worked on communicating my needs to my husband. I didn't want us to become strangers. Once I'd made this effort, I was much happier and I stopped feeling like such a martyr.

"By the time the new century rolled around, I saw that I had succeeded as a wife. Our daughter was in high school and I began to see my worth—as a mother, a wife, a working woman. Today I feel that I have my whole life ahead of me and that I have accomplished so much already."

The hopeful tale of the veteran wife with her altered views and behaviors over the decades is as filled with self-possession as is the sentiment of the young wife of the twenty-first century. The evolution of the earlier wives is one of an awakening, which creates independence. These wives pursued their personal interests as individuals, and developed a strong sense of self. The decades of change have brought a blend of tradition and progress to their role. The new wife of any of the past five decades has the opportunity today to adapt her life, as does a young wife who begins her journey now.

Enlightenment

Despite the advancement of the twenty-first-century wife, one cannot dismiss the bitterness that can creep into unhappy marriages, and the failed expectations of those wives who feel they have compromised for too long. Today, this kind of anger on the part of the wife is more visceral than in the past, since the wife presently views her sacrifices as greater than those of past decades. That is, a husband who fails in the marriage is held to a higher scrutiny today than ever before.

The emotional/physical component of marriage is explored in a *New York Times* article that ran in October of 2002, "Good and Bad Marriage, Boon and Bane to Health," by Sharon Lerner. It supports a theory we are familiar with—that marriage is more healthful for men than women.

However, Lerner also reports that for both wife and husband, when the marriage works properly, it provides a balm against loneliness and stress associated with illnesses. It is when a marriage is unhappy for the wife that her health is threatened and she is prone to depression and illness. Lerner reports that a 1998 study found that unhappily married women had higher blood pressure "just from thinking about fights they had had with their husbands." A fifteen-year study conducted in Oregon shows that "unequal decision making power in marriage" caused a greater risk of death for women than for men. The most disturbing news in Lerner's article is that "studies consistently show that the physiological effects of marital stress are stronger and last longer in women." The opposite approach to marriage can be found in Linda Waite's book *The Case For Marriage*, in which the author extols the benefits of marriage for women of any age, and tells us that, if a woman is married, the percentages for living longer are increased.

"Unless I was able to change the tempo of my marriage, I would have died," begins Adrienne, who at thirty-nine has reinvented herself as a wife. "I married a man I thought I knew well when, in fact, I did not. We both had worked such long hours in our jobs before we married that weekends were just a time to catch up on sleep and have sex. Then we were married and I hated how Stu acted about money, about friends and our social life. Suddenly, we were incompatible and I couldn't believe what a mistake I had made. I didn't want to be a homemaker or a nurturing wife; I wanted to be his partner in life and to share the day to day. I wanted space; he wanted control. I began to get sick: hives, headaches, and respiratory infections. I'd never been like this. Whatever model Stu had in his mind of how a wife should be was lost on me.

"In the end, after five years of marriage, we went into therapy. Stu was hesitant, but I insisted. We discussed where conventional roles would work and where they would not for me. I told him how sick I was getting. Stu said he was willing to try to be more flexible, and he saw it was the only way I would stay. The last year he and I have made a life together. I've given up on my expectations of romance like in the movies, and my focus is more on balance in the relationship and what I need to feel like a wife, a wife in the new century."

Being a wife is being part of a deal, a partnership. In a deal each party is expected to keep her or his part of the bargain, a sort of no-nonsense, sharp-edges-only approach. Yet we have witnessed how life's changes can alter one's initial intent. Every experience that a wife has in her role, from being a young wife, to mid-age to a seasoned wife, is colored by mothering, if this is a part of the marriage, and unexpected events and the consequences of such events.

In the recent Broadway play *Life (x) 3*, by Yasmina Reza, starring Helen Hunt and John Turturro, one evening is played out in three different versions, each depicting Hunt's role as the wife in a different light. In each scenario, the misery, resentment and twisted loyalty of a wife can be seen in Helen Hunt's character, Sonia, to varying degrees. Sonia is a lawyer with a six-year-old son. Sonia's husband, Henry, played by Turturro, is a scientist who has not published for three years. It is obvious that Sonia's work keeps bread on the table, as her husband struggles for recognition. In a gender switch that applies to twenty-first-century wives, Sonia is the rock and even has boundaries when it comes to their spoiled son, while Henry is the pushover parent, indicative of his own inadequacies in his field of work. Or so it seems to his crisp and brittle wife. We can only imagine that this couple did not marry anticipating that Sonia's career would lead and that Henry's would lag or that their approach to raising their only child would be so disparate. So while this stage couple is absorbed with their child and their parenting roles, as their unanticipated life rolls on, their resentment toward one another increases.

The stability of marriage for low-income couples is explored in Alex Kotlowitz's op-ed, which ran on November 13, 2002, in *The New York Times*. In "It Takes a Wedding," Kotlowitz writes of how low-income couples who want to be married have drawn the attention of the clergy who are, naturally, proponents of these unions. The idea of marriages as offering children security versus the traditionally single-mother families in urban neighborhoods across America has many benefits. Marriage is not only for the two adults involved, Kotlowitz points out, but a community benefits when both parents are present. This, then, reinforces how marriage anchors the society, and how spouses, the children, and the population benefit from this institution.

For Stella, who has one daughter who is three years old, the idea of being married is very important. "I have been waiting for my baby's father to marry me for years," she begins. "He gave me a ring but he kept putting off the marriage. I would feel much more secure if we were married. He has two girls from his first marriage and he visits them on weekends. I stay home with our baby, and it upsets me that I'm not married to him. It gets to me on the weekends. We've been engaged for a long time and I still hope that he'll marry me. I thought we would be married by now. I do not feel as secure without the marriage and he says he is afraid of the cost of a wedding. We both make money but not enough to throw a wedding. We both work two jobs to pay for things. I don't know why he cares so much about the party, but he is very religious and wants a big ceremony and then a celebration. I don't think about the wedding, I think about being his wife. I am very disappointed to not be his wife, and it's worse now because my friends are starting to marry their boyfriends. We are all immigrants and we live in the same area and have the same kind of jobs. I know that this should happen to me, it is one reason that I came to America.""

The desire to be a wife has not disappeared; rather, the definition of who a wife is has been taken to another level. Although the twenty-first-century wife is inherently separate from the nineties wife or wives in any prior decade in some respects, being a wife matters all the same. What makes these wives uncommon is their sense that whether they strive for a graduate degree or not, they do not feel compelled to use it once they become wives. Rather, these new wives believe that the option of resuming a career at a future point is possible. These women do not doubt themselves, as their predecessors have done, but are in charge of the relationship.

Their idealism is unlike that of any previous decade and a reflection of how each wife, a fifties wife, a sixties wife, a seventies wife, an eighties wife and a nineties wife, has adapted with the passing years. As the global situation becomes more unstable, fidelity and everlasting love are very important to the twenty-first-century wife, whether she is twenty-five, thirty-five or forty-five. For mature wives who have battled it out each decade in the role of wife, there is a sense of satisfaction in having mastered the art of marriage. From each stance, these wives have witnessed the disintegration of marriages and the loss of families. Many young wives have divorced parents and vow never to do this to their own children.

Rebecca is twenty-two and has just graduated college. She has no plan to be married immediately, although some of her friends have already chosen this path.

"I don't plan on getting married the way that women used to do it. I look at my goals in life, to have a career and to have children. I know that I can do both of those things without a husband. This means that the person I choose has to be very special, because being married is personal for me—it's about the person not the institution. I look at how the women in the seventies and eighties chose to get married and then all the upset and divorces in the nineties and I don't want any of those experiences, I don't want to process it that way. My friends who are already married seem anachronistic to me, especially the ones who are educated and have careers ahead of them. It seems like a throwback, and I don't know why they would give up the independence they have after college so quickly, to do something that can be done at any time.

"As far as equality goes in a marriage, it seems an irrelevant question. I think that 'egalitarian' is an old buzzword that doesn't apply to me or to my friends. My feeling is that I will work or I won't work, as I decide at the time. I want my husband to be successful because it will be a better life if he is. But as far as work goes, I don't see the workplace as male-dominated any more, but like it has been taken over by everyone, every minority. I can enter the workforce, make what I need to make, and marriage is a completely separate issue for me. I believe I am an individual—in the work I do and as someone's wife. I expect a gigantic amount from my husband because I will be choosing him and so he will have to give back to me. Why would I bother to be married if not? I can get lots of attention and affection from my friends and my family. I do not believe that I need a husband to have children, and many of my friends feel this way, too. That sets us apart from women who married before us."

The Generation Y female, the future wife, views herself as immersed in an era of individualism, as evidenced in Rebecca's viewpoint. While she is ready to shun the old standards that apply to marriage, underneath there remains an interest in being a wife. Young women who follow Rebecca and her peers by five or ten years have another take on the role. Yet an extraordinary self-esteem exists for both groups as a centerpiece to their adult lives.

Lux, who, at sixteen, considers herself a future twenty-first-century wife, has already contemplated what her role as wife will be.

"I want to be twenty-six when I get married and I want both children and a career. I want to be a photojournalist and that will mean I'll do freelance work and have flexibility. I don't want to be someone who gets crazy if I don't have an assignment, so I want success but not to make it into a priority. I don't plan to go to graduate school after college and I don't care if my husband has a graduate degree. What I expect out of my marriage is sex and laughter and a true friend. I never want to be divorced and I know that my husband and I will be equals. I know this because I know myself and who I choose to marry will have to meet that requirement. My husband should be successful but I don't care if he makes a lot of money, I care more that we have enough to live. Last year I cared about having a very successful husband, but I know now that his character is more important than how much money he makes.

"I don't expect my husband to share equally with me when it comes to childcare. I just don't believe it's human nature for men to want to do it the way that women do. I hope that we can get someone to clean the house, because I also can't imagine my husband cleaning up and then I would do more than he would do. This is because women won't live in filth and men will. No one person can revolutionize the standard, so I assume my marriage will be somewhat conventional, but with equality between the two of us. I look at my friends' mothers and I know they wanted it a certain way and it didn't work. I don't want to be married to an idea, but to a person. I think of my mother and her friends as women with dreams, mostly failed. So maybe subconsciously, I want it to be very different. My grandmother is my role model because she is strong and beautiful and knew what she wanted out of life. And she got it."

In Lux's interpretation of the role of wife there is a backlash—with her grandmother as heroine and her mother as fallible. Her futuristic wifing will bring in the best qualities of each decade with great expectations to be met. Becoming a twenty-first-century wife means a marriage of parity, hope and a kind of utopia. Whether we are seasoned or new wives, we can only admire the young wives to come who are able to discard the complexities and errors of the past, and draw only upon the successes of previous decades.

Afterword

I began the research for *The New Wife: The Evolving Role of the American Wife* recognizing the implications of wifedom. I was curious about the nuances, what holds true, what evolves over time, what is discarded and why women today are as interested in being a wife as women were fifty, forty or thirty years ago. As I complete this book, articles on marriage and partnering are ubiquitous, including those on sexless marriages, loveless marriages, keeping the romance alive, the hurdles of balancing work, children and husband, and the best way to find the ideal man. Further proof of our culture's belief in happy-ever-after is reflected in the public's interest in marriage. For the summer of 2003, Hollywood's major releases included the wedding movies, *American Wedding*, starring Alyson Hannigan and Jason Biggs, and *The In-Laws*, starring Albert Brooks and Michael Douglas. Love triumphant over adversity, and romance as a cure-all are intrinsic to our culture, from fiction to film to fact.

Although singlehood has become an accepted alternative lifestyle along with gay unions and cohabitation, the majority of women today are more than ready to be wives and view it as an opportunity. At the same time, in the last three decades women have been able to admit that both wifehood and motherhood, which they longed for, have been overrated. For those wives who are disappointed by the experience, there is the chance to renegotiate the marriage. They can take steps within the marriage to enhance their lives, such as going back to school or to work, or divorcing and beginning again. Although change has come slowly, because of our cultural conditioning, change is here at last. In any of these scenarios, the value of being a wife is at a premium, and it is up to the individual woman to create an environment in which she is able to succeed.

It is evident from my research that a large population of women subscribes to the program of wifing, which is proof of its value, regardless of its drawbacks. Women yearn for the right partner and the chance to be a wife. And even if it can be disillusioning, it continues to be coveted and an aspiration for women of all ages in America. The security and commitment that marriage represents is what helps the wife to get through the tough times and to hold onto the relationship.

In this exploration we have seen the expectations versus the realities of being a wife. The steady progress women have made toward the stage of the modern wife illustrates how wives of all ages, representative of the past five decades, have evolved. The advancement of the wife in America is impressive, encompassing bold steps that previous wives in previous times might not have imagined. This includes peer marriages, home offices, breadwinning wives, childless marriages by choice, shared parenting, separate finances, open communication, romance combined with best friendships, and shared goals.

Most wives who divorce will want to be a wife again; it is the nature of our society that marriage, in all social strata, represents success and warrants a repeat performance. Marriage, desired or discouraging, is in demand. For the savvy wife who gets it right the first time, a certain kind of wisdom accompanies her fortunate action. This particular kind of wife knows how to pick and choose her battles and, more importantly, how to choreograph her life. She is acutely conscious of how to sustain her own essence while embarking on one of the longest shared experiences of her life, that of marriage. The secrets of being a successful wife do not elude her and she is able to move fluidly through time, making the alterations necessary to stay in step with both her husband and the society at large.

Although I rarely interview women I know personally and the interviewees are from across the country, of disparate ages and walks of life, for this project I did interview my mother, a fifties wife, and my daughters, who are future twenty-first-century wives. My mother's interview fascinated me because of her candor, confidence and determination to get her needs met in the face of a restrictive time for the American wife. Her conventionalism was always secondary to her strong sense of caring for herself and an equality that existed within her marriage. Yet she never worked but stayed at home and raised her children, making her traditional in her actions, if not in her philosophy. My daughters' interviews echo my mother's sentiments in certain ways. Yet these young women exhibit a strong sense of self and a lack of urgency in getting their lives right. Both have the conviction that their role as a wife will be a roaring success that defies the point of view of past wives of former decades. They are representative of young future wives who view the baby boomer mother with a kind of pity. These young women do not feel pressured to prove themselves to anyone. What makes this generation of future twenty-first-century wives singular from the wives sandwiched between the fifties wives and the twenty-first-century wives is how they perceive their power. The desire to be a wife is not minimized, but immutable. For mature wives who have battled it out each decade in the role of the wife, there is a sense of satisfaction in having mastered the art of marriage. For a young wife today, there are endless possibilities.

The message for wives for the past fifty years has been mixed at best, filled with false starts and societal confusion at worst. Certain patterns emerge, even as we move backward to jump forward. The outcome of the new wife as protected, powerful and autonomous is a result of the modification of the roles of the wife over the past half-century. The lack of modelling has had repercussions, and daughters have reacted to their mothers by choosing different paths, though often, ironically, with echoes of yesterday. Yet, in revisiting past decades, the new wife has intrinsic options. The twenty-first-century wife may be reminiscent of the eighties wife in terms of status and society, but more influenced by the media than any wife to come before her. The self-confidence we have observed in the young twenty-first-century wife has not been seen before.

Long-standing marriages succeed because the couples are optimistic and have a tenacity that needs to be applied at all times. While certain interviewees believe that sharing the same religion or ethnicity counts in solidifying a marriage, sex, a sense of humor and the same values are factored into the quotient as well. If these wives worry as they age about their appeal to their husbands in a culture that emphasizes youth and beauty to such an extent, they have come to terms with the issue. A mature love enters the life of a veteran wife, and the trajectory of her marriage, universal and personal, including the way that we fall in love, build a life together, raise a family, drift apart, and come back together, makes the pieces of the mosaic. In order to be a contented wife, one navigates a path that depends on a woman's understanding of her own aspirations.

Romance will always be at a premium and a riveting part of marriage, as we have seen in earlier chapters in this study. In any decade of wife, few women embarked on the journey without a component of love in their choice of a husband. And so the twenty-first-century wife, the "new wife", stands before us, a culmination of the past fifty years of trial and error—she is filled with hope and self-esteem, more aware than ever before of her role as essential, intact and remarkable.

Bibliography

Allen, S.M. and R.A. Kalish. 1984. Professional Women and Marriage. *Journal of Marriage and the Family*. 46 (5): 356-382.

Althea, Samantha. 2003. How Long Should You Wait to Get Married? *Marie Claire*, March.

American Demographics Magazine, Marion, OH. 1994.

Andre, Rae. 1981. *Homemakers: The Forgotten Workers*. Chicago: University of Chicago Press.

Apter, Terri. 1985. *Why Women Don't Have Wives: Professional Success and Motherhood*. New York: Schocken Books.

Austen, Jane. 1983. *Pride and Prejudice*. New York: Bantam Classics.

Bank, Melissa. 2000. *The Girls' Guide to Hunting & Fishing*. New York: Penguin USA, 2000.

Barash, Susan Shapiro. 2001. *A Passion for More: Wives Reveal the Affairs that Make or Break Their Marriages*. Berkeley: Berkeley Hills Books.

Barash, Susan Shapiro. 2003. *Women of Divorce: Mothers, Daugthers, Stepmothers—The New Triangle*. Far Hills, NJ: New Horizon Press.

Barnes, Michael, and Robert J. Sternberg, eds. 1988. *The Psychology of Love*. New Haven: Yale University Press.

Bayles, Martha. 1990. Feminism and Abortion. *Atlantic Monthly*, April.
Belenky, Mary, Blythe Clinchy, Nancy Goldberger, and Jill Tarule. 1980. *Women's Ways of Knowing: The Development of Self, Voice, and Mind*. New York: Basic Books.

Benjamin, Jessica. 1988. *The Bonds of Love*. New York: Pantheon Books.

Berger, Lynn. 2002. A Death in the Family. *The New York Times*, March 10.

Bernard, Jessie. 1982. *The Future of Marriage*. 2nd ed. New York: Bantam Books.

Berman, Jennifer and Laura Berman. 2002. *For Women Only: A Revolutionary Guide to Reclaiming Your Sex Life*. New York: Henry Holt & Co.

Boston Women's Health Book Collective. 1998. *Our Bodies, Ourselves for the New Century*. Rev. ed. New York: Touchstones.

Boteach, Shmuley. 2002. *Kosher Adultery: Seduce and Sin with Your Spouse*. Avon, MA: Adams Media.

Boyles, Salyyn. 2001. Preserving Fertility. *WebMD Medical News*, September 13. www.webmd.com/.

Brooke, Jill. 2002. A Promise to Love, Honor and Bear No Children. *The New York Times*, Oct. 13.

Brown, Helen Gurley. 1983. *Sex and the Single Girl.* Reissue ed. New York: Avon.
Brownmiller, Susan. 1975. *Against Our Will: Men, Women and Rape*. New York: Fawcett.

Butterfield, Fox. 2002. Killings at Fort Reflect Growing Problem in Military. *The New York Times*, July 28.

Byars, Jackie. 1997. The Prime of Miss Kim Novak. In *The Other Fifties*, ed. Joel Foreman, 197-223. Chicago: University of Illinois Press.
Carabillo, Toni, Judith Mueli and June B. Csida. *Feminist Chronicles: 1953-1993*. Los Angeles: Women's Graphics.

Catalyst. 2001. New York. http://www.catalystwomen.org/.

Catrall, Kim, and Mark Levinson. 2003. *Satisfaction: The Art of the Female Orgasm*. New York: Warner.

Chicago: University of Chicago Press, November 4th.

Centers for Disease Control and Prevention. 1990. Atlanta, GA.

Center for International Development at Harvard University/*The Washington Post* Study. 1976.

Chen, David W. Two Wives Become Comrades in Anxiety. *The New York Times*, March 10.

Child Care Action Campaign. 1975. New York.

Collins, Patricia Hill. 1991. *Black Feminist Thought: Knowledge, Consciousness and the Politics of Empowerment*. New York: Routledge.

Collins, Patricia Hill. 1989. *Journal of Women in Culture and Society* 14: 745-773.

Concoran, Mary, and Gregory J. Duncan. 1979. Work History, Labor Force Attachment and Earnings Differences Between the Races and the Sexes. *Journal of Human Resources*. (Winter):3-20.

Cornwell, John. 2001. Bride and Gloom. *The London Times*, July 3.

Cose, Ellis. 2003. The Black Gender Gap. *Newsweek*, March 3.

Curtis, David G. Perspectives on Acquaintance Rape. The American Academy of Experts in Traumatic Stress, Inc.: Commack, NY. www.aets.org/arts/arts.org.
de Beavoir, Simone. 1953. *The Second Sex*. New York: Alfred A. Knopf.

Declaire, Joan. 2003. Your Marriage: Getting Better All the Time. *Reader's Digest*, February.

de la Cruz, Melissa. 2003. Wanted: $mart, $ingle, $uccessful Men. *Marie Claire*, March.

Drusine, Helene. 2003. Just a Housewife! In *Sisterhood is Forever*, ed. Robin Morgan, 342-348. New York: Washington Square Press.

Dunn, Irina. http://phrases.shu.ac.uk.

Eds. 2002. Good Sex Tips from Samantha. *The New York Times*, January 27.

Eds. 1990. *The New York Times*, August 16.

Eds. 2003. *People Magazine*, March 3.

Eds. 1955. The Good Housekeeping Guide. *Housekeeping Monthly*, May.

Ellis, Peter Berresford. 1996. Celtic Women: Women in Celtic Society and Literature. Philadelphia: Trans-Atlantic Publications, Inc.

Ellis, Peter Berresford. 2002. *Celtic Myths and Legends*. New York: Carroll and Graf.

Epstein, Cynthia Fuchs, Carroll Seron, Bonnie Oglensky, and Robert Saute. 1998. *The Part-Time Paradox: Time Norms, Professional Lives, Family and Gender*. New York: Routledge.

Fielding, Helen. 1999. *Bridget Jones' Diary*. New York: Penguin.

Forecasts. 2002. *Publisher's Weekly*. October 7.
Foreman-Brunell, Miriam. What Barbie Dolls Have to Say About Postwar America. www.smithsonianeducation.org/idealabs/ap/essays/barbie.htm. (accessed 12/2/03).

Forward, Susan. 1986. *Men Who Hate Women and the Women Who Love Them: When Loving Hurts and You Don't Know Why*. New York: Bantam Books.

Foss, Krita. 2002. Living Together: A Popular First Step, Data Shows. *The Globe and Mail*, July 12.

Freedman, Estelle B. 2002. *No Turning Back*. New York: Ballantine Books.

Freeman, Jo. 1984. *Women: A Feminist Perspective*. 3rd ed. New York: McGraw Hill.

French, Marilyn. 1993. *The War Against Women*. New York: Ballantine Books.

French, Marilyn. 1977. *The Women's Room*. New York: Summit Books.

Friday, Nancy. 1996. *Our Looks, Our Lives: Sex, Beauty, Power, and the Need to be Seen*. New York: Harper Paperbacks.

Friedan, Betty. 1973. *The Feminine Mystique*. New York: Dell Publishing.

Galsworthy, John. 1999. *The Forsyte Saga*. Reissue ed. New York: Oxford University Press.

Giele, Janet Z. 2001. Decline of the Family: Conservative, Liberal, and Feminist Views. In *Family in Transition*, Eds. A.S. Skolnick and Jerome H. Skolnick, 57-76. New York: Allyn and Bacon.

Gilligan, Carol. 1982. *In A Different Voice*. Cambridge: Harvard University Press.

Gilman, Charlotte Perkins. 1998. *Women and Economics: A Study of the Economic Relations Between Men and Women as a Factor in Social Evolution*. Los Angeles: University of California Press.

Gilman, Charlotte Perkins. 1996. *The Yellow Wallpaper*. New York: The Feminist Press (CUNY).

Gonzalez, Rosalinda Mendez. 1997. Distinctions in Western Women's Experience: Ethnicity, Class, and Social Change. In *The Women's West*, eds. Susan Armitage and Elizabeth Jameson, 10. Oklahoma: University of Oklahoma Press.

Gottman, John. 1995. *Why Marriages Succeed or Fail: And How You Can Make Yours Last*. New York: Simon and Schuster.

Gottman, John and Nan Silver. 2000. *The Seven Principles for Making Marriage Work*. New York: Three Rivers Press. Greer, Germaine. 1970. *The Female Eunuch*. London: MacGibbon & Kee.

Halberstam, David. 1993. *The Fifties*. New York: Fawcett. Hanauer, Cathi, ed. 2002. *The Bitch in the House*. New York: William Morrow.

Harrison, Barbara Grazutti. 1981. "What Do Women Want?" Feminism and Its Future. *Harper's Magazine* October.

Hays, Sharon. 2001. The Mommy Wars: Ambivalence, Ideological Work and the Contradictions of Motherhood. *Family in Transition*, eds. Arlene S. Skolnick and Jerome H. Skolnick, 40-56. Needham, MA: Allyn and Bacon.

Hertz, Rosanna. A Typology of Approaches to Child Care: The Centerpiece of Organizing Family Life for Dual-Earning Couples. In *Family in Transition*, eds. Arlene S. Skolnick and Jerome H. Skolnick, 266. Needham, MA: Allyn and Bacon.
Hewlett, Sylvia Ann. 2002. *Creating a Life: Professional Women and the Quest for Children*. New York: Miramax Books.

Hite, Shere. 1987. *The Hite Report: A National Study of Female Sexuality*. New York: Ballantine Books.

Hobson, Louis B. 1999. Feed the Fire: Antonio Banderas and Melanie Griffith Reveal Secret of Their Love. *Calgary Sun*, October 17.

Howe, Florence. 2003. The Proper Study of Womankind: Women's Studies. In *Sisterhood is Forever: The Women's Anthology for a New Millenium*, ed. Robin Morgan, 70-84. New York: Washington Square Press.

Hyatt, Elizabeth. 2002. It's Never too Late to Date a Virgin. *The New York Times*, August 4.

Jackson, Robert M. 1998. *Destined for Equality: The Inevitable Rise of Women's Status*. Cambridge: Harvard University Press.

Journal of American Medical Association. American Medical Association. Chicago, Illinois.

Journal of American Women's Association. American Medical Women's Association. Alexandria, Virginia.

Kamen, Paula. 2000. *Her Way: Young Women Remake the Sexual Revolution*. New York: Broadway Books.

Kaufman, Sue. 1967. *Diary of a Mad Housewife*. New York: Random House.

Kelly, Kittey. 1991. *Nancy Reagan: The Unauthorized Biography*. New York: Simon Schuster.

Kennedy, John F. 2000. *Profiles in Courage*, Reissue ed. New York: Perrenial.

Kimmel, Michael S. 2000. *The Gendered Society*. New York: Oxford University Press.

Kinsey, Alfred. 1953. *The Sexual Behavior in the Human Female*. Philadelphia: WB Saunders.

Kinsey, Alfred. 1948. *The Sexual Behavior in the Human Male*. Philadelphia: WB Saunders.

Komter, Aafke. 1989. Hidden Power in Marriage. Gender and Society, 3(2): 187-216.

Kornbluth, Karen. 2003. The Parent Trap. *Atlantic Monthly* Vol. 291 (January/February).

Koss, Mary P. 1987. Rape (study and survey). *Ms.* Magazine. Kotlowitz, Alex. 2002. It Takes a Wedding. *The New York Times*, November 13.

Kramer, Laura. 2000. *The Sociology of Gender: A Brief Introduction*. Los Angeles, CA: Roxbury Publishing Company.

Kuhn, R.D., John Guidubaldi, and John Caroll. 1997. Child Custody Policies and Divorce Rates in the United States, abstract. Washington, D.C.: Children's Rights Council.

Kurdek, Lawrence A. 1989. Relationship Quality for Newly Married Husbands and Wives: Marital History, Stepchildren, and Individual-Difference Predictors. *Journal of Marriage and the Family*. 51(4) (November): 1053-64.

Lamanna, Mary Ann and Agnes Riedmann. 2000. *Marriages and Families: Making Choices in a Diverse Society*, 7th ed. Belmont, CA: Wadsworth/Thomas Learning.

Leibowitz, Arleen, Linda J. Waite, and Christina Witsberger. 1992. Child Care for Preschoolers: Differences by Ages. *The Journal of Human Resources*, Vol. 27, N. 4: 112-133.

Lerner, Sharon. 2002. Good and Bad Marriage, Boon and Bane to Health. *The New York Times*, October 22.

Levinson, Daniel. 1996. *The Season's of a Woman's Life*. New York: Ballantine Books.

Lipton, Laura. 2003. Note To Self: Be My Valentine. *The Wall Street Journal*, February 13.

Lloyd, Carol. 2002. Why Should a Baby Get Her Father's Last Name? *Salon.com*, January 12. http://www.salon.com.

Long, B. 1983. Evaluations and Intentions Concerning Marriage Among Unmarried Female Graduates. *The Journal of Social Psychology* 119: 235-242.

Lonsway, K.A. 1996. Preventing Acquaintances Rape Through Education: What Do We Know? *Psychology of Women Quarterly* 20: 229-265.

Lyall, Sarah. 2002. For Europeans: Love, Yes. Marriages, Maybe. *The New York Times*, March 1.

Marcus, Amy Docker. 2003. Guys Your Biological Clock is Ticking Too. *The Wall Street Journal*, April 1.

Marech, Rona. 1999. With This Name... *Horizons*, February 14.

Martin, Teresa Castro and Larry Bumpass. 1989. *Trends in Marital Disruption Demography*, 26: 37-52.

McLaughlin, S.D. 1988. *The Changing Lives of American Women*. Charlotte, NC: University of North Carolina Press. Mead, Margaret. 1949. *Male and Female*. New York: William Morrow.

Mitchell, Stephen A. 2002. *Can Love Last? The Fate of Romance Over Time*. New York: W.W. Norton & Co.

Mill, Harriet Taylor and John Stuart Mill. 1970. *Essays on Sex Equality*. Alice Rossi, ed. Chicago: University of Chicago Press.

Minton, Michael H., and Jean LeBondon Block. 1983. *What is a Wife Worth? The Leading Experts Place a High Dollar Value on Homemaking*. New York: McGraw Hill.

Morgan, Robin, ed. 2003. *Sisterhood is Forever: The Woman's Anthology for a New Millennium*. New York: Washington Square Press.

Morgan, Robin, ed. 1970. *Sisterhood is Powerful: An Anthology of Writings from the Women's Liberation Movement*. New York: Random House.

Morrison, Joan and Robert Morrison. 1987. *From Camelot to Kent State*. New York: Oxford.

National Center for Health Statistics, Hyattsville, MD 1990, 2000.

National Council of Women's Organizations, Washington, D.C. 2000.

Nicholsen, Linda. 1997. *The Second Wave: A Reader in Feminist History*. New York: Routledge.

Nietzsche, Friedrich. 1999. *Thus Spake Zarathustra*, Reprint ed. New York: Dover.

Norton, Arthur J. and Jeanne E. Moorman. 1987. Current Trends in Marriage and Divorce Among American Women. *Journal of Marriage and the Family* 49: 3-14.

O'Neill, William. 1994. *Feminism in America: A History*. Princeton: Transaction Publishers.

Orth, Maureen. 2002. Fort Bragg's Deadly Summer. *Vanity Fair*, December.

Pantel, Pauline Schmitt. 1994. *A History of the Women of the West, Vol.1*. Cambridge, MA: Harvard University Press.

Pearson, Allison. 2002. *I Don't Know How She Does It: The Life of Kate Reddy, Working Woman*. New York: Alfred

Knopf.

Plath, Sylvia. 1998. *The Bell Jar*. New York: Everyman's Library.

Qian, Zhenchao. 1997. Breaking the Racial Barriers: Variations in Interracial Marriage between 1980 and 1990. *Demography* 34: 263-276.

Rider, Elizabeth A. 2002. *Our Voices: Psychology of Women*. New York: John Wiley & Sons, Inc.

Rubin, Rita. 2003. Older Moms Add a Wrinkle on Motherhood. *USA Today*, January 29.

Safran, Claire. 1976. What Men Do To Women On the Job: A Shocking Look at Sexual Harrassment. *Redbook*, November.

Samuels, Allison. 2003. The Black Gender Gap. *Newsweek*, March 3.

Samuels, Alison. 2003. Time To Tell It Like It Is. *Newsweek*, March 3.

Schnurnberger, Lynn. 2003. Our Weekend at Sex Camp. *MORE Magazine*, April.

Segal, Eric. 2002. *Love Story*, Reprint ed. New York: Avon. Shapiro, Laura. 1997. The Myth of Quality Time. *Newsweek*, May 12.

Shellenbarger, Sue. 2003. DINS. *The Wall Street Journal*, May 16.

Shulman, Alix Kates. 1993. A Marriage Contract. In *Feminist Frameworks*, eds. Alison M. Jaggar and Paula S. Rothenberg, 368. New York: McGraw-Hill.

Smith, James P. and Michael P. Ward. 1984. *Women's Wages and Work in the Twentieth Century*. R 3119. NCHD, Santa Monica, CA: Rand.

Spragins, Ellyn. 2002. His Thoughts About Her Earning Their Keep, *The New York Times*, February 3.

Tarkan, Laurie. 2002. Fertility Clinics Begin to Address Mental Health. *The New York Times*, October 8.

Tavris, Carol. 1992. *The Mismeasure of Women: Why Women are Not the Better Sex, the Inferior Sex or the Opposite Sex*. New York: Touchstone Books.

Tierney, John. 2000. New Look at the Realities of Divorce. *The New York Times*, July 22.

Taraborrelli, J. Randy. 2000. *Jackie, Ethel, Joan: Women of Camelot*. New York: Warner Books.

U.S. Department of Labor Statistics, 2000.

U. S. Department of Health and Human Services/ Office of Women's Health, Washington, D.C. 1990.

U.S. Bureau of the Census. Washington, D.C., 1990.

U.S. Bureau of the Census. Washington, D.C., 1998.

U.S. Bureau of the Census. Washington, D.C. 2000.

U.S. Bureau of Labor Statistics. Department of Labor, Washington, D.C. 1995.

U.S. Statistics/Marital Status. Washington, D.C. 1990.

Van Ogtop, Kristin. 2002. Angel at Work, Devil at Home. *Glamour Magazine*, September.
Waller, Robert James. 1997. *The Bridges of Madison County*. New York: Warner Books.

Weinstein, Laurie and Christie White. 1997. *Wives and Warriors: Women and the Military in the United States and Canada*. Westport, CT: Bergen and Garvey.

Whitehead, Barbara Dafoe. 2002. *Why There are No Good Men Left*. New York: Broadway.

Williams, Juanita H. 1985. Sexuality in Marriage. In *Psychology of Women*, 282, 306. New York: W.W. Norton & Company.

Wharton, Edith. 2000. *The House of Mirth*, Reprint ed. New York: Signet.

Wolfe, Tom. 1990. *The Bonfire of the Vanities*. New York: Farrar, Straus, & Giroux.

Women's Committee of the Director's Guild

www.iVillage.com/relationship/features

www.militarywomen.org/family/htm

www.questia.com

Yalom, Marilyn. 2001. *A History of the Wife*. New York: HarperCollins.

Zaslow, Jeffrey. 2003. Ready to Pop the Question? Hold Off Until You've Done the Interrogation. *The Wall Street Journal*, February 6.

Zigman, Laura. 2002. *Her*. New York: Alfred A. Knopf.